PowerPoint 2007

FOR

DUMMIES®

PowerPoint® 2007
FOR
DUMMIES®

by Doug Lowe

Wiley Publishing, Inc.

PowerPoint® 2007 For Dummies®

Published by
Wiley Publishing, Inc.
111 River Street
Hoboken, NJ 07030-5774
www.wiley.com

For general information on our other products and services, please contact our Customer Care Department within the U.S. at 800-762-2974, outside the U.S. at 317-572-3993, or fax 317-572-4002.

For technical support, please visit www.wiley.com/techsupport.

Wiley also publishes its books in a variety of electronic formats. Some content that appears in print may not be available in electronic books.

Library of Congress Control Number: 2006934818

ISBN-13: 978-0-470-04059-1

ISBN-10: 0-470-04059-9

Manufactured in the United States of America

10 9 8 7 6 5 4 3 2

1O/QU/RS/QW/IN

WILEY

About the Author

Doug Lowe has written enough computer books to line all the birdcages in California. His other books include *Word 2007 All-in-One Desk Reference For Dummies*, *Java All-in-One Desk Reference For Dummies,* and *Networking For Dummies, Sixth Edition.*

Although Doug has yet to win a Pulitzer Prize, he remains cautiously optimistic. He is hopeful that George Lucas will pick up the film rights to this book and suggests *PowerPoint Episode 2,007: The Phantom Presentation* as a working title.

Doug lives in sunny Fresno, California, where the motto is either "We Love Arnold!" or "We Hate Arnold!" (we can't decide which) with his wife, Debbie, and a couple of crazy dogs.

Dedication

To Debbie, Rebecca, Sarah, and Bethany.

Author's Acknowledgments

I'd like to thank the whole crew at Wiley who helped with this edition. Melody Layne got the project rolling and nudged it along when it needed nudging. Project editor Mark Enochs did a great job keeping everything afloat and was very patient as deadlines came and chapters didn't. Copy editor Virginia Sanders (with help from Jennifer Riggs) did a fantastic job with all the details, including dotting all the t's and crossing all the i's, or something like that. Stuart Stuple gave the entire manuscript a thorough technical review and made many excellent suggestions. And, of course, many other people pitched in.

I'd also like to thank everyone who helped out with previous editions of this book: Kala Schrager, Rebecca Mancilla, Doug Sahlin, Andrea Boucher, Garret Pease, Steve Hayes, Kel Oliver, Nancy DelFavero, Grace Jasmine, Rev Mengle, Tina Sims, Pam Mourouzis, Leah Cameron, Jim McCarter, Kezia Endsley, Becky Whitney, and Michael Partington.

Publisher's Acknowledgments

We're proud of this book; please send us your comments through our online registration form located at www.dummies.com/register.

Some of the people who helped bring this book to market include the following:

Acquisitions, Editorial, and Media Development

Project Editor: Mark Enochs

Acquisitions Editor: Melody Layne

Copy Editor: Virginia Sanders

Technical Editor: Stuart Stuple

Editorial Manager: Leah Cameron

Media Development Manager: Laura VanWinkle

Editorial Assistant: Amanda Foxworth

Sr. Editorial Assistant: Cherie Case

Cartoons: Rich Tennant (www.the5thwave.com)

Composition Services

Project Coordinators: Adrienne Martinez, Patrick Redmond

Layout and Graphics: Claudia Bell, Carl Byers, Lavonne Cook, Clint Lahnen, Barbara Moore, Barry Offringa, Alicia B. South, Erin Zeltner

Proofreaders: Susan Moritz, Sossity R. Smith

Indexer: Techbooks

Anniversary Logo Design: Richard Pacifico

Special Help

Jennifer Riggs

Publishing and Editorial for Technology Dummies

Richard Swadley, Vice President and Executive Group Publisher

Andy Cummings, Vice President and Publisher

Mary Bednarek, Executive Acquisitions Director

Mary C. Corder, Editorial Director

Publishing for Consumer Dummies

Diane Graves Steele, Vice President and Publisher

Joyce Pepple, Acquisitions Director

Composition Services

Gerry Fahey, Vice President of Production Services

Debbie Stailey, Director of Composition Services

Contents at a Glance

Table of Contents

Introduction

Welcome to *PowerPoint 2007 For Dummies,* the book written especially for those who are lucky enough to use this latest and greatest version of PowerPoint and want to find out just enough to finish that presentation that was due yesterday.

Do you ever find yourself in front of an audience, no matter how small, flipping through flip charts or shuffling through a stack of handwritten transparencies? You need PowerPoint! Have you always wanted to take your notebook computer with you to impress a client at lunch, but you don't know what to do with it between trips to the salad bar? You *really* need PowerPoint!

Or maybe you're one of those unfortunate folks who bought Microsoft Office because it was such a bargain and you needed a Windows word processor and spreadsheet anyway, and hey, you're not even sure what PowerPoint is, but it was free. Who can resist a bargain like that?

Whichever way, you're holding the perfect book right here in your formerly magic-marker-stained hands. Help is here, within these humble pages.

This book talks about PowerPoint in everyday — and often irreverent — terms. No lofty prose here; the whole thing checks in at about the fifth-grade reading level. I have no Pulitzer expectations for this book. My goal is to make an otherwise dull and lifeless subject at least tolerable, and maybe even kind of fun.

About This Book

This isn't the kind of book that you pick up and read from start to finish as though it were a cheap novel. If I ever see you reading it at the beach, I'll kick sand in your face. This book is more like a reference — the kind of book you can pick up, turn to just about any page, and start reading. It has 26 chapters, each one covering a specific aspect of using PowerPoint — such as printing, animating your slides, or using clip art.

Each chapter is divided into self-contained chunks, all related to the major theme of the chapter.

For example, the chapter on using charts contains nuggets like these:

- ✔ Understanding charts
- ✔ Adding a chart to your presentation
- ✔ Pasting a chart from Excel
- ✔ Changing the chart type
- ✔ Working with chart data

You don't have to memorize anything in this book. It's a need-to-know book: You pick it up when you need to know something. Need to know how to create an organization chart? Pick up the book. Need to know how to override the Slide Master? Pick up the book. After you find what you're looking for, put it down and get on with your life.

How to Use This Book

This book works like a reference. Start with the topic that you want to find out about: To get going, look for it in the Table of Contents or in the Index. The Table of Contents is detailed enough that you should be able to find most of the topics that you look for. If not, turn to the index, where you find even more detail.

When you find your topic in the Table of Contents or the index, turn to the area of interest and read as much or as little as you need or want. Then close the book and get on with it.

This book is loaded with information, of course, so if you want to take a brief excursion into your topic, you're more than welcome. If you want to know all about Slide Masters, read the chapter on templates and masters. If you want to know all about animation, read the chapter on animation. Read whatever you want. This is *your* book — not mine.

On occasion, this book directs you to use specific keyboard shortcuts to get things done. When you see something like Ctrl+Z, this instruction means to hold down the Ctrl key while pressing the Z key and then release both together. Don't type the plus sign.

Sometimes I tell you to use a command that resides on the new ribbon interface like this: choose Home⇨Editing⇨Find. That means to click the Find button, which you'll find in the Editing group on the Home tab.

Whenever I describe a message or information that you see on-screen, it looks like this:

```
Are we having fun yet?
```

Anything you're instructed to type appears in bold like so: Type **a:setup** in the Run dialog box. Type exactly what you see, with or without spaces.

Another nice feature of this book is that whenever I discuss a certain button that you need to click in order to accomplish the task at hand, the button appears either in the margin or in a helpful table that summarizes the buttons that apply to a particular task. This way, you can easily locate it on your screen.

What You Don't Need to Read

Some parts of this book are skippable. I carefully place extra-technical information in self-contained sidebars and clearly mark them so that you can give them a wide berth. Don't read this stuff unless you just gots to know. Don't worry; I won't be offended if you don't read every word.

Foolish Assumptions

I make only three assumptions about you:

- ✔ You use a computer.
- ✔ It's a Windows computer — not a Macintosh.
- ✔ You use or are thinking about using PowerPoint 2007.

Nothing else. I don't assume that you're a computer guru who knows how to change a controller card or configure memory for optimal use. These types of computer chores are best handled by people who like computers. Hopefully, you are on speaking terms with such a person. Do your best to stay there.

How This Book Is Organized

Inside this book are chapters arranged in six parts. Each chapter is broken down into sections that cover various aspects of the chapter's main subject. The chapters have a logical sequence, so it makes sense to read them in order if you want. But you don't have to read the book that way; you can flip it open to any page and start reading.

Here's the lowdown on what's in each of the five parts:

Part 1: Basic PowerPoint 2007 Stuff

In this part, you review the basics of using PowerPoint. This is a good place to start if you're clueless about what PowerPoint is, let alone how to use it.

Part II: Creating Great-Looking Slides

The chapters in this part show you how to make presentations that look good. Most important are the chapters about themes (Chapter 9), and masters and templates (Chapter 11). Get the theme, template, and masters right, and everything else falls into place.

Part III: Embellishing Your Slides

One of the nifty new features of PowerPoint 2007 is the Insert tab on the Ribbon. It's loaded with things you can insert into your presentations. The chapters in this part explore the various goodies to be found here, such as pictures, clip art, charts, SmartArt objects, sounds, movies, tables, ginsu knives, and more!

Part IV: Working with Others

The chapters in this part show you how to use PowerPoint's many collaboration features, such as using revision tracking tools, creating slide libraries, and working with SharePoint.

Part V: The Part of Tens

This wouldn't be a *For Dummies* book without lists of interesting snippets: ten PowerPoint commandments, ten tips for creating readable slides, ten ways to keep your audience awake, ten things that often go wrong (my all-time favorite), and ten new features for 2007.

Icons Used in This Book

As you're reading all this wonderful prose, you occasionally see the following icons. They appear in the margins to draw your attention to important information. They are defined as follows:

Watch out! Some technical drivel is just around the corner. Read it only if you have your pocket protector firmly attached.

Pay special attention to this icon — it tells you that some particularly useful tidbit is at hand, perhaps a shortcut or a way of using a command that you might not have considered.

Danger! Danger! Danger! Stand back, Will Robinson!

Did I tell you about the memory course I took? Paragraphs marked with this icon simply point out details that are worth committing to memory.

Where to Go from Here

Yes, you can get there from here. With this book in hand, you're ready to charge full speed ahead into the strange and wonderful world of desktop presentations. Browse through the Table of Contents and decide where you want to start. Be bold! Be courageous! Be adventurous! Above all else, have fun!

Part I
Basic PowerPoint 2007 Stuff

In this part . . .

Once upon a time, the term *presentation software* meant poster board and marker pens. Now, however, programs such as Microsoft PowerPoint enable you to create spectacular presentations on your computer.

The chapters in this part compose a bare-bones introduction to PowerPoint. You find out exactly what PowerPoint is and how to use it to create simple presentations. More-advanced stuff, such as adding charts or using fancy text fonts, is covered in later parts. This part is just the beginning. As a great king once advised, it is best to begin at the beginning and go on until you come to the end; then stop.

Chapter 1

Welcome to PowerPoint 2007

*T*his chapter is a grand and gala welcoming ceremony for PowerPoint 2007, the all-new and thoroughly revamped version of Microsoft's popular slide-presentation program.

This chapter is sort of like the opening ceremonies of the Olympics, in which all the athletes parade around the stadium and people make speeches in French. In much the same way, this chapter marches PowerPoint 2007 around the stadium so you can get a bird's-eye view of what the program is and what you can do with it. I might make a few speeches, but not in French (unless, of course, you're reading the French edition of this book).

What in Sam Hill Is PowerPoint?

PowerPoint is a program that comes with Microsoft Office (although you can buy it separately, as well). Most people buy Microsoft Office because it's a great bargain: You get Word, Excel, and Outlook all together in one inexpensive package. And PowerPoint is thrown in for good measure. Of course, depending on which edition of Office you buy, you might get other goodies as well, such as Access, Publisher, a complete set of Ginsu knives, and a Binford VegaPneumatic Power Slicer and Dicer (always wear eye protection).

You know what Word is — it's the world's most loved and most hated word processor, and it's perfect for concocting letters, term papers, and great American novels. Excel is a spreadsheet program used by bean counters the world over. Outlook is that program you use to read your e-mail. But what the heck is PowerPoint? Does anybody know or care? (And as long as I'm asking questions, who in Sam Hill was Sam Hill?)

PowerPoint is a *presentation* program, and it's one of the coolest programs I know. It's designed to work with a projector to display presentations that will bedazzle your audience and instantly sway them to your point of view, even if you're selling real estate on Mars, season tickets for the Mets, or a new Medi-care plan to Congress. If you've ever flipped a flip chart, you're going to love PowerPoint.

Here are some of the many uses of PowerPoint:

- ✔ **Business presentations:** PowerPoint is a great timesaver for anyone who makes business presentations, whether you've been asked to speak in front of hundreds of people at a shareholders' convention, a group of sales reps at a sales conference, or your own staff or co-workers at a business meeting.

- ✔ **Sales presentations:** If you're an insurance salesperson, you can use PowerPoint to create a presentation about the perils of not owning life insurance and then use your laptop to show it to hapless clients.

- ✔ **Lectures:** PowerPoint is also useful for teachers or conference speakers who want to back up their lectures with slides.

- ✔ **Homework:** PowerPoint is a great program to use for certain types of homework projects, such as those big history reports that count for half your grade.

- ✔ **Church:** People use PowerPoint at churches to display song lyrics on big screens so everyone can sing or to display sermon outlines so everyone can take notes. If your church still uses hymnals or prints the outline in the bulletin, tell the minister to join the 21st century.

- ✔ **Information stations:** You can use PowerPoint to set up a computerized information kiosk that people can walk up to and use. For example, you can create a museum exhibit about the history of your town or set up a trade-show presentation to provide information about your company and products.

- ✔ **Internet presentations:** PowerPoint can even help you to set up a pre-sentation that you can broadcast over the Internet so people can join in on the fun without having to leave the comfort of their own homes or offices.

Introducing PowerPoint Presentations

PowerPoint is similar to a word processor such as Word, except that it's geared toward creating *presentations* rather than *documents*. A presentation is kind of like those Kodak Carousel slide trays that your father used to load up with 35-mm slides of your family trip to the Grand Canyon. The main difference is that you don't have to worry about dumping all the slides in your PowerPoint presentation out of the tray and onto the floor.

Word documents consist of one or more pages, and PowerPoint presentations consist of one or more *slides*. Each slide can contain text, graphics, and other information. You can easily rearrange the slides in a presentation, delete slides that you don't need, add new slides, or modify the contents of existing slides.

You can use PowerPoint both to create your presentations and to actually present them.

You can use several different types of media to actually show your presentations:

- **Computer monitor:** Your computer monitor, either a CRT monitor or an LCD, is a suitable way to display your presentation when you're showing it to just one or two other people.

- **Computer projector:** A computer projector projects an image of your computer monitor onto a screen so large audiences can view it.

- **Overhead transparencies:** Overhead transparencies can be used to show your presentation using an overhead projector.

- **Printed pages:** Printed pages allow you to distribute a printed copy of your entire presentation to each member of your audience. (When you print your presentation, you can print one slide per page, or you can print several slides on each page to save paper.)

- **35-mm slides:** For a fee, you can have your presentation printed onto 35-mm slides either by a local company or over the Internet. Then, your presentation really is like a Kodak Carousel slide tray!

Presentation files

A presentation is to PowerPoint what a document is to Word or a worksheet is to Excel. In other words, a presentation is a file that you create with PowerPoint. Each presentation that you create is saved on the hard drive as a separate file.

PowerPoint 2007 presentations have the special extension .pptx added to the end of their filenames. For example, Sales Conference.pptx and History Day.pptx are both valid PowerPoint filenames. When you type the filename for a new PowerPoint file, you don't have to type the .pptx extension, because PowerPoint automatically adds the extension for you. Windows may hide the .pptx extension, in which case a presentation file named Conference.pptx often appears as just Conference.

Previous versions of PowerPoint saved presentations with the extension .ppt instead of .pptx. The *x* at the end of the new file extension denotes that the new file format is based on XML, a popular data format that makes it easier to exchange files among different programs. PowerPoint 2007 can save files in the old .ppt format, but I recommend you do so only if you need to share presentations with people who haven't yet upgraded to PowerPoint 2007. (You can download a program called the Microsoft Office Compatibility Pack from www.microsoft.com that enables PowerPoint 2002 or 2003 to read and write files in .pptx format. This program enables you to share your .pptx files with people who haven't yet upgraded.)

PowerPoint is set up initially to save your presentation files in the My Documents folder, but you can store PowerPoint files in any folder of your choice on your hard drive or on any other drive. You can write a presentation to a CD-RW drive or to a removable USB flash drive if you want to take it home with you to work on or if you need to give it to other people so they can use it on their computers.

What's in a slide?

PowerPoint presentations comprise one or more slides. Each slide can contain text, graphics, and other elements. A number of PowerPoint features work together to help you easily format attractive slides:

- ✔ **Slide layouts:** Every slide has a slide layout that controls how information is arranged on the slide. A slide layout is simply a collection of one or more placeholders, which set aside an area of the slide to hold information. Depending on the layout that you choose for a slide, the placeholders can hold text, graphics, clip art, sound or video files, tables, charts, graphs, diagrams, or other types of content.

- ✔ **Background:** Every slide has a background, which provides a backdrop for the slide's content. The background can be a solid color; a blend of two colors; a subtle texture, such as marble or parchment; a pattern, such as diagonal lines, bricks, or tiles; or an image file. Each slide can have a different background, but you usually want to use the same background for every slide in your presentation to provide a consistent look.

- ✔ **Themes:** Themes are combinations of design elements such as color schemes and fonts that make it easy to create attractive slides that don't look ridiculous. You can stray from the themes if you want, but you should do so only if you have a better eye than the design gurus that work for Microsoft.

- ✔ **Slide Master:** The Slide Master is a special type of slide that controls the basic design and formatting options for slides in your presentation. The Slide Master includes the position and size of basic title and text placeholders; the background and color scheme used for the presentation; and font settings, such as typefaces, colors, and sizes. In addition, the Slide Master can contain graphic and text objects that you want to appear on every slide.

  You can edit the Slide Master to change the appearance of all the slides in your presentation at once. This helps to ensure that the slides in your presentation have a consistent appearance.

All the features described in the previous list work together to control the appearance of your slides in much the same way that style sheets and templates control the appearance of Word documents. You can customize the appearance of individual slides by adding any of the following elements:

- ✔ **Title and body text:** Most slide layouts include placeholders for title and body text. You can type any text that you want into these placeholders. By default, PowerPoint formats the text according to the Slide Master, but you can easily override this formatting to use any font, size, style, or text color that you want.

- ✔ **Text boxes:** You can add text anywhere on a slide by drawing a text box and then typing text. Text boxes allow you to add text that doesn't fit conveniently in the title or body text placeholders.

- ✔ **Shapes:** You can use PowerPoint's drawing tools to add a variety of shapes on your slides. You can use predefined AutoShapes, such as rectangles, circles, stars, arrows, and flowchart symbols. Alternatively, you can create your own shapes by using basic line, polygon, and freehand drawing tools.

- ✔ **Illustrations:** You can illustrate your slides by inserting clip art, photographs, and other graphic elements. PowerPoint also comes with a large collection of clip art pictures you can use, and Microsoft provides an even larger collection of clip art images online.

- ✔ **Charts and diagrams:** PowerPoint includes a new diagramming feature called *SmartArt* that enables you to create several common types of diagrams, including organization charts, cycle diagrams, and others. In addition, you can insert pie charts, line or bar charts, and many other chart types.

- ✔ **Media clips:** You can add sound clips or video files to your slides.

Starting PowerPoint

Here's the procedure for starting PowerPoint:

1. **Get ready.**

   Light some votive candles. Take two Tylenol. Put on a pot of coffee. If you're allergic to banana slugs, take an allergy pill. Sit in the lotus position facing Redmond, Washington, and recite the Windows creed three times:

   Bill Gates is my friend. Resistance is futile. No beer and no TV make Homer something something . . .

2. **Click the Start button.**

   The Start button is ordinarily found in the lower-left corner of the Windows display. When you click it, the famous Start menu appears. The Start menu works pretty much the same, no matter which version of Windows you're using.

   If you can't find the Start button, try moving the cursor all the way to the bottom edge of the screen and holding it there a moment. With luck on your side, you see the Start button appear. If not, try moving the cursor to the other three edges of the screen: top, left, and right. Sometimes the Start button hides behind these edges.

3. **Point to All Programs on the Start menu.**

   After you click the Start button to reveal the Start menu, move the cursor up to the word *All Programs* and hold it there a moment. Yet another menu appears, revealing a bevy of commands.

4. **Choose Microsoft Office⇨Microsoft Office PowerPoint 2007.**

   Your computer whirs and clicks and possibly makes other unmentionable noises while PowerPoint comes to life.

   If you use PowerPoint frequently, it might appear in the *Frequently Used Programs List* directly on the Start menu so you don't have to choose All Programs⇨Microsoft Office to get to it. If you want Power-Point to always appear at the top of the Start menu, choose Start⇨All Programs⇨Microsoft Office. Then, right-click Microsoft Office Power-Point 2007 and choose the Pin to Start Menu command.

Navigating the PowerPoint Interface

When you start PowerPoint, it greets you with a screen that's so cluttered with stuff that you're soon ready to consider newsprint and markers as a viable alternative for your presentations. The center of the screen is mercifully blank, but the top part of the screen is chock-full of little icons and buttons and doohickies. What is all that stuff?

Figure 1-1 shows the basic PowerPoint screen in all its cluttered glory. The following list points out the more important parts of the PowerPoint screen:

Office button (a.k.a. the File menu)

Quick Access toolbar

Slides and Outline tabs

The Ribbon

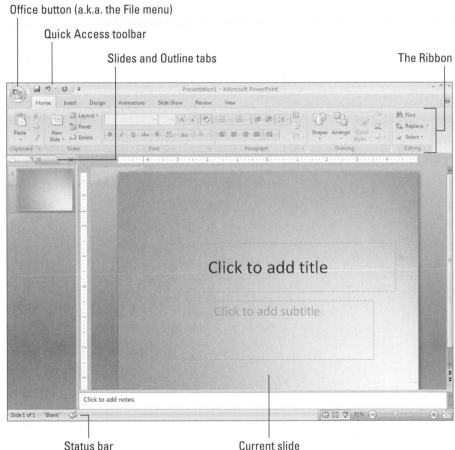

Figure 1-1:
PowerPoint's
cluttered
screen.

Status bar

Current slide

> ✔ **The Ribbon:** Across the top of the screen, just below the Microsoft PowerPoint title, is PowerPoint's main user-interface gadget, called the *Ribbon*. If you've worked with previous versions of PowerPoint, you were probably expecting to see a menu followed by one or more toolbars in this general vicinity. After meticulous research, Microsoft gurus decided that menus and toolbars are hard to use. So they replaced the menus and toolbars with the Ribbon, which combines the functions of both. The Ribbon takes some getting used to, but after you figure it out,

it actually does become easier to use than the old menus and toolbars. The deepest and darkest secrets of PowerPoint are hidden on the Ribbon. Wear a helmet when exploring it.

Note that the exact appearance of the Ribbon varies a bit depending on the size of your monitor. On smaller monitors, PowerPoint may compress the Ribbon a bit by using smaller buttons and arranging them differently (for example, stacking them on top of one another instead of placing them side by side).

For more information about working with the Ribbon, see the section "Unraveling the Ribbon," later in this chapter.

Although PowerPoint 2007 has done away with the menus, the keyboard shortcuts (technically called *accelerators*) that were associated with the PowerPoint 2003 menu commands still work. However, instead of pressing Alt and the accelerator key at the same time, you press them separately. For example, to call up the Open dialog box, press Alt, F, and O (for the old File⇨Open command). And to insert clip art, press Alt, I, P, and C (for the old Insert⇨Picture⇨Clip Art command).

✔ **The Office button (also known as the File menu):** The big colorful logo in the top-left corner of the PowerPoint window is called the Office button. You can click it to reveal the program's one and only traditional menu. This is the place to come when you need to open or save files, create new presentations, print a document, and do other file-related chores.

✔ **Quick Access toolbar:** Just to the right of the Office button is the *Quick Access toolbar,* also called the *QAT* for short. Its sole purpose in life is to provide a convenient resting place for the PowerPoint commands you use the most often.

Initially, this toolbar contains just four buttons: Save, Undo, Redo, and Print. However, you can add additional buttons if you want. To add any button to the QAT, right-click the button and choose Add to Quick Access Toolbar. You'll also find a pull-down menu at the end of the QAT that lists several frequently used commands. You can use this menu to add these common commands to the QAT.

✔ **Current slide:** Right smack in the middle of the screen is where your current slide appears.

✔ **Slides tab and Outline tab:** To the left of the slide is an area that has two tabs, labeled Outline and Slides. The Slides tab shows thumbnail icons of your slides, and the Outline tab shows your presentation arranged as an outline. You can switch between the two tabs by clicking the tab you want to view. (For more information on working in Outline View, see Chapter 3.) The Slides tab, shown in Figure 1-1, shows little thumbnail images of your slides.

✔ **Notes pane:** Beneath the slide is a small area called the *Notes pane,* which you can use to add notes to your slides. For more information on using this feature, see Chapter 5.

✔ **Task pane:** To the right of the slide is an area called the *task pane.* The task pane is designed to help you complete common tasks quickly. When you first start PowerPoint, the task pane isn't visible, so you can't see it in Figure 1-1. However, it will appear whenever it's needed, and you'll see plenty of examples of it throughout this book.

✔ **Status bar:** At the very bottom of the screen is the *status bar,* which tells you the slide that is currently displayed (for example, Slide 1 of 1).

You can configure the status bar by right-clicking anywhere on it. This reveals a list of options that you can select or deselect to determine which elements appear on the status bar.

You'll never get anything done if you feel that you have to understand every pixel of the PowerPoint screen before you can do anything. Don't worry about the stuff that you don't understand; just concentrate on what you need to know to get the job done and worry about the bells and whistles later.

Unraveling the Ribbon

The Ribbon is Microsoft's new user-interface gadget for not just PowerPoint 2007, but also Word 2007, Excel 2007, and Access 2007. The Ribbon replaces the menus and toolbars found in earlier versions of these programs.

Across the top of the Ribbon is a series of tabs. You can click one of these tabs to reveal a set of controls specific to that tab. For example, the Ribbon in Figure 1-1 (earlier in the chapter) shows the Home tab. Figure 1-2 shows the Ribbon with the Insert tab selected.

Figure 1-2:
The Ribbon with the Insert tab selected.

Initially, the Ribbon displays the following seven tabs:

- **Home:** Basic commands for creating and formatting slides
- **Insert:** Commands for inserting various types of objects on slides
- **Design:** Commands that let you tweak the layout of a slide
- **Animations:** Commands that let you add animation effects
- **Slide Show:** Commands for presenting your slide show
- **Review:** Commands for proofing and adding comments to your presentations
- **View:** Commands that let you change the view

Besides these basic tabs, additional tabs appear from time to time. For example, if you select a picture, a Picture Tools tab appears with commands that let you manipulate the picture.

The commands on a Ribbon tab are organized into groups. Within each group, most of the commands are simple buttons that are similar to toolbar buttons in previous versions of PowerPoint.

The View from Here Is Great

Near the right edge of the status bar is a series of three View buttons. These buttons enable you to switch among the various *views,* or ways of looking at your presentation. Table 1-1 summarizes what each View button does.

Table 1-1	View Buttons
Button	*What It Does*
	Switches to Normal View, which shows your slide, outline, and notes all at once. This is the default view for PowerPoint.
	Switches to Slide Sorter View, which enables you to easily rearrange slides and add slide transitions and other special effects.
	Switches to Slide Show View, which displays your slides in an on-screen presentation.

Creating a New Presentation

When you first start PowerPoint, a new, blank presentation is created. The simplest way to create a new presentation is to start PowerPoint and then edit the blank presentation to your liking.

An alternative is to use the Office➪New command, which brings up the big dialog box shown in Figure 1-3. This dialog box presents several ways to create a new presentation:

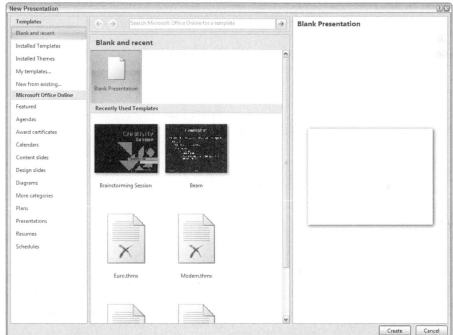

✔ **Blank Presentation:** Double-click Blank Presentation to start a new presentation from scratch.

✔ **Recently Used Templates:** This section of the New Presentation dialog box lists templates you've recently used to create presentations. You can double-click any of these templates to create another presentation based on the template.

✔ **Installed Templates:** Click this item to display a list of all the templates installed on your computer. When you create a presentation from a template, the presentation inherits various design elements (collectively called the *theme*) as well as pre-written content that's stored in the template.

✔ **Installed Themes:** Click this item to display a list of all the themes installed on your computer. Creating a presentation from a theme is similar to creating a presentation from a template, except that the new presentation doesn't contain any pre-written content.

✔ **My Templates:** Double-click My Templates to bring up a separate dialog box that lets you locate templates to create your presentation from.

✔ **New From Existing:** Double-click New From Existing to create a new presentation based on an existing one. Use this option if you want to create a presentation that is similar to one that you created previously.

✔ **Microsoft Office Online:** Use this section of the dialog box to select a template from Microsoft's online Web site. Note that the templates are arranged into categories, such as Agendas, Plans, and Presentations.

Zooming in

PowerPoint automatically adjusts its zoom factor so that Slide View displays each slide in its entirety. You can change the size of your slide by using the zoom control slider that appears at the bottom right of the window.

Editing text

In PowerPoint, slides are blank areas that you can adorn with various objects. The most common type of object is a *text object,* a rectangular area that is specially designated for holding text. (Other types of objects include shapes, such as circles or triangles; pictures imported from clip art files; and graphs.)

Most slides contain two text objects: one for the slide's title and the other for its body text. However, you can add more text objects if you want, and you can remove the body text or title text object. You can even remove both to create a slide that contains no text.

Whenever you move the cursor over a text object, the cursor changes from an arrow to the *I-beam,* which you can use to support bridges or build aircraft carriers. Seriously, when the cursor changes to an I-beam, you can click the mouse button and start typing text.

When you click a text object, a box appears around the text, and an insertion pointer appears at the spot where you clicked. PowerPoint then becomes like a word processor. Any characters that you type are inserted into the text at the insertion pointer location. You can press Delete or Backspace to demolish text, and you can use the arrow keys to move the insertion pointer around in the text object. If you press Enter, a new line of text begins within the text object.

When a text object contains no text, a placeholder message appears in the object. For example, a title text object displays the message Click to add title. Other placeholders display similar messages. The placeholder message magically vanishes when you click the object and begin typing text.

If you start typing without clicking anywhere, the text that you type is entered into the title text object — assuming that the title text object doesn't already have text of its own. If the title object is not empty, any text that you type (with no text object selected) is simply ignored.

After you finish typing text, press Esc or click anywhere outside the text object.

In Chapter 2, you find many details about playing with text objects, but hold your horses. You have more important things to attend to first.

Adding a new slide

When you first create a presentation, it has just one slide, which is useful only for the shortest presentations. Fortunately, PowerPoint gives you about 50 ways to add new slides to your presentation. You see only three of them here:

- ✔ On the Home tab, click the New Slide button in the Slides group.
- ✔ Press Ctrl+M.
- ✔ Right-click in the Slides or Outline tab on the left and then choose New Slide.

In all three cases, PowerPoint adds a blank slide with a standard layout that includes a title and content area as shown in Figure 1-4. If you want to choose a different layout, click the Layout button in the Home tab to display the gallery of slide layouts. This pane enables you to pick from several different types of slide layouts. Just click the one that you want to use, and PowerPoint sets the new slide to the layout of your choosing.

Figure 1-4:
Choosing a
slide layout.

Each slide layout has a name. For example, the *Title and Content* layout includes a text object in addition to the title area. This is probably the layout you'll use most. It's the best format for presenting a topic along with several supporting points. For example, Figure 1-5 shows a typical bulleted list slide, in which a list of bulleted items describes signs that your son is headed down the road toward moral decay.

Moving from slide to slide

You have several ways to move forward and backward through your presentation, from slide to slide:

- **Click one of the double-headed arrows at the bottom of the vertical scroll bar.** Doing so moves you through the presentation one slide at a time.
- **Press the Page Up and Page Down keys.** Using these keys also moves one slide at a time.

Figure 1-5:
A typical
text slide.

> ✔ **Use the scroll bar.** When you drag the box in the scroll bar, a ToolTip appears to display the number and title of the current slide. Dragging the scroll bar is the quickest way to move directly to any slide in your presentation.
>
> ✔ **In the list of slides on the left side of the window, click the thumbnail for the slide that you want to display.** If the thumbnails are not visible, click the Slides tab above the outline.

Choosing a design

In Parts II and III of this book, you'll learn many different ways to create great-looking slides. However, you don't have to wait until then to apply some basic style to your presentation. I've already mentioned that Office 2007 comes pre-loaded with a handful of professionally-designed themes that are designed to create polished presentations with just the click of a mouse. To apply one of these themes, just select the Design ribbon tab, then click the theme you want to apply in the Themes group. Figure 1-6 shows a presentation after a theme has been applied.

Figure 1-6:
A slide
after a
design
has been
applied.

Due to space constraints, PowerPoint doesn't display all of the available themes in the Ribbon at the same time. But just to the right of the themes is a scroll bar you can use to scroll through the themes. And the button at the bottom of the scroll bar brings up a gallery that displays all of the themes that come with Office 2007.

Displaying Your Presentation

When your masterpiece is ready, you can show it on the screen. Just follow these steps:

1. **Choose the Slide Show tab on the Ribbon and then click the From Beginning button in the Start Slide Show group (shown in the margin).**

   There are several shortcuts to this command. You can also start the show by pressing F5 or by clicking the Slide Show button, located with the other view buttons in the lower-right corner of the screen.

2. **Behold the first slide.**

   The slide fills the screen. Isn't it pretty?

3. **Press Enter to advance to the next slide.**

   You can keep pressing Enter to call up each slide in the presentation. If you don't like the Enter key, you can use the spacebar instead.

   If you want to go back a slide, press Page Up.

4. **Press Esc when you're done.**

   You don't have to wait until the last slide is shown. If you find a glaring mistake in a slide or if you just get bored, you can press Esc at any time to return to PowerPoint.

For the complete lowdown on showing your presentation, kindly turn to Chapter 6.

Saving Your Work

Now that you've spent hours creating the best presentation since God gave Moses the Ten Commandments, it's time to save your work to a file. If you make the rookie mistake of turning off your computer before you've saved your presentation, *poof!* Your work vanishes as if David Copperfield were in town.

Like everything else in PowerPoint, you have at least four ways to save a document:

✔ Click the Save button on the Quick Access toolbar.

✔ Click the Office button and then choose Save.

✔ Press Ctrl+S.

✔ Press Shift+F12.

If you haven't yet saved the file to your hard drive, the magical Save As dialog box appears. Type the name that you want to use for the file in the Save As dialog box and click OK to save the file. After you save the file once, subsequent saves update the hard drive file with any changes that you made to the presentation since the last time you saved it.

Also note that after you save a file for the first time, the name in the presentation window's title area changes from *Presentation* to the name of your file. This is simply proof that the file has been saved.

Keep the following tips in mind when saving files:

- Put on your Thinking Cap when assigning a name to a new file. The file-name is how you can recognize the file later on, so pick a meaningful name that suggests the file's contents.

- Don't work on your file for hours at a time without saving it. I've learned the hard way to save my work every few minutes. After all, I live in California, so I never know when a rolling blackout will hit my neighborhood. Get into the habit of saving every few minutes, especially after making a significant change to a presentation, such as adding a covey of new slides or making a gaggle of complicated formatting changes.

Opening a Presentation

After you save your presentation to your hard drive, you can retrieve it later when you want to make additional changes or to print it. As you might guess, PowerPoint gives you about 2,037 ways to accomplish the retrieval. Here are the three most common:

- Click the Office button and then choose the Open command.
- Press Ctrl+O.
- Press Ctrl+F12.

All three retrieval methods pop up in the Open dialog box, which gives you a list of files to choose from. Click the file that you want and then click OK or press Enter.

The Open dialog box has controls that enable you to rummage through the various folders on your hard drive in search of your files. If you know how to open a file in any Windows application, you know how to do it in PowerPoint (because the Open dialog box is pretty much the same in any Windows program).

If you seem to have lost a file, rummage around in different folders to see whether you can find it. Perhaps you saved a file in the wrong folder by accident. Also, check the spelling of the filename. Maybe your fingers weren't on the home row when you typed the filename, so instead of `River City.pptx`, you saved the file as `Eucwe Xurt.pptx`. I hate it when that happens. If all else fails, you can use Windows' built-in Search feature. For Windows XP, click the Start button and then choose Search and follow the instructions that appear in the Search Results window. If you're using Vista, you can simply type some or all of the filename in the Instant Search box that appears in the Start menu.

The fastest way to open a file from the Open dialog box is to double-click the file. This spares you from having to click the file once and then click OK. Double-clicking also exercises the fast-twitch muscles in your index finger.

PowerPoint keeps track of the last nine files that you've opened and displays them on the File menu. To open a file that you recently opened, click the File menu and inspect the list of files on the right side of the menu. If the file that you want is in the list, click it to open it.

Closing a Presentation

Having finished and saved your presentation, you have come to the time to close it. Closing a presentation is kind of like gathering your papers, putting them neatly in a file folder, and returning the folder to its proper file drawer. The presentation disappears from your computer screen. Don't worry: It's tucked safely away on your hard drive where you can get to it later if you need to.

To close a file, click the Close button that appears at the top right of the PowerPoint window. Alternatively, you can click the Office button and then choose Close, or use the keyboard shortcut Ctrl+W. But clicking the Close button is the easiest way to close a file.

You don't have to close a file before exiting PowerPoint. If you exit Power-Point without closing a file, PowerPoint graciously closes the file for you. The only reason that you might want to close a file is that you want to work on a different file and you don't want to keep both files open at the same time.

If you've made changes since the last time you saved the file, PowerPoint offers to save the changes for you. Click Yes to save the file before closing or click No to abandon any changes that you've made to the file.

If you close all the open PowerPoint presentations, you might discover that most of the PowerPoint commands have been rendered useless (they are grayed on the menu). Fear not. If you open a presentation or create a new one, the commands return to life.

Exiting PowerPoint

Had enough excitement for one day? Use any of these techniques to shut PowerPoint down:

- ✔ Click the Office button and then click the Exit PowerPoint button.
- ✔ Click the X box at the top-right corner of the PowerPoint window.
- ✔ Press Alt+F4.

Bam! PowerPoint is history.

You should know a couple things about exiting PowerPoint (or any application):

- ✔ PowerPoint doesn't let you abandon ship without first considering whether you want to save your work. If you've made changes to any presentation files and haven't saved them, PowerPoint offers to save the files for you. Lean over and plant a fat kiss right in the middle of your monitor — PowerPoint just saved you your job.
- ✔ Never, never, never, ever, never turn off your computer while PowerPoint or any other program is running. Bad! Always exit PowerPoint and all other programs that are running before you turn off your computer.

Chapter 2

Editing Slides

*I*f you're like Mary Poppins ("Practically Perfect in Every Way"), you can skip this chapter. Perfect people never make mistakes, so everything that they type in PowerPoint comes out right the first time. They never have to press Backspace to erase something they typed incorrectly, or go back and insert a line to make a point they left out, or rearrange their slides because they didn't add them in the right order to begin with.

If you're more like Jane ("Rather Inclined to Giggle; Doesn't Put Things Away") or Michael ("Extremely Stubborn and Suspicious"), you probably make mistakes along the way. This chapter shows you how to go back and correct those mistakes.

Reviewing your work and correcting it if necessary is called *editing*. It's not a fun job, but it has to be done. A spoonful of sugar usually helps.

This chapter focuses mostly on editing text objects. Many of the techniques apply to editing other types of objects, such as clip art pictures or drawn shapes. For more information about editing other types of objects, see Part III.

Moving from Slide to Slide

The most common way to move in a PowerPoint presentation is to press the Page Down and Page Up keys:

- ✔ **Page Down:** Press Page Down to move forward to the next slide in your presentation.

- ✔ **Page Up:** Press Page Up to move backward to the preceding slide in your presentation.

You can also use the vertical scroll bar on the right side of the window to navigate through your presentation:

- ✔ **Double-headed arrows:** You can move forward or backward through your presentation one slide at a time by clicking the double-headed arrows at the bottom of the vertical scroll bar.

- ✔ **Single-headed arrows:** You can also scroll forward or backward through your presentation by clicking and holding the single-headed arrow at the top or bottom of the vertical scroll bar. (Note that if the zoom factor is set so that a single slide is visible in the presentation window, clicking the single-headed arrows moves to the next or previous slide.)

- ✔ **Scroll box:** Another way to move quickly from slide to slide is to click the scroll box within the vertical scroll bar and drag it up or down by left-clicking. When you drag the box, a little ToolTip pops up next to the slide bar to tell you which slide will be displayed if you release the button at that position.

Working with Objects

In the beginning, the User created a slide. And the slide was formless and void, without meaning or content. And the User said, "Let there be a Text Object." And there was a Text Object. And there was evening and there was morning, one day. Then the User said, "Let there be a Picture Object." And there was a Picture Object. And there was evening and there was morning, a second day. This continued for forty days and forty nights, until there were forty objects on the slide, each after its own kind. And the User was laughed out of the auditorium by the audience who could not read the slide.

I present this charming little parable solely to make the point that Power-Point slides are nothing without objects. *Objects* are items — such as text, pictures, and charts — that give meaning and content to otherwise formless and empty slides. When it comes to objects, however, sometimes less is more. Don't overdo it by cluttering your slides with so many objects that the main point of the slide is obscured.

Most of the objects on your slides are text objects, which let you type text on your slides. For more information about working with text objects, see Chapter 8.

Every slide has a slide layout that consists of one or more placeholders. A *placeholder* is simply an area on a slide that is reserved for text, clip art, a graph, or some other type of object. For example, a slide that uses the Title layout has two placeholders for text objects: one for the title and the other for the subtitle. You use the Slide Layout task pane to select the layout when you create new slides. You can change the layout later, and you can add more objects to the slide. You can also delete, move, or resize objects if you want. For more information about slide layouts, see Chapter 1.

You can add many different types of objects, such as clip art, charts, graphs, shapes, and so on. You can add additional objects to your slide with one of the tools that appears on the Drawing toolbar at the bottom of the screen or by using the icons that appear in the center of slides created using the Content layouts. For more information about adding additional objects to your slides, see Chapters 12 through 17.

Each object occupies a rectangular region on the slide. The contents of the object might or might not visually fill the rectangular region, but you can see the outline of the object when you select it (see the section "Selecting objects," later in this chapter).

Objects can overlap. Usually, you don't want them to, but sometimes doing so creates a jazzy effect. You may lay some text on top of some clip art, for example.

Selecting objects

Before you can edit anything on a slide, you have to select the object that contains whatever it is that you want to edit. For example, you can't start typing away to edit text on-screen. Instead, you must first select the text object that contains the text you want to edit. Likewise, you must select other types of objects before you can edit their contents.

Here are some guidelines to keep in mind when selecting objects:

> ✔ **Text objects:** To select a text object so that you can edit its text, move the insertion point over the text that you want to edit and then click. A rectangular box appears around the object, and a text insertion point appears so that you can start typing away.

✔ **Non-text objects:** Other types of objects work a little differently. Click an object, and the object is selected. The rectangular box appears around the object to let you know that you have hooked it. After you have hooked the object, you can drag it around the screen or change its size, but you can't edit it.

✔ **Click and drag:** Another way to select an object — or more than one object — is to use the insertion point to drag a rectangle around the objects that you want to select. Point to a location above and to the left of the object(s) that you want to select, and then click and drag the mouse down and to the right until the rectangle surrounds the objects. When you release the button, all the objects within the rectangle are selected.

✔ **The Tab key:** Also, you can press the Tab key to select objects. Press Tab once to select the first object on the slide. Press Tab again to select the next object. Keep pressing Tab until the object that you want is selected.

✔ **The Ctrl key:** You can select more than one object by selecting the first object and then holding down the Ctrl key while clicking to select additional objects.

Pressing Tab to select objects is handy when you can't easily point to the object that you want to select. This problem can happen if the object that you want is buried underneath another object or if the object is empty or otherwise invisible and you're not sure of its location.

Resizing or moving an object

When you select an object, an outline box appears around it. If you look closely at the box, you can see that it has love handles, one on each corner and one in the middle of each edge. You can use these love handles to adjust the size of an object. You can also grab the box between the love handles to move the object on the slide.

In addition, for many types of objects, a green dot called the *rotate handle* appears, floating above the object. You can rotate the object by grabbing this handle and dragging it around in a circle. (Not all types of objects can be rotated, however. For example, you can't rotate charts.)

To change the size of an object, click the object to select it and then grab one of the love handles by clicking. Hold down the mouse button and then move the mouse to change the object's size.

The various handles on an object give you different ways to change the object's size:

- The handles at the corners allow you to change both the height and width of the object.
- The handles on the top and bottom edges allow you to change just the object's height.
- The handles on the right and left edges change just the width of the object.

If you hold down the Ctrl key while you drag one of the love handles, the object stays centered at its current position on the slide. Try it to see what I mean. Also, try holding down the Shift key while you drag an object by using one of the corner love handles. This combination maintains the object's proportions when you resize it.

Changing a text object's size doesn't change the size of the text in the object; it changes only the size of the *frame* that contains the text. Changing the width of a text object is equivalent to changing margins in a word processor: It makes the text lines wider or narrower. To change the size of the text within a text object, you must change the font size. For more information, see Chapter 8.

To move an object, click anywhere in the outline box — except on a love handle — and then drag the object to its new locale.

The outline box can be hard to see if you have a fancy background on your slides. If you select an object and have trouble seeing the outline box, try squinting or cleaning your monitor screen. Or, in severe weather, try selecting the View tab on the Ribbon and then choosing one of the Color/Grayscale options:

- **Color:** Displays slides in full color
- **Grayscale:** Displays colors as shades of gray
- **Pure Black and White:** Shows the slides in black and white

Viewing the slide in Grayscale or Pure Black and White might make the love handles easier to spot. To switch back to full-color view, click Back to Color View.

Editing a Text Object

When you select a text object for editing, PowerPoint transforms into a baby word processor so you can edit the text. Note that PowerPoint automatically wraps text so that you don't have to press Enter at the end of every line. Press Enter only when you want to begin a new paragraph.

Text in a PowerPoint presentation is usually formatted with a *bullet character* at the beginning of each paragraph. The default bullet character depends on the theme you've applied to the slide. But if you don't like the bullet provided by the theme, you can change it to just about any shape that you can imagine. The point to remember here is that the bullet character is a part of the paragraph format, and not a character that you have to type in your text.

Most word-processing software enables you to switch between *Insert mode* and *Typeover mode* by pressing the Insert key on the right side of your keyboard. In Insert mode, any characters that you type are inserted at the insertion point (the blinking vertical line that appears within the text.) In Typeover mode, each character that you type replaces the character at the insertion point. However, PowerPoint always works in Insert mode, so any text that you type is inserted at the insertion point. Pressing Insert has no effect on the way text is typed.

You can move around within a text object by pressing the arrow keys or by using the mouse. You can also use the End and Home keys to take the insertion point to the start or end of the line that you're on. Additionally, you can use the arrow keys in combination with the Ctrl key to move around even faster. For example, press the Ctrl key and the left- or right-arrow key to move left or right an entire word at a time.

You delete text by pressing the Delete or Backspace key. To delete from the insertion point to the start or end of a word, use the Ctrl key along with the Delete or Backspace key. If you first select a block of text, the Delete and Backspace keys delete the entire selection. (The next section, "Selecting Text," has some tips for selecting text.)

Selecting Text

Some text-editing operations — such as amputations and transplants — require that you first select the text on which you want to operate. The following list shows you the methods for selecting blocks of text:

> ✔ **When you use the keyboard,** hold down the Shift key while you press any of the arrow keys to move the insertion point.

> ✔ **When you use the mouse,** point to the beginning of the text that you want to mark and then click and drag over the text. Release the mouse button when you reach the end of the text that you want to select.

PowerPoint has an automatic word-selection option that tries to guess when you intend to select an entire word. If you use the mouse to select a block of text that spans the space between two words, you notice that the selected text jumps to include entire words while you move the mouse. If you don't like this feature, you can disable it by clicking the PowerPoint Options button on the Office menu. Click the Advanced tab and then deselect the When Selecting, Automatically Select Entire Word check box.

You can use the following tricks to select different amounts of text:

> ✔ **A single word:** To select a single word, point the insertion point anywhere in the word and double-click.

> ✔ **An entire paragraph:** To select an entire paragraph, point the insertion point anywhere in the paragraph and triple-click.

After you have selected text, you can edit it in the following ways:

> ✔ **Delete text:** To delete the entire block of text that you've selected, press Delete or Backspace.

> ✔ **Replace text:** To replace an entire block of text, select it and then begin typing. The selected block vanishes and is replaced by the text that you're typing.

> ✔ **Cut, Copy, and Paste:** You can use the Cut, Copy, and Paste commands from the Clipboard group with selected text blocks. The following section describes these commands.

Using Cut, Copy, and Paste

Like any good Windows program, PowerPoint uses the standard Cut, Copy, and Paste commands. These commands work on text that you've selected, or if you've selected an entire object, the commands work on the object itself. In other words, you can use the Cut, Copy, and Paste commands with bits of text or with entire objects.

Cut, Copy, and Paste all work with one of the greatest mysteries of Windows — the *Clipboard.* The Clipboard is where Windows stashes stuff so that you can get to it later. The Cut and Copy commands add stuff to the Clipboard, and the Paste command copies stuff from the clipboard to your presentation.

The Ribbon buttons for working with the Clipboard are found in the Clipboard group of the Home tab. Three of the four buttons in this section are for working with the Clipboard:

 Cut

 Copy

 Paste

Notice that the Paste button includes a drop-down arrow. If you click the Clipboard icon, the object you most recently cut or copied is pasted. If you click the arrow, a menu with additional pasting options appears.

The keyboard shortcuts for Cut, Copy, and Paste are the same as they are for other Windows programs: Ctrl+X for Cut, Ctrl+C for Copy, and Ctrl+V for Paste. Because these three keyboard shortcuts work in virtually all Windows programs, memorizing them pays off.

You can use the Copy and Paste commands together to duplicate information. If you want to repeat an entire sentence, for example, copy the sentence to the Clipboard, place the insertion point where you want the sentence duplicated, and then use the Paste command. Or if you want to create a slide that has five identical rectangles on it, start by drawing one rectangle. Then copy the rectangle to the Clipboard and paste it to the slide four times. You end up with five rectangles — the original one you drew, plus the four copies that you pasted.

PowerPoint has a Duplicate command you can use to quickly create copies of objects. First, select the object you want to duplicate. Then, press Ctrl+D to create a duplicate of the object. You'll probably need to move the duplicate object to its correct location.

An even easier way to duplicate an object is to hold down the Ctrl key, click, and then drag the object to a new location on the slide. After you release the mouse button, a duplicate copy of the object is created.

If you want to blow away an entire object permanently, select it and then press Delete or Backspace. This step removes the object from the slide but doesn't copy it to the Clipboard. It's gone forever. Well, sort of — you can still get it back by using the Undo command, but only if you act fast. See the section, "Oops! I Didn't Mean It (The Marvelous Undo Command)" for more information.

To include the same object on each of your slides, you can use a better method than copying and pasting: Add the object to the *Slide Master,* which governs the format of all the slides in a presentation (see Chapter 11).

Using the Clipboard Task Pane

The Clipboard task pane lets you gather up to 24 items of text or graphics from any Office program and then selectively paste them into your presentation. To summon the Clipboard task pane, click the Dialog Box Launcher in the Home tab on the Ribbon at the bottom right of the Clipboard group. Then, the Clipboard task pane appears, as shown in Figure 2-1. Here, you can see the Clipboard task pane at the left side of the PowerPoint window, with several objects held in the clipboard.

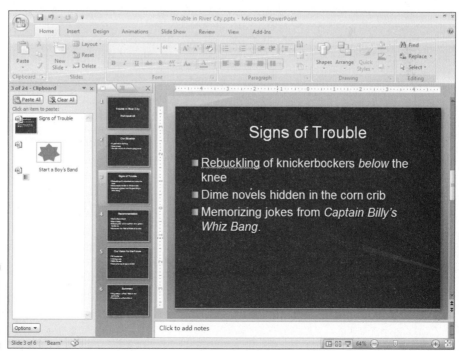

Figure 2-1:
The Clipboard task pane.

To paste an item from the Clipboard task pane, simply click the item you want to insert.

Oops! I Didn't Mean It (The Marvelous Undo Command)

Made a mistake? Don't panic. Use the Undo command. Undo is your safety net. If you mess up, Undo can save the day.

You have two ways to undo a mistake:

✔ Click the Undo button in the Quick Access toolbar.

✔ Press Ctrl+Z.

Undo reverses whatever you did last. If you deleted text, Undo adds it back. If you typed text, Undo deletes it. If you moved an object, Undo puts it back where it was. You get the idea.

Undo is such a useful command that committing the Ctrl+Z keyboard short-cut to memory is a good idea. If you want, think of the word *Zip!* to help you remember how to zip away your mistakes.

Undo remembers up to 20 of your most recent actions. You can undo each action one at a time by repeatedly using the Undo command. Or you can click the down arrow next to the Undo button on the Quick Access Toolbar and then choose the actions you want to undo from the list that appears. However, as a general rule, you should correct your mistakes as soon as possible. If you make a mistake, feel free to curse, kick something, or fall on the floor in a screaming tantrum if you must, *but don't do anything else on your computer!* If you use the Undo command immediately, you can reverse your mistake and get on with your life.

PowerPoint also offers a Redo command, which is sort of like an Undo for Undo. In other words, if you undo what you thought was a mistake by using the Undo command and then decide that it wasn't a mistake after all, you can use the Redo command. Here are two ways to use the Redo command:

✔ Click the Redo button on the Quick Access toolbar.

✔ Press Ctrl+Y.

Note that if the last action you performed wasn't an Undo command, the Redo button is replaced by a Repeat button. You can click the Repeat button to repeat the last command.

Deleting a Slide

Want to delete an entire slide? No problem. Simply move to the slide that you want to delete and click the Delete button in the Slides group of the Home tab on the Ribbon. Zowie! The slide is history.

Another way to delete a slide is to click the miniature of the slide in the Slide Preview pane (on the left side of the screen) and then press the Delete key or the Backspace key.

Deleted the wrong slide, eh? No problem. Just press Ctrl+Z or click the Undo button to restore the slide.

Duplicating a Slide

PowerPoint sports a Duplicate Slide command that lets you duplicate an entire slide; text, formatting, and everything else included. That way, after you toil over a slide for hours to get its formatting just right, you can create a duplicate to use as the basis for another slide.

To duplicate a slide — or slides — select the slide(s) you want to duplicate. Then open the Home tab on the Ribbon, click the arrow at the bottom of the Add Slide button in the Slides group, and choose the Duplicate Selected Slides button. A duplicate of the slide is inserted into your presentation.

If you're a keyboard shortcut fanatic, all you have to do is select the slide that you want to duplicate in the Slides pane (located on the left side of the screen) and then press Ctrl+D.

Finding Text

You know that buried somewhere in that 60-slide presentation is a slide that lists the options available on the Vertical Snarfblat, but where is it? This sounds like a job for the PowerPoint Find command!

The Find command can find text buried in any text object on any slide. These steps show you the procedure for using the Find command:

1. **Think of what you want to find.**

   Snarfblat will suffice for this example.

Find

2. **Click the Find button in the Editing group of the Home tab (as shown in the margin). Or use the keyboard shortcut Ctrl+F.**

   The Find dialog box appears, as shown in Figure 2-2, which contains the secrets of the Find command.

Figure 2-2: The Find dialog box.

3. **Type the text that you want to find.**

   It displays in the Find What box.

4. **Press Enter.**

   Or click the Find Next button. Either way, the search begins.

If the text that you type is located anywhere in the presentation, the Find command zips you to the slide that contains the text and highlights the text. You can then edit the text object or search for the next occurrence of the text within your presentation. If you edit the text, the Find dialog box stays on-screen to make it easy to continue your quest.

Here are some facts to keep in mind when using the Find command:

✔ **Find the next occurrence:** To find the next occurrence of the same text, press Enter or click the Find Next button again.

✔ **Edit the text:** To edit the text you found, click the text object. The Find dialog box remains on-screen. To continue searching, click the Find Next button again.

✔ **Start anywhere:** You don't have to be at the beginning of your presentation to search the entire presentation. When PowerPoint reaches the end of the presentation, it automatically picks up the search at the beginning and continues back to the point at which you started the search.

✔ **Give up:** You might receive the following message:

```
PowerPoint has finished searching the presentation.
        The search item wasn't found.
```

This message means that PowerPoint has given up. The text that you're looking for just isn't anywhere in the presentation. Maybe you spelled it wrong, or maybe you didn't have a slide about Snarfblats after all.

✔ **Match case:** If the right mix of uppercase and lowercase letters is important to you, select the Match Case check box before beginning the search. This option is handy when you have, for example, a presentation about Mr. Smith the Blacksmith.

✔ **Find whole words:** Use the Find Whole Words Only check box to find your text only when it appears as a whole word. If you want to find the slide on which you discuss Smitty the Blacksmith's mitt, for example, type **mitt** for the Find What text and select the Find Whole Words Only check box. That way, the Find command looks for *mitt* as a separate word. It doesn't stop to show you the *mitt* in *Smitty*.

✔ **Replace text:** If you find the text that you're looking for and decide that you want to replace it with something else, click the Replace button. This step changes the Find dialog box to the Replace dialog box, which is explained in the following section.

✔ **Close the Find dialog box:** To make the Find dialog box go away, click the Close button or press Esc.

Replacing Text

Suppose that the Rent-a-Nerd company decides to switch to athletic consulting, so it wants to change the name of its company to Rent-a-Jock. Easy. Just use the handy Replace command to change all occurrences of the word *Nerd* to *Jock*. The following steps show you how:

1. **Click the Replace button (found in the Editing group on the Home tab on the Ribbon) or use the keyboard shortcut Ctrl+H.**

   The Replace dialog box, as shown in Figure 2-3, appears.

Figure 2-3:
The Replace
dialog box.

2. **In the Find What box, type the text that you want to find.**

   Enter the text that you want to replace with something else (**Nerd**, in this example).

3. **Type the replacement text in the Replace With box.**

   Enter the text you want to use to replace the text that you typed in the Find What box (**Jock**, in this example).

4. **Click the Find Next button.**

   PowerPoint finds the first occurrence of the text.

5. **Click the Replace button to replace the text.**

   Read the text first to make sure that it found what you're looking for.

6. **Repeat the Find Next and Replace sequence until you're finished.**

   Click Find Next to find the next occurrence, click Replace to replace it, and so on. Keep going until you finish.

If you're absolutely positive that you want to replace all occurrences of your Find What text with the Replace With text, click the Replace All button. This step dispenses with the Find Next and Replace cycle. The only problem is that you're bound to find at least one spot where you didn't want the replacement to occur. Replacing the word *mitt* with *glove,* for example, results in *Sglovey* rather than *Smitty.* Don't forget that you can also use the Find Whole Words Only option to find and replace text only if it appears as an entire word.

If you totally mess up your presentation by clicking Replace All, you can use the Undo command to restore sanity to your presentation.

Rearranging Your Slides in Slide Sorter View

Normal View is the view that you normally work in to edit your slides, move things around, add text or graphics, and so on. However, Normal View has one serious limitation: It doesn't give you a big picture of your presentation. You can see the details of only one slide at a time, and the Slide Preview pane lets you see snapshots of only a few slides. To see an overall view of your presentation, you need to work in Slide Sorter View.

You can switch to Slide Sorter View in two easy ways:

- ✔ Click the Slide Sorter button at the right side of the status bar.
- ✔ Select the View tab on the Ribbon and then click the Slide Sorter button in the Presentation Views group.

The PowerPoint Slide Sorter View is shown in Figure 2-4.

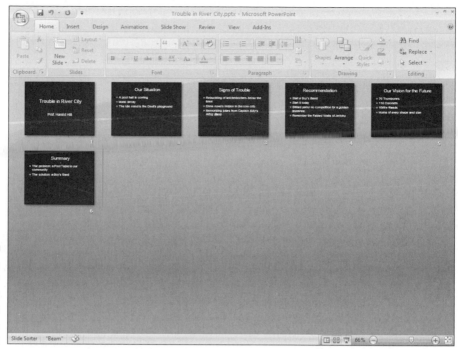

Figure 2-4:
Slide Sorter
View lets
you see the
big picture.

The following list tells you how to rearrange, add, or delete slides from Slide Sorter View:

- **Move a slide:** To move a slide, click and drag it to a new location. Point to the slide and then hold down the left mouse button. Drag the slide to its new location and release the button. PowerPoint adjusts the display to show the new arrangement of slides.

- **Delete a slide:** To delete a slide, click the slide to select it and then press Delete or Backspace. This works only in Slide Sorter View.

- **Add a new slide:** To add a new slide, click the slide that you want the new slide to follow and then click the New Slide button. The Slide Layout task pane appears so that you can select the layout for the new slide. To edit the contents of the slide, return to Slide or Outline View via the view buttons (located at the right side of the status bar) or the View tab on the Ribbon.

If your presentation contains more slides than can fit on-screen at one time, you can use the scroll bars to scroll through the display. Or you can use the zoom slider at the bottom right corner of the screen to make the slides smaller.

Slide Sorter View might seem kind of dull and boring, but it's also the place where you can add jazzy transitions, build effects, or add cool animation effects to your slides. For example, you can make your bullets fall from the top of the screen like bombs and switch from slide to slide by using strips, wipes, or blinds. Chapter 10 describes all this cool stuff.

Chapter 3

Working in Outline View

In This Chapter

▶ Understanding the outline

▶ Focusing on substance instead of form

▶ Promoting, demoting, and the lateral arabesque

▶ Adding a slide in the Outline tab

▶ Collapsing and expanding the outline

*M*ost presentations consist of slide after slide of bulleted lists. You might see a chart here or there and an occasional bit of clip art thrown in for comic effect, but the bread and butter of presentations is the bulleted list. It sounds boring, but it's often the best way to make sure that your message gets through.

For this reason, presentations lend themselves especially well to outlining. Good presentations are light on prose but heavy in the point and subpoint department — and that's precisely where outlines excel. The Outline tab that appears to the left of your slides in Normal View lets you focus on your presentation's main points and subpoints. In other words, it enables you to focus on content without worrying about appearance.

Calling Up the Outline

At the left side of the PowerPoint window is a pair of tabs — Slides and Outline. Normally, the Slides tab is active, showing you thumbnail images of your slides. To work with the presentation in Outline mode, click the Outline tab. Then, your presentation appears as an outline, with the title of each slide as a separate heading at the highest level of the outline, and the text on each slide appears as lower-level headings subordinate to the slide headings. See Figure 3-1. (Note that if a slide doesn't have a title, the slide will still appear in the outline, but the top-level heading for the slide will be blank.)

Figure 3-1:
Viewing the
outline.

You can expand the area devoted to the outline by clicking and dragging the border of the Outline pane.

The following list highlights a few important things to notice about the outline:

- **The outline is comprised of the titles and body text of each slide.** Any other objects that you add to a slide — such as pictures, charts, and so on — are not included in the outline. Also, if you add any text objects to the slide in addition to the basic title and body text objects that are included automatically when you create a new slide, the additional text objects are not included in the outline.

- **Each slide is represented by a high-level heading in the outline.** The text of this heading is taken from the slide's title, and an icon that represents the entire slide appears next to the heading. Also, the slide number appears to the left of the Slide icon.

- **Each text line from a slide's body text appears as an indented heading.** This heading is subordinate to the slide's main title heading.

- **An outline can contain subpoints that are subordinate to the main points on each slide.** PowerPoint enables you to create as many as five heading levels on each slide, but your slides will probably get too complicated if you go beyond two headings. You can find more about working with heading levels in the section "Promoting and Demoting Paragraphs," later in this chapter.

Selecting and Editing an Entire Slide

When you work with the Outline tab, you often have to select an entire slide. You can do that by clicking the icon for the slide. This selects the slide title and all its body text. In addition, any extra objects, such as graphics, that are on the slide are also selected even though those objects don't appear in the outline.

You can delete, cut, copy, or duplicate an entire slide:

- **Delete:** To delete an entire slide, select it and then press Delete.
- **Cut or copy:** To cut or copy an entire slide to the Clipboard, select the slide and then press Ctrl+X (Cut) or Ctrl+C (Copy), or use the Cut or Copy buttons on the Home tab on the Ribbon. You can then move the cursor to any location in the outline and press Ctrl+V or use the Paste button to paste the slide from the Clipboard. (You can also cut or copy a slide by right-clicking the slide and choosing Cut or Copy from the menu that appears.)
- **Duplicate:** To duplicate a slide, select it and then press Ctrl+D. This step places a copy of the selected slide immediately after it. (Actually, you don't have to select the entire slide to duplicate it. Just click anywhere in the slide's title or body text.)

Selecting and Editing One Paragraph

You can select and edit an entire paragraph along with all its subordinate paragraphs. To do so, just click the bullet next to the paragraph that you want to select. To delete an entire paragraph along with its subordinate paragraphs, select it and then press Delete.

To cut or copy an entire paragraph to the Clipboard along with its subordinates, select it and then press Ctrl+X (Cut) or Ctrl+C (Copy). You can then press Ctrl+V to paste the paragraph anywhere in the presentation.

Promoting and Demoting Paragraphs

To *promote* a paragraph is to move it up one level in the outline. If you promote the "Memorizes jokes from *Captain Billy's Whiz Bang*" paragraph in Figure 3-1, for example, that paragraph becomes a separate slide rather than a bullet paragraph under "Signs of Trouble."

To promote a paragraph, place the cursor anywhere in the paragraph and then press Shift+Tab or click the Decrease List Level button in the Paragraph group.

To *demote* a paragraph is just the opposite: The paragraph moves down one level in the outline. If you demote the "Dime novel hidden in the corn crib" paragraph in Figure 3-1, it becomes a subpoint under "Rebuckles knicker-bockers *below* the knee" rather than a separate main point.

To demote a paragraph, place the cursor anywhere in the paragraph and then either press the Tab key or click the Increase List Level button in the Paragraph group. Note that you can't promote a slide title. Slide title is the highest rank in the outline hierarchy. If you demote a slide title, the entire slide is *subsumed* into the preceding slide. In other words, the slide title becomes a main point in the preceding slide.

You can promote or demote paragraphs by using the mouse, but the technique is a little tricky. When you move the cursor over a bullet (or the Slide button), the pointer changes from a single arrow to a four-cornered arrow. This arrow is your signal that you can click to select the entire paragraph (and any subordinate paragraphs). Then, you can use the mouse to promote or demote a paragraph along with all its subordinates by dragging the selected paragraph left or right.

Be sensitive when you demote paragraphs. Being demoted can be an emotionally devastating experience.

Adding a New Paragraph

To add a new paragraph to a slide with the outline that appears on the Outline tab, move the insertion point to the end of the paragraph that you want the new paragraph to follow and then press Enter. PowerPoint creates a new paragraph at the same outline level as the preceding paragraph

Note that if you move the insertion point to the end of the title line and press Enter, PowerPoint creates a new slide. However, you can then press the Tab key to change the new slide to a paragraph on the previous slide.

If you position the insertion point at the beginning of a paragraph and press Enter, the new paragraph is inserted above the cursor position. If you position the cursor in the middle of a paragraph and press Enter, the paragraph is split in two.

After you add a new paragraph, you might want to change its level in the outline. To do that, you must promote or demote the new paragraph. To create a subpoint for a main point, for example, position the cursor at the end of the main point and press Enter. Then, demote the new paragraph by pressing the Tab key.

Adding a New Slide

You can add a new slide in many ways when you're working with the outline. This list shows the most popular methods:

- **Promote existing text:** Promote an existing paragraph to the highest level. This method splits a slide into two slides.

- **Promote new text:** Add a new paragraph and then promote it to the highest level.

- **Press Enter:** Place the cursor in a slide's title text and press Enter. This method creates a new slide before the current slide. Whether the title text stays with the current slide, goes with the new slide, or is split between the slides depends on the location of the cursor within the title when you press Enter.

- **Press Ctrl+Enter:** Place the cursor anywhere in a slide's body text and press Ctrl+Enter. This method creates a new slide immediately following the current slide. The position of the cursor within the existing slide doesn't matter; the new slide is always created after the current slide. (The cursor must be in the slide's body text, however, in order for this method to work. If you put the cursor in a slide title and press Ctrl+Enter, the cursor jumps to the slide's body text without creating a new slide.)

- **Insert a new slide:** Place the cursor anywhere in the slide and use the keyboard shortcut Ctrl+M or click the Add Slide button in the Slides group of the Home Ribbon tab.

- **Duplicate an existing slide:** Select an existing slide by clicking the slide's icon or triple-clicking the title and then press Ctrl+D to duplicate it.

Because the outline focuses on slide content rather than on layout, new slides receive the basic Bulleted List layout, which includes title text and body text formatted with bullets.

Moving Text Up and Down

The outline is a handy way to rearrange your presentation. You can easily change the order of individual points on a slide, or you can rearrange the order of the slides.

You can rearrange your presentation by right-clicking the paragraphs that you want to move and then clicking the Move Up or Move Down buttons in the menu that appears. Or you can point to the bullet next to the paragraph that you want to move. Then, when the cursor changes to the four-cornered arrow, click and drag the paragraph up or down. A horizontal line appears, showing the horizontal position of the selection. Release the mouse button when the horizontal line is positioned where you want the text.

Be careful when you're moving text in a slide that has more than one level of body text paragraphs. Notice the position of the horizontal line when you drag the selection; the entire selection is inserted at that location, which might split up subpoints. If you don't like the result of a move, you can always undo it by pressing Ctrl+Z or clicking the Undo button.

Collapsing and Expanding the Outline

If your presentation has many slides, you might find that grasping its overall structure is difficult, even when looking at the outline. Fortunately, PowerPoint enables you to *collapse* the outline so that only the slide titles are shown. Collapsing an outline doesn't delete the body text; it merely hides the body text so that you can focus on the order of the slides in your presentation.

Expanding a presentation restores the collapsed body text to the outline so that you can once again focus on details. You can collapse and expand an entire presentation, or you can collapse and expand one slide at a time.

To collapse the entire presentation, right-click anywhere in the outline and then choose Collapse⇨Collapse All or use the keyboard shortcut Alt+Shift+1. To expand the presentation, right-click and choose Expand⇨Expand All or press Alt+Shift+9.

To collapse a single slide, right-click anywhere in the slide and then choose Collapse⇨Collapse from the menu that appears. To expand a single slide, right-click the collapsed slide and choose Expand⇨Expand.

Chapter 4

Proofing Your Presentations

I was voted Worst Speller in the sixth grade. Not that being Worst Speller qualifies me to run for president or anything, but it shows how much I appreciate computer spell checkers. Spelling makes no sense to me. I felt a little better after watching *The Story of English* on public television. Now at least I know whom to blame for all the peculiarities of English spelling — the Anglos, the Norms (including the guy from *Cheers*), and the Saxophones.

Fortunately, PowerPoint 2007 has a pretty decent spell checker. In fact, the spell checker in PowerPoint is so smart that it knows that you've made a spelling mistake almost before you make it. The spell checker watches over your shoulder as you type and helps you to correct your spelling errors as you work.

Checking Spelling As You Go

Spelling errors in a word-processing document are bad, but at least they're small. In a PowerPoint presentation, spelling errors are small only until you use a projector to throw your presentation onto a 30-foot screen. Then they get all blown out of proportion. Nothing is more embarrassing than a 3-foot-tall spelling error. And if you're like me, you probably try to look for mistakes in other people's presentations just for kicks. Thank goodness for Power-Point's on-the-fly spell checker.

The PowerPoint spell checker doesn't make you wait until you finish your presentation and run a special command to point out your spelling errors. It boldly points out your mistakes right when you make them by underlining any mistake with a wavy red line, as shown in Figure 4-1.

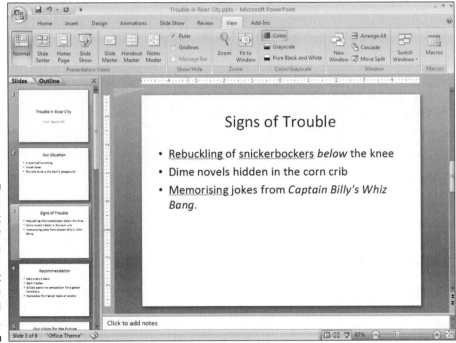

Figure 4-1: PowerPoint usually knows before you do that you've misspelled a word.

In Figure 4-1, three words have been marked as misspelled: *Rebuckling, snickerbockers* (isn't that a kind of cookie?), and *Memorising.* When you see the telltale wavy red line, you have several options:

✔ **Make the correction:** You can retype the word using the correct spelling.

✔ **Let PowerPoint help:** You can right-click the word to call up a menu that lists suggested spellings for the word. In most cases, PowerPoint can figure out what you meant to type and suggests the correct spelling. To replace the misspelled word with the correct spelling, just click the correctly spelled word in the menu.

✔ **Ignore the misspelling:** Sometimes, you want to misspell a word on purpose (for example, if you run a restaurant named "The Koffee Kup"). More likely, the word is correctly spelled, but PowerPoint just doesn't know about the word.

The spell checker can't tell you when you've used the wrong word but spelled it correctly. For example, the second bullet point in Figure 4-1 mentions *dime navels* instead of *dime novels.* Cheap literature might be a bad thing, but cheap citrus certainly is not.

Spell Checking After-the-Fact

If you prefer to ignore the constant nagging by PowerPoint about your spelling, you can always check your spelling the old-fashioned way: by running the spell checker after you finish your document. The spell checker works its way through your entire presentation, looking up every word in its massive list of correctly spelled words and bringing any misspelled words to your attention. It performs this task without giggling or snickering. As an added bonus, the spell checker even gives you the opportunity to tell it that you're right and it's wrong and that it should discern how to spell words the way you do.

The following steps show you how to check the spelling for an entire presentation:

1. **If the presentation that you want to spell check is not already open, open it.**

2. **Open the Review tab on the Ribbon and then click the Spelling button found in the Proofing group (shown in the margin).**

3. **Tap your fingers on your desk.**

   PowerPoint is searching your presentation for embarrassing spelling errors. Be patient.

4. **Don't be startled if PowerPoint finds a spelling error.**

   If PowerPoint finds a spelling error in your presentation, it switches to the slide that contains the error, highlights the offensive word, and displays the misspelled word along with a suggested correction, as shown in Figure 4-2.

5. **Choose the correct spelling and click the Change button. Alternatively, click Ignore and laugh in PowerPoint's face.**

   If you agree that the word is misspelled, scan the list of corrections that PowerPoint offers and select the one that you like. Then click the Change button.

   If you like the way that you spelled the word in the first place (maybe it's an unusual word that isn't in the PowerPoint spelling dictionary, or maybe you like to spell the way Chaucer did), click the Ignore button. Watch as PowerPoint turns red in the face.

Figure 4-2:
The Power-
Point spell
checker
points out a
boo-boo.

If you want PowerPoint to ignore all occurrences of a particular mis-spelling, click the Ignore All button. Likewise, if you want PowerPoint to correct all occurrences of a particular misspelling, click the Change All button.

6. Repeat Steps 4 and 5 until PowerPoint gives up.

When you see the following message, you're finished:

```
The spelling check is complete
```

PowerPoint always checks spelling in the entire presentation, beginning with the first slide — unless you specify a single word or group of words by high-lighting them first. PowerPoint checks the spelling of titles, body text, notes, and text objects added to slides. It doesn't check the spelling in embedded objects, however, such as charts or graphs.

If PowerPoint can't come up with a suggestion or if none of its suggestions are correct, you can type your own correction and click the Change button. If the word that you type isn't in the dictionary, PowerPoint asks whether you're sure that you know what you're doing. Double-check and click OK if you really mean it.

If you get tired of PowerPoint always complaining about a word that's not in its standard dictionary, click Add to add the word to the custom dictionary. If you can't sleep at night until you know more about the custom dictionary, read the following sidebar titled "Don't make me tell you about the custom dictionary."

The speller can't tell the difference between *your* and *you're, ours* and *hours, angel* and *angle,* and so on. In other words, if the word is in the dictionary, PowerPoint passes it by regardless of whether you used the word correctly. Consequently, PowerPoint spell checker is no substitute for good, old-fashioned proofreading. Print your presentation, sit down with a cup of cappuccino, and *read* it.

Don't make me tell you about the custom dictionary

The PowerPoint spell checker can use more than one spelling dictionary. Besides the standard dictionary, which contains untold thousands of words that were all reviewed for correctness by Noah Webster himself (just kidding), you can have one or more custom dictionaries, which contains words that you have added by clicking the Add button when the spell checker found a spelling error.

Custom dictionaries are shared by other Microsoft programs that use spell checkers — most notably Microsoft Word. So if you add a word to a custom dictionary in Word, the PowerPoint spell checker knows about the word, too.

What if you accidentally add a word to the dictionary? Then you have a serious problem. You have two alternatives. You can petition Noah Webster to have your variant spelling officially added to the English language, or you can edit the `Custom.dic` file, search through the file until you find the bogus word, and then delete it. The easiest way to edit the `Custom.dic` file is to choose PowerPoint Options from the Office button, click Proofing, and then click the Custom Dictionaries button. You can then select the `Custom.dic` file and click Edit Word List to edit its contents.

Using the Thesaurus

PowerPoint includes a built-in thesaurus that can quickly show you synonyms for a word that you've typed. Using it is easy:

1. **Right-click a word that you've typed and choose Synonyms from the menu that appears.**

   A menu listing synonyms for the word appears. (Sometimes PowerPoint throws an antonym into the list just to be contrary.)

2. **Select the word that you want to use to replace your word.**

   PowerPoint replaces the original word with your selection.

If you choose Thesaurus from the Synonyms menu, the Thesaurus section of the Research task pane appears with the synonyms listed, as shown in Figure 4-3. The Thesaurus lets you look up words to find even more synonyms. For example, if you select *shocking* from the list of synonyms, you get another set of words. You can keep clicking words to find other synonyms as long as you'd like, until you're ready to get back to real work.

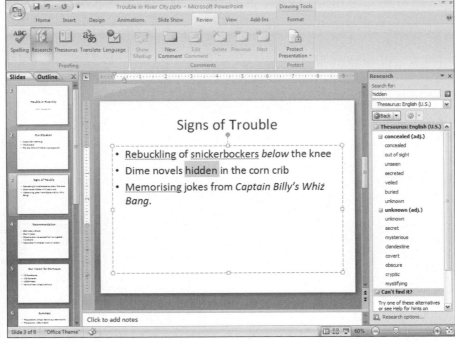

Capitalizing Correctly

The PowerPoint Change Case command enables you to capitalize the text in your slides properly. These steps show you how to use it:

1. **Select the text that you want to capitalize.**

2. **Choose the Home tab on the Ribbon and then click Change Case button in the Font section (shown in the margin).**

   This reveals a menu of Change Case choices.

3. **Study the options for a moment and then click the one that you want.**

   Here are the case options:

   - **Sentence case:** The first letter of the first word in each sentence is capitalized. Everything else is changed to lowercase.

   - **lowercase:** Everything is changed to lowercase.

   - **UPPERCASE:** Everything is changed to capital letters.

- **Capitalize Each Word:** The first letter of each word is capitalized.

- **tOGGLE cASE:** This option turns capitals into lowercase and turns lowercase into capitals, for a ransom-note look.

4. **Check the results.**

Always double-check your text after using the Change Case command to make sure that the result is what you intended. This is especially true when you select Capitalize Each Word. In most cases, you should *not capitalize* articles (like *a* and *the*) and prepositions (like *of* and *from*). The Capitalize Each Word option capitalizes every word in the title, so you'll have to manually change articles and prepositions back to lowercase.

Slide titles should almost always use title case. The first level of bullets on a slide can use title or sentence case. Lower levels usually should use sentence case.

Avoid uppercase if you can. It's hard to read and LOOKS LIKE YOU'RE SHOUTING.

Using the AutoCorrect Feature

PowerPoint includes an AutoCorrect feature that can automatically correct spelling errors and style errors as you type them. For example, if you accidentally type `teh`, PowerPoint automatically changes your text to `the`. And if you forget to capitalize the first word of a sentence, PowerPoint automatically capitalizes it for you.

Any time PowerPoint makes a correction that you don't like, just press Ctrl+Z to undo the correction. For example, if you really intended to type `teh`, press Ctrl+Z immediately after PowerPoint corrects it to `the`.

If you move the insertion pointer back to a word that has been corrected (or if you click the word), a small blue line appears beneath the first letter of the word. Point the mouse at this blue line, and the button with a lightning bolt in it appears. You can then click this button to bring up a menu that enables you to undo the correction that was made, tell PowerPoint to stop making that type of correction, or summon the AutoCorrect options dialog box to adjust your AutoCorrect settings.

To control PowerPoint's AutoCorrect feature, click the Office button and then choose PowerPoint options. This summons the PowerPoint Options dialog box. Next, choose the Proofing tab on the left side of the PowerPoint Options dialog box, and then click the AutoCorrect Options button to display the dialog box shown in Figure 4-4.

As you can see, the AutoCorrect Options dialog box contains check boxes for a variety of options that govern how AutoCorrect works:

- **Show AutoCorrect Options buttons:** This option displays the Auto-Correct button beneath words that were changed by the AutoCorrect feature, which allows you to undo the change or tell PowerPoint to stop making that particular type of correction.

- **Correct TWo INitial CApitals:** Looks for words with two initial capitals and changes the second one to lowercase. For example, if you type BOther, PowerPoint changes it to Bother. However, if you type three or more capitals in a row, PowerPoint assumes that you did it on purpose, so no correction is made.

- **Capitalize first letter of sentences:** Automatically capitalizes the first word of a new sentence if you forget.

- **Capitalize first letter of table cells:** Automatically capitalizes the first word in table cells.

- **Capitalize names of days:** You know, Monday, Tuesday, Wednesday, and so forth.

- **Correct accidental use of the cAPS LOCK key:** This is an especially cool feature. If PowerPoint notices that you're capitalizing everything backwards, it assumes that you accidentally pressed the Caps Lock key. So it turns off Caps Lock and corrects the words that you capitalized backwards.

✔ **Replace text as you type:** This option is the heart of the AutoCorrect feature. It consists of a list of words that are frequently typed wrong, along with the replacement word. For example, `teh` is replaced by `the` and `adn` is replaced by `and`. The AutoCorrect list also contains some shortcuts for special symbols. For example, `(c)` is replaced by the copyright symbol (©) and `(tm)` is replaced by the trademark symbol (™).

You can add your own words to this list. In the Replace text box, type the word that you want PowerPoint to watch for. In the With text box, type the word that you want PowerPoint to substitute for the first word. Then click Add.

The AutoCorrect feature also includes several formatting options that can automatically apply formats as you type. To set these options, click the AutoFormat As You Type tab. The options shown in Figure 4-5 appear. These options let you control formatting features, such as automatically converting straight quotes to curly quotes, changing fractions such as 1/2 to fraction symbols such as ½, and so on.

Figure 4-5:
The
AutoFormat
As You Type
options.

Chapter 5

Don't Forget Your Notes!

In This Chapter

▶ Creating speaker notes to get you through your presentation

▶ Adjusting the notes page to make long notes fit

▶ Adding a new slide from Notes Pages View

▶ Printing your notes pages

*E*ver had the fear — or maybe the actual experience — of showing a beautiful slide, complete with snappy text and perhaps an exquisite chart, and suddenly forgetting why you included the slide in the first place? You stumble for words. "Well, as you can see, this is a beautiful chart, and, uh, this slide makes the irrefutable point that, uh, well, I'm not sure — are there any questions?"

Fear not! One of the slickest features in PowerPoint 2007 is its ability to create speaker notes to help you get through your presentation. You can make these notes as complete or as sketchy as you want or need. You can write a complete script for your presentation or just jot down a few key points to refresh your memory.

The best part about speaker notes is that you're the only one who sees them. They don't actually show up on your slides for all the world to see. Instead, notes pages are printed separately. One notes page is allocated for each slide in the presentation, and each notes page includes a reduced version of the slide so that you can keep track of which notes page belongs to which slide.

One great feature of PowerPoint is that, assuming your computer has the hardware to pull it off, you can display your slides on a computer projector and your notes on a separate monitor so only you can see them. For more information about this feature, see the section "Displaying Notes on a Separate Monitor," later in this chapter.

Don't you think that it's about time for a short chapter? Although notes pages are one of the slickest features in PowerPoint, creating notes pages isn't all that complicated — hence the brevity of this chapter.

Understanding Notes

Notes are like an adjunct attachment to your slides. They don't appear on the slides themselves but are displayed separately. Each slide in your presentation has its own page of notes.

Notes are usually hidden at the bottom of the screen in a tiny Notes pane that's just large enough to display a line or two of text. To work with notes, you must first enlarge the Notes pane to give yourself some room to work. For more information, see the section "Adding Notes to a Slide," later in this chapter.

PowerPoint also has a separate view designed for working with notes pages, called (you guessed it) Notes Page View. To call up Notes Page View, choose the View tab on the Ribbon and then click the Notes Page button found in the Presentation Views group. Each notes page consists of a reduced version of the slide and an area for notes, as shown in Figure 5-1.

Of course, these notes are too small to see or work with in Notes Page View unless you increase the zoom setting. If you want to work in Notes Page View, you'll need to zoom in so you can see your work.

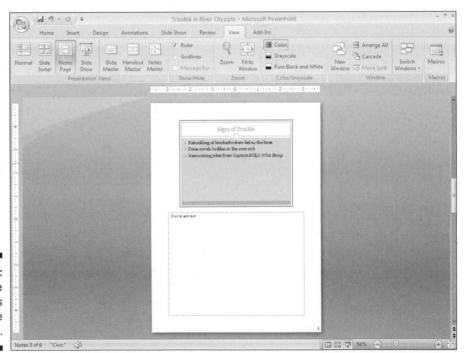

Figure 5-1:
Notes Page
View lets
you see
your notes.

Unfortunately, no keyboard shortcut is available to switch directly to Notes Page View. Earlier versions of PowerPoint included a button for this alongside the other view buttons in the lower-left corner of the screen. But for some mysterious reason, Microsoft decided to omit this button in recent versions of PowerPoint. So the only way to get to Notes Page View now is to use the Ribbon's Notes Page button.

Adding Notes to a Slide

To add notes to a slide, follow this procedure:

1. **In Normal View, move to the slide to which you want to add notes.**

2. **Click and drag the Notes pane border, if necessary, to bring the notes text into view.**

3. **Click the notes text object, where it reads** `Click to add notes`**.**

4. **Type away.**

The text that you type appears in the notes area. As you create your notes, you can use any of the PowerPoint standard word-processing features, such as Cut, Copy, and Paste. Press Enter to create new paragraphs.

Figure 5-2 shows a slide with the Notes pane enlarged to a comfortable size and some notes typed.

Adding an Extra Notes Page for a Slide

PowerPoint doesn't provide a way to add more than one page of notes for each slide. However, these steps show you a trick that accomplishes essentially the same thing:

1. **Create a duplicate slide immediately following the slide that requires two pages of notes.**

   To duplicate the slide, move to the slide that you want to duplicate in Normal View and press Ctrl+D to duplicate the slide.

2. **Click the Notes Page button in the Presentation Views group of the View tab.**

   The notes page for the new duplicate slide appears.

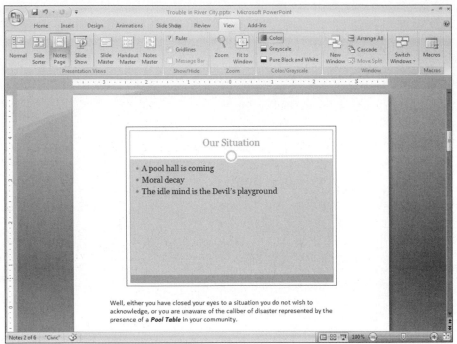

Figure 5-2:
A slide
with notes.

3. **Delete the slide object at the top of the duplicate notes page.**

   To do so, click the slide object at the top of the page and press Delete.

4. **Extend the notes text area up so that it fills the page.**

   To extend the notes area, just drag the top-center love handle of the notes text area up.

5. **Type the additional notes for the preceding slide on this new notes page.**

   Add a heading, such as "Continued from slide 23," at the top of the text to help you remember that this portion is a continuation of notes from the preceding slide.

6. **Return to Normal View.**

   Click the Normal button in the Presentation Views group of the View tab.

7. **Open the Slide Show tab on the Ribbon and then click the Hide Slide button in the Set Up group.**

   The Hide Slide button hides the slide, which means that it isn't included in an on-screen slide show.

Random thoughts about notes

Here are some random ideas that might help you make the most of your notes pages.

✔ If you're giving an important presentation for a large audience, consider using notes pages to write a complete script for your presentation. For less formal presentations, more succinct notes are probably better.

✔ Use notes pages to jot down any anecdotes, jokes, or other asides that you want to remember to use in your presentation.

✔ If you prefer to handwrite your notes, you can print blank notes pages. Don't bother adding notes to your presentation. Instead, just print the notes pages as described in the section "Printing Notes Pages," later in this chapter. The resulting notes pages have a reduced image of the slide at the top and a blank space in which you can handwrite your notes later.

✔ Consider providing blank notes pages for your audience.

The result of this trick is that you now have two pages of notes for a single slide, and the second notes page doesn't have an image of the slide on it and is not included in your slide show.

If you're printing overhead transparencies, you might want to deselect the Print Hidden Slides check box in the Print dialog box. This way, the hidden slide isn't printed. Be sure to select the check box when you print the notes pages, though. Otherwise, the notes page for the hidden slide isn't printed either — and the reason you created the hidden slide in the first place was to print a notes page for it!

Think twice before creating a second page of notes for a slide. Do you really have that much to say about a single slide? Maybe the slide contains too much to begin with and should be split into two slides.

Adding a New Slide from Notes Page View

If you're working in Notes Page view and realize that you want to create a new slide, you don't have to return to Normal View. Just click the Add Slide button in the Slides group on the Home tab to add the new slide. Or press Ctrl+M.

If you want to work on the slide's appearance or contents, however, you must switch back to Normal View. You can't modify a slide's appearance or contents from Notes Page View.

Printing Notes Pages

If you don't have a computer that can show your slides on a projector and your notes on a separate monitor, you can always print your notes on paper and then use the printed notes while you give your presentation. These steps show you how to print your notes:

1. **Choose the Print command from the Office button menu.**

   The Print dialog box appears.

2. **Use the Print What list box to choose the Notes Pages option.**

3. **Make sure that the Print Hidden Slides check box is selected if you want to print notes pages for hidden slides.**

   The Print Hidden Slides check box is dimmed if the presentation doesn't have any hidden slides.

4. **Click OK or press Enter.**

You can find more information about printing in Chapter 6.

Displaying Notes on a Separate Monitor

If you're lucky enough to have a computer that can use two monitors, you can display your notes on one monitor and connect a projector as the other monitor to show your slides. This way, you can see your notes on the monitor while your audience sees only the projected slides.

To enable this feature, select the Slide Show tab and click the Set Up Show button (found in the Set Up group). This summons the Set Up Show dialog box. In the Multiple Monitors section of the dialog box, change the Display Slide Show On setting to Secondary Monitor. Switch to Notes View on the primary monitor to view your notes and then start the slide show on the secondary monitor to show the slides on the projector.

Chapter 6

Show Time!

Overture, curtains, lights. This is it — the night of nights.
No more rehearsing and nursing a part,
We know every part by heart.
Overture, curtains, lights. This is it, you'll hit the heights.
And Oh, what heights we'll hit,
On with the show, this is it.

The old Bugs Bunny theme song (written by Mack David and Jerry Livingston) strikes a chord when your presentation is all finished and all that remains is to present it to your audience.

This chapter shows you how to finish the final preparations by printing copies of your slides, notes, and handouts. Then the chapter delves into the task of setting up a projector and actually presenting your show.

This is it!

The Quick Way to Print

The Print command. The Printmeister. Big presentation comin' up. Printin' some slides. The Printorama. The Mentor of de Printor. Captain Toner of the Good Ship Laseroo.

Don't worry — when you print a PowerPoint presentation, no one's waiting to ambush you with annoying one-liners like that guy who used to be on *Saturday Night Live.* Just a handful of boring dialog boxes with boring check boxes. Point-point, click-click, print-print.

The fastest way to print your presentation is to click the Quick Print button. Click the Office button, click the arrow immediately to the right of Print, and then click Quick Print. Clicking this button prints your presentation without further ado, using the current settings for the Print dialog box, which I explain in the remaining sections of this chapter. Usually, this action results in printing a single copy of all the slides in your presentation. But if you have altered the Print dialog box settings, clicking the Print button uses the altered settings automatically.

Using the Print Dialog Box

For precise control over how you want your presentation to be printed, you must conjure up the Print dialog box shown in Figure 6-1. To summon this dialog box, choose Office➪Print or press Ctrl+P.

Figure 6-1:
Behold the
Print dialog
box.

After you call up the Print dialog box, click OK or press Enter to print all the slides in your presentation. Fiddle around with the settings to print a select group of slides, to print more than one copy, or to print handouts, speaker notes, or an outline. The following sections show you the treasures that lie hidden in this dialog box.

Printing can be es-el-oh-double-ewe, so don't panic if your presentation doesn't start printing right away. PowerPoint printouts tend to demand a great deal from the printer, so sometimes the printer has to work for a while before it can produce a finished page. Be patient. The Printer Wizard has every intention of granting your request.

Changing printers

If you're lucky enough to have two or more printers at your disposal, you can use the Name field to pick which printer you want to use. Each printer must first be successfully installed in Windows — a topic that's beyond the reach of this humble book. However, you can find plenty of information about installing printers in the appropriate version of Andy Rathbone's _Windows For Dummies_ (Wiley Publishing, Inc.).

Printing part of a presentation

When you first use the Print command, the All option is selected so that your entire presentation prints. The other options in the Print Range area of the Print dialog box enable you to tell PowerPoint to print distinct portions of your presentation:

- **Current Slide:** Prints just the current slide. Before you invoke the Print command, you should move to the slide that you want to print. Then select this option in the Print dialog box and click OK. This option is handy when you make a change to one slide and don't want to reprint the entire presentation.

- **Selection:** Prints just the portion of the presentation that you selected before invoking the Print command. First, select the slides that you want to print. Then call up the Print command, click the Selection option, and click OK. (Note that this option is grayed out if nothing is selected when you call up the Print dialog box.)

- **Custom Show:** If you set up one or more custom slide shows, you can use this option to select the show that you want to print. (See "Using Custom Shows" later in this chapter.)

✔ **Slides:** Lets you select specific slides for printing. You can print a range of slides by typing the beginning and ending slide numbers, separated by a hyphen, as in *5–8* to print slides 5, 6, 7, and 8. Or you can list individual slides, separated by commas, as in *4,8,11* to print slides 4, 8, and 11. And you can combine ranges and individual slides, as in *4,9–11,13* to print slides 4, 9, 10, 11, and 13.

Printing more than one copy

The Number of Copies field in the Print dialog box lets you print more than one copy of your presentation. You can click one of the arrows next to this field to increase or decrease the number of copies, or you can type directly in the field to set the number of copies.

Below the Number of Copies field is a check box labeled Collate. If this check box is selected, PowerPoint prints each copy of your presentation one at a time. In other words, if your presentation consists of ten slides and you select three copies and select the Collate check box, PowerPoint first prints all ten slides of the first copy of the presentation, then all ten slides of the second copy, and then all ten slides of the third copy. If you don't select the Collate check box, PowerPoint prints three copies of the first slide, followed by three copies of the second slide, followed by three copies of the third slide, and so on.

The Collate option saves you from the chore of manually sorting your copies. If your presentation takes forever to print because it's loaded down with heavy-duty graphics, however, you can probably save time in the long run by deselecting the Collate check box. Why? Because many printers are fast when it comes to printing a second or third copy of a page. The printer might spend ten minutes figuring out how to print a particularly complicated page, but after it figures it out, the printer can print additional copies in ten seconds each. If you print collated copies, the printer must labor over each page separately for each copy of the presentation that it prints.

Choosing what to print

The Print What drop-down list in the Print dialog box enables you to select the type of output that you want to print. The following choices are available:

✔ **Slides:** Prints slides. (Duh.)

✔ **Notes Pages:** Prints speaker notes pages, which are covered in Chapter 5.

✔ **Handouts (With Slides per Page):** Prints audience handout pages. Select the number of slides that you want to appear on each handout page by clicking the Slides per Page drop-down list (to the right of the Print What drop-down list). You can also order the slides to appear horizontally or vertically on the handout.

✔ **Outline View:** Prints an outline of your presentation.

Select the type of output that you want to print and then click OK or press Enter. Off you go!

When you're printing slides to be used as overhead transparencies, print a proof copy of the slides on plain paper before committing the output to transparencies. Transparencies are too expensive to print on until you're sure that your output is just right.

If you are printing on transparencies, make absolutely sure you have the right type of transparencies for your printer. Transparencies designed for laser printers won't look good if you use them in an ink-jet printer. And transparencies designed for ink-jet printers might melt under the intense heat generated inside a laser printer.

To change the orientation of your printed output from Landscape to Portrait mode (or vice versa), use the Slide Orientation button in the Page Setup group of the Design tab on the Ribbon. Clicking this button reveals a menu that lets you choose between Landscape and Portrait orientation.

To print handouts with two, three, or six slides per page, PowerPoint naturally must shrink the slides to make them fit. Because slides usually have outrageously large type, the handout slides are normally still readable, even at their reduced size.

Exploring the other printing options

The Print command has several additional options, which hide out near the bottom of the dialog box, hoping to slip by unnoticed. This list shows you what they do:

✔ **Color/Grayscale:** This drop-down list lets you choose whether to print your slides in color, black and white, or with shades of gray.

✔ **Scale to Fit Paper:** This option adjusts the size of the printed output to fit the paper in the printer. Leave this option deselected to avoid bizarre printing problems.

✔ **Frame Slides:** This feature draws a thin border around the slides.

✔ **Print Comments and Ink Markup:** If you've added comments to your slides, you can print the comments on separate pages by choosing this option. This option is grayed out if the presentation has no comments.

✔ **Print Hidden Slides:** You can hide individual slides by clicking the Hide Slide button on the Slide Show tab. When a slide is hidden, it doesn't print unless you select the Print Hidden Slides check box in the Print dialog box. This option is grayed out if the presentation has no hidden slides.

Using the Print Preview Command

The Print Preview feature lets you see how your pages will appear before committing them to paper (or transparencies). To use the Print Preview feature, choose Office⇨Print⇨Print Preview. Or you can click the Preview button from the Print dialog box. Either way, a preview of the printed page appears, as shown in Figure 6-2.

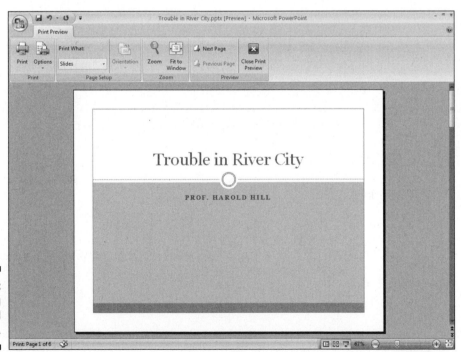

Figure 6-2:
Previewing
your printed
output.

From the Print Preview screen, you can zoom in to examine the preview more closely by clicking anywhere in the preview area. Or you can scroll through the pages by using the scroll bar, the Page Up and Page Down keys, or the Prev Page and Next Page buttons located on the Ribbon.

When you're satisfied that the printout will be to your expectations, click the Print button to print the presentation. If you discover a mistake in the preview, click Close Print Preview to return to PowerPoint so you can correct the mistake before printing your slides.

Starting a Slide Show

PowerPoint's printing features are useful, but PowerPoint is really designed to create slides that are presented directly on a screen rather than printed out. The screen can be either your computer's own monitor, a projector, or an external monitor such as a giant-screen Plasma or LCD display. Either way, this section and the sections that follow show you how to set up and show a presentation.

When you want to do a slide show in a one-on-one or small group setting without a projector, beginning the show is just a click away. To start a slide show immediately, click the Slide Show button located (along with the other View buttons) in the lower-right corner of the screen. If you have set up a full-screen slide show, PowerPoint fills the entire screen with the first slide of the slide show. To advance to the next slide, click the mouse, or press Enter, the down arrow, Page Down, or the spacebar.

You can also start a slide show by opening the Slide Show tab on the Ribbon and clicking either From Beginning or From Current Slide, depending on how you want to start the show. Or, if you're in a hurry and have a good memory for keyboard shortcuts, just press F5.

If you've configured PowerPoint to display the slide show on a secondary monitor, the slide show runs on the secondary monitor. The primary monitor still displays the presentation in Normal View. If you want, you can switch to Notes View on the primary monitor to display your notes while the slides are displayed on the secondary monitor.

Setting Up a Slide Show

In most cases, the default settings for showing a presentation are adequate. However, in some cases you may need to change the default settings. To do so, first open the presentation that you want to set up and then open the Slide Show tab on the Ribbon and click Set Up Slide Show (found in the Set Up group). This summons the Set Up Show dialog box, which is shown in Figure 6-3. With this dialog box, you can twiddle with the various options that are available for presenting slide shows.

Figure 6-3:
The Set Up
Show dialog
box.

With the options on the Set Up Show dialog box, you can do the following:

- ✔ **Configure the presentation:** You can configure the presentation for one of three basic slide show types: Presented by a Speaker (Full Screen), Browsed by an Individual (Window), or Browsed at a Kiosk (Full Screen).

- ✔ **Loop through slides:** Select the Loop Continuously until 'Esc' check box if you want the show to run indefinitely. If you enable this setting, the show jumps back to the first slide after the last slide is shown, and the show continues to repeat until you press Esc.

- ✔ **Simplify the presentation:** Deselect the Show Without Narration and Show Without Animation options if you want to simplify the presentation by not playing narrations that you've recorded or animations that you've created.

- ✔ **Select pen color:** Select the color to use for the pen. (See the section "Scribbling on Your Slides," later in this chapter, for more information about using the pen.)

- ✔ **Select slides:** In the Show Slides area, select All to include all slides in the slide show or choose From and supply starting and ending slide numbers if you want to display just some of the slides in the presentation.

- **Set up custom shows:** Choose Custom Show if you have set up any custom shows within your presentation. (See the section "Using Custom Shows," later in this chapter, for more information.)

- **Choose to change slides manually:** In the Advance Slides area, choose Manually to advance from slide to slide by pressing Enter, pressing the spacebar, or clicking. Or, if you want the show to proceed automatically, select the Using Timings, If Present option if it's available.

- **Select a monitor:** If your computer has two monitors, select the monitor to use for the slide show by using the drop-down list in the Multiple Monitors area.

- **Set performance options:** You can enable or disable graphics acceleration features of your hardware; you should check the "Use hardware graphics acceleration" option unless you find that your presentation isn't working properly. You can also change the screen resolution to use for the presentation.

Setting Up a Projector

If you're going to present your show using a computer projector and a laptop, you need to know how to connect the computer to your laptop as well as how to set up the projector, turn it on, focus it, and so on. Most of these details vary from one projector to the next, so you have to consult the manual that came with the projector or bribe someone to set up the projector for you. The following list provides a few general tips that might help:

- **Connecting the projector:** Most laptops have an external video port on the back or side, and most projectors have a video input connection. A standard VGA or DVI (depending on the type of connector on the PC and the projector) cable works to connect the computer to the projector.

- **Activating the external video port:** To use the laptop with a projector, you must first activate the external video port. Some laptops have a key that you can press to accomplish this; others require that you twiddle with the display settings to activate the external video port. If you can't figure out how to make the switch, try right-clicking an empty area of the desktop and choose Properties from the menu that appears. This brings up a Properties dialog box. Click the Settings tab in this dialog box and then click the Advanced button and look for a setting to enable the external video port. (On my Toshiba laptop, this setting is located in the Display Device tab of the dialog box that appears when I click the Advanced button.)

✔ **Resuming normal video:** When your presentation is finished, be sure to switch your computer back to its normal video port setting *before* you disconnect the projector. It's never a good idea to unplug a video cable while the video port is active. Plus, if your laptop disables its built-in display while the external port is active, you won't be able to see anything!

✔ **Selecting the projector's video input:** Most projectors can accept input from more than one source. For example, you might be able to connect a computer and a VCR to the projector. The projector should have some buttons or perhaps a menu setting that let you select the input that is used to display the projected image. If you connect your computer to the projector and everything else seems okay but you still don't get a picture, make sure that the projector is set to the correct input.

✔ **Using the projector's remote control:** If you want to use the projector's remote control to operate your presentation, you need the appropriate cable to connect the projector to your laptop's mouse port or USB. The correct cable should come with the projector.

✔ **Using sound:** If your presentation has sound, you need to connect your computer's sound outputs to a set of amplified speakers or, if you're showing the presentation in a large auditorium, a PA system. The correct cable to connect to a PA system depends on the PA system, but a cable with a mini-stereo plug on one end and a ¼-inch plug on the other will probably do the trick.

Keyboard and Mouse Tricks for Your Slide Show

During an on-screen slide show, you can use the keyboard and mouse to control your presentation. Tables 6-1 and 6-2 list the keys and clicks that you can use.

If the cursor is hidden, you can summon it by jiggling the mouse. Then, when the cursor is visible, a faint menu appears in the lower-left corner of the slide. You can use this menu to activate various slide show features.

Table 6-1	Keyboard Tricks for Your Slide Show
To Do This	*Press Any of These Keys*
Display next slide	Enter, spacebar, Page Down, or N
Display preceding slide	Backspace, Page Up, or P
Display first slide	1+Enter

To Do This	Press Any of These Keys
Display specific slide	Slide number+Enter
Toggle screen black	B or . (period)
Toggle screen white	W or , (comma)
Show or hide pointer	A or = (equal sign)
Erase screen doodles	E
Stop or restart automatic show	S, or + (plus sign)
Display next slide even if hidden	H
Display specific hidden slide	Slide number of hidden slide+Enter
Change pen to arrow	Ctrl+A
Change arrow to pen	Ctrl+P
End slide show	Esc, Ctrl+Break (the Break key doubles as the Pause key), or – (minus)

Table 6-2	Mouse Tricks for Your Slide Show
To Do This	**Do This**
Display next slide	Click.
Move through slides	Roll the wheel on your mouse (if your mouse has a wheel).
Call up menu of actions	Right-click.
Display first slide	Hold down both mouse buttons for two seconds.
Doodle	Press Ctrl+P to change the mouse arrow to a pen and then draw on-screen like John Madden.

Scribbling on Your Slides

If you've always wanted to diagram plays on-screen the way John Madden does during a football game, try using the pen during a slide show:

1. **Start a slide show.**

2. **When you want to doodle on a slide, press Ctrl+P.**

The arrow cursor changes to a pen shape.

3. **Draw away.**

   Figure 6-4 shows an example of a doodled-upon slide.

4. **To erase your doodles, press E.**

5. **To stop drawing, press Esc.**

   This returns the normal cursor.

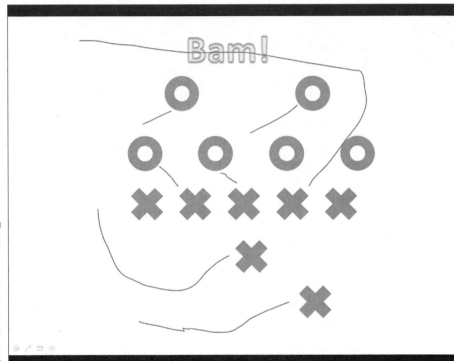

Figure 6-4:
John
Madden
would love
to scribble
on Power-
Point slides
like this.

Drawing doodles like this requires good mouse dexterity. With practice, you can create all kinds of interesting doodles. Work on circling text or drawing exclamation points or question marks, smiley faces, and so on.

Keep these tasty tidbits in mind when doodling:

▸ **Hiding the cursor:** To hide the cursor temporarily during a slide show, press A or the equal sign (=). The cursor returns the moment you move the mouse, or you can press A or the equal sign again to summon it back.

✔ **Adding emphasis:** If you use the pen, be sure to say "Bam" and "Pow" a lot.

✔ **Changing the pen color:** If you don't like the pen color, you can change it by using the faint Show menu that appears in the bottom-left corner of the slide. This menu has four little icons, and the second icon from the left displays a list of pen options: a ballpoint pen, a felt-tipped pen that draws a somewhat heavier line, and a highlighter, which draws in broad lines that are semitransparent, just like a real highlighter. (The Show menu disappears after a few seconds if you don't use it, but you can get it to reappear by moving the mouse around a bit.)

You can also right-click for a floating menu of the preceding choices; how-ever, this might be a little more distracting for your audience than the key-strokes because the audience will suddenly be privy to all your fancy footwork. Notice, though, that the menu allows you to change pen colors and a few other tricks. You can set up the pen color by clicking Set Up Slide Show in the Set Up group of the Slide Show tab before you begin your presentation so as not to distract your audience. If you have a remote mouse and you won't have access to your keyboard during your presentation, I suggest that you investi-gate the floating menu method.

When you finish your presentation, you're given the option to keep your doo-dles as annotations in your presentation. Then you won't have to draw the doodles next time.

Rehearsing Your Slide Timings

You can use the PowerPoint Rehearsal feature to rehearse your presentation. The Rehearsal feature lets you know how long your presentation takes, and it can even set slide timings so that the slides automatically advance based on the timings you set during the rehearsal.

To rehearse a slide show, choose Slide Show➪Set Up➪Rehearse Timings. This starts the slide show, with a special Rehearsal dialog box visible, as shown in Figure 6-5.

Figure 6-5:
Rehearsing
a slide show.

Now rehearse your presentation. Click or use keyboard shortcuts to advance slides. As you rehearse, the Rehearse dialog box keeps track of how long you display each slide and the total length of your presentation.

When you dismiss the final slide, PowerPoint displays a dialog box that gives you the option of applying or ignoring the timings recorded during the rehearsal to the slides in the presentation. If you were satisfied with the slide timings during the rehearsal, click Yes.

If you mess up during a rehearsal, click the Repeat button. Clicking this button restarts the rehearsal from the beginning.

Using Custom Shows

The Custom Shows feature in PowerPoint lets you create several similar slide shows stored in a single presentation file. For example, suppose that you're asked to give presentations about company benefits to management and non-management staff. You can create a presentation containing slides for all the company benefits and then create a custom show containing only those slides describing benefits that are available to non-management staff. (This custom slide show can leave out slides such as "Executive Washrooms," "Golf Days," and "Boondoggles.") You may then show the complete presentation to management but show the custom show to non-management staff.

A presentation can contain as many custom shows as you want. Each custom show is simply a subset of the complete presentation — comprised of selected slides from the complete presentation.

Creating a custom show

To create a custom show, follow these steps:

1. **On the Slide Show tab on the Ribbon, click Custom Slide Show (located in the Start Slide Show group), then choose Custom Shows from the menu that appears.**

   This displays the Custom Shows dialog box.

2. **Click the New button.**

   The Define Custom Show dialog box appears, as shown in Figure 6-6.

3. **Type a name for the custom show in the Slide Show Name field.**

Figure 6-6:
Defining a
custom
show.

4. **Add the slides that you want to appear in the custom slide show.**

All the slides available in the presentation are listed in the list box on the left side of the Define Custom Show dialog box. To add a slide to the custom show, click the slide that you want to add and then click Add. The slide appears in the list box on the right side of the Define Custom Show dialog box.

You don't have to add slides to the custom show in the same order that the slides appear in the presentation. Slides for a custom show can appear in any order you want. You can also include a slide from the original presentation more than once in a custom show.

To remove a slide that you've added by mistake, click the slide that you want to remove in the list box on the right side of the Define Custom Show dialog box, and then click Remove.

You can use the up or down arrows near the right edge of the Define Custom Show dialog box to change the order of the slides in the custom show.

5. **Click OK.**

You return to the Custom Shows dialog box.

6. **Click Close to dismiss the Custom Shows dialog box.**

Showing a custom show

To show a custom show, first open the presentation that contains the custom show. Then choose Slide Show➪Start Slide Show➪Custom Slide Show➪Custom Show on the Ribbon to summon the Custom Shows dialog box. Click the custom show that you want and then click the Show button.

Hiding slides

If you don't want to go to all the trouble of creating a custom show, but you want to exclude a few slides from a presentation, you don't have to delete the slides. Instead, you can hide them. To hide a slide, select the slide and then choose Slide Show⇨Set Up⇨Hide Slide on the Ribbon. To unhide a slide, select the slide and click the button again. (You can determine which slides have been hidden by looking at the slide in the Slides tab on the left. If the slide number has a slash through it, the slide is hidden.)

Chapter 7

Getting Help!

*T*he ideal way to use PowerPoint would be to have a PowerPoint expert sitting patiently at your side, answering your every question with a straightforward answer, gently correcting you when you make silly mistakes, and otherwise minding his or her own business. All you'd have to do is occasionally toss the expert a Twinkie and let him or her outside once a day.

Short of that, the next best thing is to find out how to coax PowerPoint itself into giving you the answers you need. Fortunately, PowerPoint includes a nice built-in help feature that can provide the answers you're looking for. No matter how deeply you're lost in the PowerPoint jungle, help is never more than a few mouse clicks or keystrokes away.

Several Ways to Get Help

As with everything else in Office, more than one method is available for calling up help when you need it. The easiest thing to do would be to yell, "Skipper!!!" in your best Gilligan voice. Otherwise, you have the following options:

✔ Press F1 at any time, and help is on its way. If you press F1 when you're in the midst of doing something, odds are PowerPoint will offer suggestions for help with just the task you're trying to accomplish. This slick little bit of wizardry is called *context-sensitive help.*

✔ Click the Help button, located just above the right edge of the Ribbon. This activates PowerPoint's main Help system, shown in Figure 7-1.

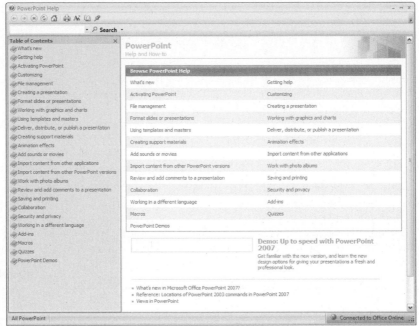

Figure 7-1:
Help!

✔ Whenever a dialog box is displayed, you can click the question mark button in the top-right corner of the dialog box to get help specific to that dialog box.

✔ When you hover the mouse over an item in the Ribbon, a ToolTip appears explaining what the item does. Many of these ToolTips include the phrase "Press F1 for more help." In that case, you can press F1 to get help specific to that item.

Finding Your Way Around in Help

The Help dialog box, shown in Figure 7-1, offers several ways to access the help you need. The following paragraphs describe the various ways you can work your way through PowerPoint's help feature:

✔ **Help window links:** You can click any of the links that appear in the Help window to display help on a particular topic. For example, if you click the What's New link, you'll find a page of useful information about the new features of PowerPoint 2007.

What happened to Clippy?

Alexander Graham Bell had Thomas Watson, Batman had Robin, and Dr. Frankenstein had Igor. Everybody needs an assistant, and Office users are no exception. That's why Microsoft decided to bless previous versions of Office with Clippy, a helpful little fellow who offered helpful assistance as you worked with Office programs.

Clippy was an animated paperclip who would suddenly morph onto your desktop with sage advice and suggestions and even a little idea light that lets you know a tip is available. You could also ask Clippy questions when you weren't sure what to do.

Unfortunately, Clippy wasn't always as helpful as he could have been. In fact, more often than not, he was just annoying. Whenever you typed the word *Dear* in the vicinity of anything that looked like it might be an address, Clippy would pop up and ask whether you were trying to type a letter. And if you asked him a question, many times his answers didn't seem remotely related to the question you were asking.

Microsoft tried to improve on Clippy with each successive version of Office, but with Office 2007, they finally threw in the towel. Clippy has gone to the paper clip pile in the sky.

✔ **Hide Table of Contents button:** You can click the Hide Table of Contents button (shown in the margin) to hide the Table of Contents, which gives you an organized overview of the various help topics. If the Table of Contents is hidden, click this button again to show it.

✔ **Search feature:** If you can't find what you're looking for, try entering a word or phrase in the Search text box and clicking the Search button. This displays a list of topics that pertain to the word or phrase you entered.

✔ **Pushpin icon:** Normally, the Help window always displays on top. In many cases, this obscures your access to the PowerPoint window. If you don't want the Help window to always stay on top, you can click the button with the pushpin icon. Then the Help window will minimize like any other window.

✔ **Back button:** You can retrace your steps by clicking the Help window's Back button. You can use the Back button over and over again, retracing all your steps if necessary.

Getting Help on the Internet

In addition to the help that's built into PowerPoint, you can get PowerPoint help from Microsoft's Office Web site. At the bottom of the Help window, you can find three helpful links to online help:

- ✔ **Training:** This link takes you to Microsoft's Training home page. Here you can find online training tutorials that teach you how to use specific aspects of PowerPoint or other Office programs.

- ✔ **Templates:** This link takes you to a page from which you can download helpful templates.

- ✔ **Check for Updates:** This link takes you to the Office Update home page, where you can download the latest updates to Office programs.

Part II
Creating Great-Looking Slides

The 5th Wave   By Rich Tennant

"Okay-looks like the 'Dissolve' transition in my presentation needs adjusting."

In this part . . .

The chapters in this part are devoted to helping you create fantastic-looking slides. I start with tips for refining the text format so your slides are readable as well as attractive. Then I launch into other refinements, such as working with themes and colors, adding animation effects, and using Master slide layouts and templates.

Enjoy!

Chapter 8

All about Fonts and Text Formatting

A good presentation is like a fireworks show: At every new slide, the audience gasps, "O-o-o-h. A-a-a-h." The audience is so stunned by the spectacular appearance of your slides that no one really bothers to read them.

This chapter gets you on the road toward ooohs and aaahs by showing you how to format text. If you use PowerPoint templates as the basis for your presentations, your text is already formatted acceptably. To really pull out the pyrotechnic stops, however, you have to know a few basic formatting tricks.

Many PowerPoint text-formatting capabilities work the same as in Microsoft Word. If you want to format text a certain way and you know how to do it in Word, try formatting the same way in PowerPoint. Odds are that it works.

Changing the Look of Your Text

The theme that's applied to your presentation determines the basic look of the presentation's text. However, you'll often want to change that look, sometimes subtly and sometimes dramatically.

You can control the most commonly used font settings by using the Font group in the Home tab on the Ribbon, as shown in Figure 8-1.

Figure 8-1:
The Font group on the Home tab on the Ribbon.

If the Font group in the Home tab doesn't provide enough options for formatting your text, you can call up the Font dialog box for additional options. To summon this dialog box, just select the dialog launcher for the Font Group (the dialog launcher is the cursor at the bottom-right corner of the group). Figure 8-2 shows this dialog box.

Figure 8-2:
The Font dialog box.

Many font formatting options also have handy keyboard shortcuts. Table 8-1 lists the buttons and equivalent keyboard shortcuts.

Table 8-1	Character-Formatting Shortcuts	
Button	**Keyboard Shortcut**	**Formatting Command**
Georgia (Body)	(none)	Font
27	(none)	Size

Button	Keyboard Shortcut	Formatting Command
A▲	Ctrl+Shift+>	Increase font size
A▼	Ctrl+Shift+<	Decrease font size
Aa	Ctrl+spacebar	Clear all formatting
B	Ctrl+B	Bold
I	Ctrl+I	Italic
U	Ctrl+U	Underline
abc	(none)	Strikethrough
S	(none)	Text shadow
AV ▾	(none)	Character spacing
Aa ▾	Shift+F3	Change case
A ▾	(none)	Font color

It's true — PowerPoint has many keyboard shortcuts for character formatting. You don't have to know them all, though. The only ones I know and use routinely are the shortcuts for bold, italic, underline, and clear all formatting. Study these and you'll be in good shape. You get the added bonus that these keyboard shortcuts are the same as the shortcuts that many other Windows programs use. If you're mouse-happy and keyboard-annoyed, click away for goodness' sake. What matters most is that you can easily find and use what you need.

Two ways to apply formatting

You can format text in two basic ways:

- **To format existing text,** highlight the text that you want to format. Then, click the toolbar button or use the keyboard shortcut for the format that you want. For example, to make existing text bold, highlight it and then click the Bold button or press Ctrl+B.

- **To type new text using a fancy format,** click the toolbar button or use the keyboard shortcut for the format. Then, type away. The text that you type is given the format you selected. To return to normal formatting, click the button or use the keyboard shortcut again. Or press Ctrl+spacebar.

Changing the size of characters

Whether text is difficult to read or you simply want to draw attention to it, you can make part of the text bigger than the surrounding text. The easiest way to change the size of your text is to use the Font Size drop-down list that appears next to the font name in the Font group on the Home tab. Just choose among the sizes that appear in the Font Size drop-down list or click in the Font Size box and type whatever size you want to use.

You can also change the size of your text by using the Increase Font Size or Decrease Font Size buttons, or by using the Ctrl+Shift+> or Ctrl+Shift+< keyboard shortcuts. These commands increase or decrease the font size in steps.

Choosing text fonts

If you don't like the looks of a text font, you can switch easily to a different font. To change the font for existing text, select the text. Then, click the arrow next to the Font control (found in the Font group of the Home tab) and choose the font that you want to use. If you're allergic to the mouse, you can get to the font list by pressing Ctrl+Shift+F. Then you can use the up- or down-arrow keys to choose the font you want to use.

Here are a gaggle of additional points to ponder concerning fonts:

- ✔ Although you can change the font from the Font dialog box, the Font control on the Ribbon has one major advantage over the Font dialog box: It displays each of your fonts by using the font itself, so you can see what each font looks like before you apply it to your text. In contrast, the Font dialog box displays the name of each font by using the standard Windows system font.

- ✔ If you want to change the font for all the slides in your presentation, switch to Slide Master View and then change the font. Details on how to do so are covered in Chapter 11.

- ✔ PowerPoint automatically moves the fonts that you use the most to the head of the font list. This feature makes picking your favorite font even easier.

- ✔ Don't overdo it with fonts! Just because you have many different font choices doesn't mean that you should try to use them all on the same slide. Don't mix more than two or three typefaces on a slide, and use fonts consistently throughout the presentation.

- ✔ You can also set the font for the presentation's theme. For more information, see Chapter 9.

Adding color to your text

Color is an excellent way to draw attention to text in a slide. To change text color, first select the text whose color you want to change. Then click the Font Color button and choose the color that you want to use from the color menu that appears.

 If you don't like any color that the Font Color button offers, click More Colors. A bigger dialog box with more color choices appears. If you still can't find the right shade of teal, click the Custom tab and have at it. Check out Chapter 10 if you need further help with colors.

If you want to change the text color for your entire presentation, do so in the Slide Master View (see Chapter 11 for details). And you can refer to Chapter 7 for information about changing font colors via the theme.

Adding shadows

Adding a shadow behind your text can make the text stand out against its background, which makes the entire slide easier to read. For that reason, many of the templates supplied with PowerPoint use shadows.

You can apply a shadow to any text by first selecting the text and then clicking the Text Shadow button, found in the Font section of the Home tab. If you want all of the text on a slide to be shadowed, however, you should use the Slide Master View to create the shadow format. For more information, peek ahead to Chapter 11.

Embossing text

Embossed text looks like it has been chiseled in stone. PowerPoint achieves the embossed effect by adding a light shadow above the text rather than the dark shadow that appears below the text when you create shadowed text. Note that you can't create text that is both shadowed and embossed; you can use only one effect or the other.

When you emboss text, PowerPoint changes the text color to the background color in order to enhance the embossed effect. As a result, the text appears to sink into the background.

Unfortunately, PowerPoint doesn't have a button for creating embossed text. Instead, you have to bring up the Font dialog box by clicking the Dialog Launcher button at the bottom-right corner of the Font group in the Home tab. Then, you can select the Emboss option and click OK.

Embossed text is difficult to read in smaller font sizes. This effect is best reserved for large titles. Also, embossed text is nearly invisible with some color schemes. You may have to fiddle with the color scheme or switch templates in order to make the embossed text visible.

Big Picture Text Formatting

The Paragraph group on the Home tab on the Ribbon, as shown in Figure 8-3, has several buttons that apply formats to entire paragraphs. The following sections describe the most common uses for the buttons in this group.

Figure 8-3:
The Paragraph group on Home tab on the Ribbon.

Biting the bulleted list

Most presentations have at least some slides that include a bulleted list, which is a series of paragraphs accented by special characters lovingly known as *bullets*. In the old days, you had to add bullets one at a time. Nowadays, PowerPoint comes with a semi-automatic bullet shooter that is illegal in 27 states.

PowerPoint lets you create fancy bullets that are based on bitmap pictures rather than simple dots and check marks. Before you go crazy with picture bullets, take a look at the basic way to bite the bullet.

To add bullets to a paragraph or series of paragraphs

1. **Highlight the paragraphs to which you want to add bullets.**

   To add a bullet to just one paragraph, you don't have to highlight the entire paragraph. Just place the cursor anywhere in the paragraph.

2. **Click the Bullets button found in the Paragraph group of the Home tab.**

   PowerPoint adds a bullet to each paragraph that you select.

The Bullets button works like a toggle: Press it once to add bullets and press it again to remove bullets. To remove bullets from previously bulleted text, therefore, you select the text and click the Bullets button again.

If you don't like the appearance of the bullets that PowerPoint uses, you can select a different bullet character, picture, or even a motion clip by clicking the down arrow at the right side of the Bullets button. This reveals a list of choices for various types of bullets.

If none of the bullets in this list are acceptable, you can bring up the Bullets and Numbering dialog box by clicking the arrow at the right of the Bullets button and then choosing Bullets and Numbers. This summons the Bullets and Numbering dialog box, as shown in Figure 8-4. From this dialog box, you can choose a different bullet character, change the bullet's color, or change its size relative to the text size.

The following paragraphs point out some important tidbits to keep in mind when you use bullets:

✔ **Customize bullet characters:** You can choose from among several collections of bullet characters that are available. If you don't like any of the bullet characters displayed for you in the dialog box, click Customize in the lower-right corner of the dialog box. This brings up a dialog box that lists a variety of useful alternative bullet characters, such as pointing fingers, a skull and crossbones, and a time bomb. Pick the bullet that you want to use and then click OK. If you can't find a bullet that suits your fancy, choose a different font in the Font control drop-down list.

✔ **Change the size of bullet characters:** If the bullet characters don't seem large enough, increase the size in the Bullets and Numbering dialog box. The size is specified as a percentage of the text size.

✔ **Change the color of bullet characters:** To change the bullet color, use the Color drop-down list to choose the color that you want to use. Colors from the current color scheme appear in the drop-down menu that appears. For additional color choices, choose More Colors to call up a dialog box that offers a complete range of color choices. (For more information about using colors, see Chapter 9.)

✔ **Use images for your bullet characters:** To use a picture bullet, click the Picture button located in the lower right of the Bullets and Numbering dialog box. This brings up the Picture Bullet dialog box, as shown in Figure 8-5. Select the picture that you want to use for your bullet and then click OK. (You can use the Import button in this dialog box to use your own bitmap file for a bullet.)

You can use certain bullet characters for good comic effect in your presentations. Be creative, but also be careful. A thumbs-down bullet next to the name of your boss might get a laugh, but it might also get you fired. One cool thing to do with bullets when you pitch a product or service is to use your logo as a bullet. It subliminally grinds your image in their brains until they submit to your will.

Creating numbered lists

If you want your slide to include a numbered list, use the Numbering button, which appears next to the Bullets button on the Home tab. When you click the Numbering button, PowerPoint adds simple numbers to the selected paragraphs.

Figure 8-5:
Using a
picture
bullet.

If you want to change the numbering format, click the arrow next to the Numbering button to display a list of number style choices. Then you can select the style that suits your fancy.

If none of the styles in the list are right, choose Bullets and Numbering to reveal the numbering options shown on the Numbered tab of the Bullets and Numbering dialog box. See Figure 8-6.

Figure 8-6:
More ways
to format
numbers.

Normally, the starting number for each list reverts to 1 for each new slide. What if you have a list that has more items than will fit on one slide, such as a David Letterman–style Top Ten list? In that case, you can type the first half of the list on one slide and then type the second half of the list on a second slide. Next, right-click the first item on the second slide and choose Bullets and Numbering from the menu that appears. Then, change the Start At value to the number at which you want the second part of the list to begin. For example, if the first slide has five numbered items, change the Start At value for the first item on the second slide to 6.

Setting tabs and indents

PowerPoint enables you to set tab stops to control the placement of text within a text object. For most presentations, you don't have to fuss with tabs. Each paragraph is indented according to its level in the outline, and the template that you use to create the presentation presets the amount of indentation for each outline level.

If you're stubborn about tabs, you can mess with the indent settings and tab stops — that is, if you're adventurous and have no real work to do today. Here's how you do it:

1. **Click the Slide button to switch to Normal View.**

   You can't mess with tabs or indents in Notes Page View or Slide Sorter View.

2. **If the rulers aren't visible, summon it by clicking the View tab on the Ribbon and then selecting the Ruler check box in the Show/Hide group.**

   Rulers appear above and to the left of the presentation window and show the current tab and indentation settings.

3. **Select the text object whose tabs or indents you want to change.**

   Each text object has its own tabs and indents setting. After you click a text object, the ruler shows that object's tabs and indents.

4. **Click the ruler to add a tab stop.**

   Move the cursor to the ruler location where you want to add a tab stop and then click. A tab stop appears.

5. **Grab the indentation doohickey and then drag it to change the indentation.**

   The Indentation Doohickey (that's not its official name) is the control that looks like an hourglass sitting on a little box, normally positioned at the left side of the ruler. It actually consists of three parts: the top upside-down triangle sets the indentation for the first line of the paragraph, the middle triangle sets the indentation for the remaining lines of the paragraph, and the box at the bottom sets the indentation for the paragraph. Try dragging the different parts of the indentation doohickey to see what happens. Have fun. Good luck.

Tabs and indents can be pretty testy, but fortunately you don't have to mess with them for most presentations. If you're one of the unlucky ones, keep these pointers in mind:

Don't even bother with this stuff about tab types

PowerPoint isn't limited to just boring left-aligned tabs. In all, it has four distinct types of tabs: left, right, center, and decimal. The square button that appears at the far-left side of the ruler when you select text tells you which type of tab is added when you click the ruler. Click this button to cycle through the four types of tabs:

✔ **Standard left-aligned tab:** Press Tab to advance the text to the tab stop.

✔ **Right-aligned tab:** Text is aligned flush right with the tab stop.

✔ **Contored tab:** Text lines up centered over the tab stop.

✔ **Decimal tab:** Numbers line up with the decimal point centered over the tab stop.

✔ **Each text object has its own tab settings.** The tab settings for an object apply to all the paragraphs within the object, so you can't change tab settings for individual paragraphs within a text object. This is different from how Word works — in Word, each paragraph has its own tab settings.

✔ **The ruler shows as many as five different indentation levels, one for each outline level.** Only those levels used in the text object are shown, so if the object has only one outline level, only one indent is shown. To see additional indents, demote text within the object by pressing the Tab key.

Each text object is initially set up with default tab stops set at every inch. When you add a tab stop, any default tab stops located to the left of the new tab stop disappear.

To remove a tab stop, use the mouse to drag the tab stop off the ruler. (For instance, click the tab stop, drag it off the ruler, and then release the mouse button.)

Spacing out

Feeling a little spaced out? Try tightening the space between text lines. Feeling cramped? Space out the lines a little. These steps show you how to do it all:

1. **Highlight the paragraph — or paragraphs — whose line spacing you want to change.**

2. **Click the Line Spacing button and then select the amount of line spacing you want.**

The Line Spacing button displays the most common line spacing options: 1.0, 1.5, 2.0, 2.5, and 3.0. If you want to set the line spacing to a value that's not shown on the Line Spacing button, select Line Spacing Options to display the Paragraph dialog box, as shown in Figure 8-7.

Figure 8-7:
Change the line spacing.

Lining things up

PowerPoint enables you to control the way your text lines up on the slide. You can center text, line it up flush left or flush right, or justify it. You can change these alignments by using the alignment buttons in the Paragraph group in the Home tab. You can also use the keyboard shortcuts described in Table 8-2.

Table 8-2	Paragraph Alignment Shortcuts	
Button	*Keyboard Shortcut*	*Alignment*
	Ctrl+E	Align Left
	Ctrl+L	Center
	Ctrl+R	Align Right
	Ctrl+J	Justify

Here are some semi random thoughts on aligning paragraphs:

- **Centered text lines up right down the middle of the slide.** Actually, text lines up down the middle of the text object that contains the text; a text line appears centered on the slide only if the text object is centered on the slide.

- **Bulleted lists look best when left-aligned.** Otherwise, the bullets don't line up.

Making columns

Most slides place all their text in a single column. However, you can easily create multiple columns by using the Columns button, found in the Paragraph section of the Home tab. To create a one-, two-, or three-column layout, just click the Columns button and then choose one, two, or three columns from the menu that appears. If you want more than three columns, select the More Columns command and then choose the number of columns you want to use.

Creating Fancy Text with WordArt

Previous versions of PowerPoint included a feature called *WordArt* that let you insert special objects that could incorporate fancy text effects such as gradient fills or curved paths. For PowerPoint 2007, Microsoft has integrated WordArt into PowerPoint, so that you can apply WordArt formatting to any bit of text in your presentation just by highlighting the text and applying the WordArt formats. Figure 8-8 is an example of what you can do with WordArt in just a couple of minutes.

Follow these steps to transform mundane text into something worth looking at:

1. **Select the text you want to apply WordArt formatting to.**

   The text can be anywhere in your presentation. For example, you can apply WordArt formatting to a slide title or body text.

2. **Click the Drawing Tools Format tab.**

   The Drawing Tools Format tab includes a WordArt Styles group, shown in Figure 8-9.

3. **Click the Quick Styles button (found in the WordArt Styles group of the Drawing Tools Format tab).**

   The WordArt Quick Styles gallery appears, as shown in Figure 8-10.

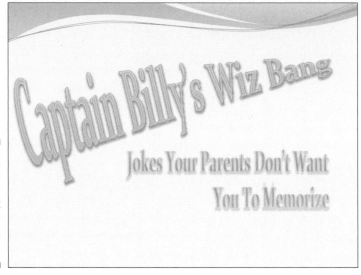

Figure 8-8:
You, too, can create fancy text effects like this using WordArt.

Figure 8-9:
The WordArt Styles group in the Drawing Tools Format tab.

4. **Select the WordArt style that most closely resembles the formatting you want to apply.**

   Don't worry if none of the gallery choices exactly match the effect you want; you can tweak the text's appearance later.

5. **Fool around with other WordArt controls in the WordArt Styles group of the Drawing Tools Format tab.**

   Table 8-3 describes the other controls in the WordArt Styles group. Experiment with these controls as much as you want until you get the text to look just right.

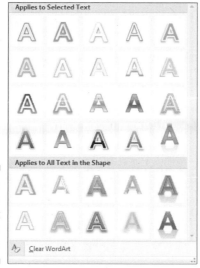

Figure 8-10:
The
WordArt
Quick Styles
gallery.

Table 8-3	Buttons on the WordArt Drawing Tools Format tab	
Control	*What It's Called*	*What It Does*
Text Fill button	Text Fill	Sets the fill color. The fill can be a simple color, a gradient (which blends two colors), a picture, a pattern, or a texture.
Text Outline button	Text Outline	Sets the properties of the text outline. You can select a color, a pattern, and a thickness.
Text Effects button	Text Effects	Lets you apply fancy text effects such as shadows, reflections, glowing text, beveled text, and 3-D rotations, and transforms.

The Text Effects button is the key to creating fancy logos, such as text that wraps around circles or text that has a three-dimensional look. Be sure to play with each of the options under this command to see what they can do.

Chapter 9

Designing Your Slides

*O*ne of the most bothersome tasks of putting together a good PowerPoint presentation is making the presentation look good. In previous versions of PowerPoint, you had to labor carefully over every aspect of your slide's design to come up with a slide that looked less than awful. However, PowerPoint 2007 introduces a new feature — *themes* — that helps you create good-looking slides in minutes.

The main access to PowerPoint themes is from the Design tab on the Ribbon. This entire chapter is devoted to this Design tab. To keep things simple, I approach this most useful tab from left to right even though that's not always the order in which you use the controls it contains.

Looking at the Design Tab

To get things started, Figure 9-1 shows the Design tab on the Ribbon. As you can see, the Design tab contains several groups of controls that let you set various aspects of the slide design used within your presentation. You can summon the Design tab by clicking it on the Ribbon or by using the handy keyboard shortcut Alt+G.

Figure 9-1:
The Design
tab.

The following list describes the general purpose of each group of controls on the Design tab:

- ✓ **Page Setup:** Lets you change the orientation of your slides from Landscape to Portrait and control other page setup options.
- ✓ **Themes:** Lets you apply a theme to the presentation. This is the group you work with most while you play with the design of your slides.
- ✓ **Background:** Lets you apply a color effect or a picture to the slide background.

Designing the Page Setup

The Page Setup group consists of a Slide Orientation control that lets you flip the slide from Landscape mode (the default) to Portrait mode. You should use Portrait mode only if you intend to print the slides on transparency masters and project them with an old-fashioned overhead projector, or if you intend to present the slide show on a tablet computer or other PC that has a screen with portrait orientation.

If you click the Page Setup button in the Page Setup group, you're rewarded with the Page Setup dialog box, as shown in Figure 9-2. This dialog box gives you extra control over your presentation's page setup.

Figure 9-2:
The Page
Setup dialog
box.

The following list describes the controls in this dialog box:

- ✔ **Slides Sized For:** This drop-down list lets you set the size of your slides based on how you plan to present them. The most common is to present the slides on a standard computer screen, which has an aspect ratio of 4:3. (*Aspect ratio* is the ratio of the screen's width to its height. Although 4:3 is a common aspect ratio, many newer computers use wide-screen displays.) Other options on this drop-down list include different screen ratios (suitable for wide-screen displays), standard sized paper, and even 35-mm slides. A Custom option even lets you set whatever width and height you want for your slides.

- ✔ **Width:** Lets you set a custom width for your slides.

- ✔ **Height:** Lets you set a custom height for your slides.

- ✔ **Number Slides From:** If your slides include numbers, this option lets you set the number for the first slide. The default is 1.

- ✔ **Orientation:** Lets you set the orientation to *portrait* (tall and skinny) or *landscape* (short and fat). You can set the setting separately for your slides, handouts, and notes. The most common setting is for the slides to use landscape orientation and the notes and handouts to use portrait.

Working with Themes

The Themes group of the Design tab lets you select a theme to apply to your slides. PowerPoint 2007 comes with a ton of carefully crafted themes that give a professional look to your presentations. If you're somewhat artsy, you can design your own themes as well.

A *theme* is a set of design elements that are applied to one or more slides in a presentation. Each theme includes several basic components:

✓ A set of **colors** that work well together. Each theme has four colors that can be used for text or backgrounds and six colors that can be used for accents.

✓ A set of **fonts** that looks good when used together. Each theme has a font used for headings and a font used for regular text.

✓ A set of **background styles**, which are a combination of background colors and effects such as patterns or gradient fills.

✓ A set of **design effects** such as bullet styles and line styles.

Office ships with 20 predefined themes. These themes are named, as shown in the following table:

Office Theme	*Apex*	*Aspect*	*Civic*
Concourse	Currency	Deluxe	Equity
Flow	Foundry	Median	Metro
Opulent	Oriel	Origin	Solstice
Technic	Trek	Urban	Verve

Applying themes

To apply a theme to an entire presentation, simply click the theme you want to apply in the Themes group on the Design tab. If the theme you want to apply isn't visible, use the scroll buttons on the right side of the Themes group to display additional themes.

You can click the down arrow in the scroll bars in the Theme gallery, which displays an expanded list of themes, as shown in Figure 9-3. As you can see, this window displays PowerPoint's built-in themes and also includes links that let you search online for additional themes. A link even lets you save the current combination of theme elements as a new theme.

Not all the slides in a presentation have to follow the same theme. To apply a theme to a single slide — or a set of slides — select the slide(s). Then, right-click the theme you want to apply and choose Apply to Selected Slides.

Using theme colors

Each PowerPoint theme includes a built-in *color scheme,* which consists of sets of colors chosen by color professionals. Microsoft paid these people enormous sums of money to debate the merits of using mauve text on a teal background. You can use these professionally designed color schemes, or you can create your own if you think that you have a better eye than the Microsoft-hired color guns.

As far as I'm concerned, the color schemes in PowerPoint themes are the best things to come along since Peanut M&Ms. Without color schemes, people like me are free to pick and choose from among the 16 million or so colors that PowerPoint lets you incorporate into your slides. The resulting slides can easily appear next to Cher and Roseanne in *People* magazine's annual "Worst Dressed of the Year" issue.

Each color scheme has 12 colors, with each color designated for a particular use, as shown in this list:

- ✔ **Four Text/Background colors:** These four colors are designed to be the primary colors for the presentation. One from each pair is used for text, and the other for the background. (You could use the same color for both, but that would make the slides impossible to read!)

- ✔ **Six accent colors:** These colors are used for various bits and pieces of your slides that complement the basic text and background colors.

- ✔ **Two hyperlink colors:** These colors are used only when your presentation includes hyperlinks.

When you apply a theme, the color scheme for that theme is applied along with the other elements of the theme. However, PowerPoint lets you change the color scheme from the scheme that comes with the theme. For example, you can apply a theme such as Opulent but then change the color scheme to the scheme from the Verve theme.

Applying a color scheme

To apply a color scheme without applying a different theme, click the Theme Colors button at the top-right of the Themes group. This reveals the drop-down list, as shown in Figure 9-4. Then you can choose the scheme you want to apply.

Figure 9-4:
The drop-down list in the Theme gallery.

Creating your own color scheme

If you don't like any color schemes that come with the built-in themes, you can create your own color scheme. Here are the steps:

1. **Select a color scheme that's close to the one you want to use.**

   Be warned that after you deviate from the preselected color scheme combinations, you better have some color sense. If you can't tell chartreuse from lime, you better leave this stuff to the pros.

2. **Click the Theme Colors button and then choose Create New Theme Colors.**

   The Create New Theme Colors dialog box appears, as shown in Figure 9-5.

Figure 9-5:
Creating new theme colors.

3. **Click the button for the color you want to change.**

   For example, to change the first accent color, click the Accent 1 button. (Note that the name of this button may vary slightly.) This summons a gallery of color choices, as shown in Figure 9-6.

Figure 9-6:
Changing a color.

4. **Pick a color you like.**

   As you can see, a plethora of color choices are available. This gallery reminds me of the shelf of paint color chips in the paint section of a hardware store.

5. **If you don't like any of the choices, click the More Colors button.**

This brings up the Colors dialog box, as shown in Figure 9-7. As you can see, PowerPoint displays what looks like a tie-dyed version of Chinese checkers. (Note that this dialog box comes up with the Standard tab selected. If you used the Custom tab the last time you used this dialog box, the Custom tab will be selected instead.)

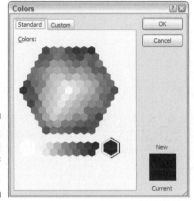

Figure 9-7:
A wonderful
world of
color.

6. **Click the color that you want and then click OK.**

    After you click OK, you're whisked back to the Create New Theme Colors dialog box.

7. **(Optional) Repeat steps 3 through 6 for any other colors you want to change.**

8. **Choose Save.**

    The new color scheme is saved.

The Standard tab of the Colors dialog box (refer to Figure 9-7) shows 127 popular colors, plus white, black, and shades of gray. If you want to use a color that doesn't appear in the dialog box, click the Custom tab. This step draws forth the custom color controls, as shown in Figure 9-8. From this tab in the dialog box, you can construct any of the 16 million colors that are theoretically possible with PowerPoint. You need a PhD in physics to figure out how to adjust the Red, Green, and Blue controls, though. Mess around with this stuff if you want, but you're on your own.

Using theme fonts

Theme fonts are similar to theme colors, but theme fonts have fewer choices. Although there are 12 colors per theme, there are only two fonts: one for headings, the other for body text.

Figure 9-8:
PowerPoint
offers 16
million
colors from
which you
can choose.

If you don't want to use the fonts associated with the theme you've chosen for your presentation, you can use the Theme Fonts button at the right side of the Themes group in the Design tab on the Ribbon to choose fonts from a different theme. Then the fonts you select are applied throughout your presentation.

Note that changing the theme font is not the same as changing the font via the Font controls found in the Font group of the Home tab. When you use the Font controls on the Home tab, you're applying *direct formatting.* Direct formatting temporarily overrides the font setting specified by the theme. As a general rule, you should use theme fonts to set the fonts used throughout a presentation. Use direct formatting sparingly — when you want to create a word or two in a font that differs from the rest of the presentation.

You can change the font used in a theme by clicking the Theme Fonts button and then choosing Create New Theme Fonts. This brings up the Create New Theme Fonts dialog box, as shown in Figure 9-9. Here you can change the font used for headings and body text.

Figure 9-9:
Changing
theme fonts.

Applying theme effects

Another major component of PowerPoint themes are the *theme effects,* which apply subtle variations to the graphical look of your presentations. Theme effects are applied automatically whenever you apply a theme. However, you can apply theme effects from a different theme by clicking the Theme Effects button at the right side of the Themes group on the Design tab on the Ribbon. This brings up the Theme Effects gallery, as shown in Figure 9-10. You can choose any of the theme effects listed.

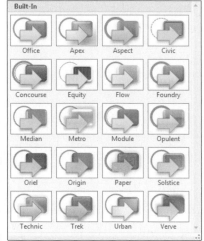

Figure 9-10: Changing theme effects.

Using Background Styles

A *background style* is a combination of a background color chosen from a theme color scheme and a background fill effect. The color scheme always includes four colors that can be used for the background — two light colors and two dark colors. In addition, you can choose from three background fill effects. These three fills are Subtle, Moderate, and Intense. For example, the Subtle fill might be a solid color, the Moderate fill might be a gentle pattern applied to the color, and the Intense fill might be a bold gradient fill.

Each combination of the four background colors and three background fills is a *background style.* Thus, each theme provides a total of 12 background styles.

To apply one of the theme's background styles to your presentation, use the Background Styles control in the Background group on the Design tab. This control reveals the Background Styles gallery, as shown in Figure 9-11.

Figure 9-11:
Changing
the
background
style.

Using a gradient fill

You may have noticed that the slide background used in many PowerPoint templates is not a solid color. Instead, the color is gradually shaded from top to bottom. This type of shading — *gradient fill* — creates an interesting visual effect. For example, look at the slide shown in Figure 9-12. This slide was based on the standard Office Theme that comes with PowerPoint 2007. The background is a dark blue at the top of the screen but gradually fades to near white by the bottom of the slide.

You can create your own custom gradient fill by following these steps:

1. **Choose the slide that you want to shade.**

   This step isn't necessary if you want to apply the shading to all slides in the presentation.

2. **Click the Background Styles button in the Background group of the Design tab on the Ribbon.**

   The Background Styles gallery appears.

3. **Click Format Background.**

   This brings up the Format Background dialog box, as shown in Figure 9-13.

4. **Select the Fill tab if it isn't already selected.**

5. **Select the Gradient Fill radio button if it isn't already selected.**

6. **Set the gradient fill options the way you want them.**

   You have to play with the controls until you get a feel for how they work. Start by selecting the present colors, which let you choose one of several predefined fill patterns. Then play with the controls until you get the fill to look the way you want. You can choose the colors to use for the fill, the transparency level, the direction, and several variants for each option.

7. **Click OK.**

Figure 9-12:
Using a
gradient fill
to create an
interesting
background.

Trouble in River City

Professor Harold Hill

Figure 9-13:
The Format
Background
dialog box.

Using other background effects

Besides gradient fills, you can use the Format Background dialog box to create several other interesting types of backgrounds. For example, you can assign a picture of your choosing, or you can use one of several predefined patterns supplied with PowerPoint.

To use a texture, click the Picture or Texture Fill radio button. Then click the Texture button to reveal the Texture gallery, as shown in Figure 9-14.

Figure 9-14:
Using a textured background.

You can also use the Picture or Texture Fill radio button to select an image file of your own. Just click the File button and then select the file you want to use. Or, you can import an image from the Clipboard or select a clip art image. The remaining controls on this dialog box let you further tweak the appearance of the picture or text you select.

Chapter 10

Animating Your Slides

*I*f you plan to run your presentation on your computer's screen or on a computer projector, you can use (or abuse) a bagful of exciting on-screen PowerPoint animations. The audience members probably won't be fooled into thinking that you hired Disney to create your slides, but they'll be impressed all the same. Animations are just one more example of how PowerPoint can make even the dullest content look spectacular.

This chapter begins with slide transitions, which are not technically animations because they don't involve movement of individual items on a slide. However, slide transitions are usually used in concert with animations to create presentations that are as much fun to watch as they are informative.

Using the Animations Tab

PowerPoint's animation effects fall into two categories: *slide transitions*, which provide interest for the movement from one slide to the next; and *animations*, which add movement to individual objects on a slide. Both types of animations are controlled from the Animations tab on the Ribbon, as shown in Figure 10-1.

Figure 10-1:
The
Animations
tab.

The Animations tab consists of three groups of controls, as described in the following list:

✔ **Preview:** This group includes a single control — a Preview button — that displays a preview of the animation effects you selected for the current slide.

✔ **Animations:** This group lets you create animation effects. You can select a predefined effect from the Animate drop-down list, or you can click the Custom Animation button to specify a custom animation. For more information, see the section, "Customizing Your Animation," later in this chapter.

✔ **Transition to This Slide:** This group lets you set the transition effect that's used when the slide is displayed. For more information, see the next section, "Using Slide Transitions."

Using Slide Transitions

A *transition* is how PowerPoint gets from one slide to the next during an on-screen slide show. The normal way to segue from slide to slide is simply cutting to the new slide — effective, yes, but also boring. PowerPoint enables you to assign any of the more than 50 different special effects to each slide transition. For example, you can have the next slide scoot over the top of the current slide from any direction, or you can have the current slide scoot off the screen in any direction to reveal the next slide. You can have slides fade out, dissolve into each other, open up like Venetian blinds, or spin in like spokes on a wheel.

To use a slide transition, follow these steps:

1. Move to the slide to which you want to apply the transition.

Note that the transition applies when you come to the slide you apply the transition to, not when you go to the next slide. For example, if you apply a transition to slide 3, the transition is displayed when you move from slide 2 to slide 3, not when you move from slide 3 to slide 4.

If you want to apply the animation scheme to all your slides, you can skip this step because it won't matter which slide you start from.

If you want to apply different transitions to different slides, you might prefer to work in Slide Sorter View (click the Slide Sorter View button near the bottom-right corner of the screen), which allows you to see more slides at once. If you're going to use the same transition for all your slides, though, no benefit comes from switching to Slide Sorter View.

2. **Open the Transitions gallery by clicking the More button that appears to the right of the six slide transition buttons.**

   The Transitions gallery appears, as shown in Figure 10-2.

Figure 10-2:
The
Transitions
gallery.

3. **Click the slide transition that you want to use.**

   PowerPoint previews the transition by animating the current slide. If you want to see the preview again, just click the transition again.

   The following list includes options that you can choose from when you create your slide transition:

   • Adjust the transition speed. You can choose from Slow, Medium, and Fast. Choose the setting that looks best on your computer.

   • Add a sound. The Sound drop-down menu lists a collection of standard transition sounds, such as applause, a cash register, and the standard whoosh. You can also choose Other Sound to use your own .wav file.

- To advance the slide automatically, select the Automatically check box and then set the number of seconds. If you leave this check box deselected, PowerPoint waits for you to press a key or click the mouse (if "On Mouse Click" is selected) to advance to the next slide.

- To apply the animation to the entire presentation, click Apply to All. This applies the animation to all the slides in the presentation.

Here are some additional points to keep in mind when using slide transitions:

✔ **Consider computer speed:** Transition effects look better on faster computers, which have more raw processing horsepower to implement the fancy pixel dexterity required to produce good-looking transitions. If your computer is a bit slow, change the speed setting to Fast so the transition won't drag.

✔ **Select sets of transitions:** Some of the transition effects come in matched sets that apply the same effect from different directions. You can create a cohesive set of transitions by alternating among these related effects from slide to slide. For example, set up the first slide with Wipe Right, the second slide with Wipe Left, the third with Wipe Down, and so on.

✔ **Use random transitions:** PowerPoint has a Random Transition option that picks a different transition effect randomly for each slide. Although you might be tempted by indecision to use this option, I recommend against it. Your presentation looks more cohesive when you pick a transition effect and stick to it. Using a different transition for every slide can be tacky.

✔ **Choose effective transitions:** If the next slide has the same color scheme as the current slide, even the most bizarre transition effects, such as "Wheel Clockwise, 8 Spokes" or "Wedge" look pretty tame. To maximize the impact of the transitions, use slides with contrasting color schemes.

✔ **Preview transitions:** When you work in Slide Sorter View, you can click the little star icon beneath each slide to preview the transition for that slide. Also, the automatic slide timing is shown beneath the slide if you set the slide to advance automatically.

Animating Text with Entrance and Exit Effects

Besides slide transitions, the most common type of animation in PowerPoint is adding entrance and exit effects to the text that appears on the slide. This is especially useful for bullet lists because it lets you display the list one item at a time. You can have each item appear out of nowhere, drop from the top of the screen, march in from the left or right, or do a back somersault followed by two cartwheels and a double-twist flip (talc, please!).

This type of animation is often called a *build effect* because it lets you build your points one by one.

To apply a build effect, first select the text box that you want to animate. Then, choose the animation style from the Animate drop-down list in the Animations group in the Animations tab on the Ribbon. You can apply three distinct text animations via this drop-down:

✔ Fade

✔ Wipe

✔ Fly In

For more complex animations, you need to use custom animations as described in the next section, "Customizing Your Animation."

Customizing Your Animation

Custom animation is the nitty-gritty of PowerPoint animation. Custom animation is the only way to apply text animation that's more complicated than the predefined Fade, Wipe, or Fly In styles of the Animate drop-down list. In addition to animating text, custom animation lets you animate other objects on your slides, such as pictures, shapes, and charts.

Understanding custom animation

Before I get into the details of setting up custom animation, you need to understand some basic concepts. Don't worry — this won't get too technical. But you need to know this stuff.

For starters, you can apply custom animations to any object on a slide, whether it's a text placeholder, a drawing object such as an AutoShape or a text box, or a clip art picture. For text objects, you can apply the animation to the text object as a whole or to individual paragraphs within the object. You can also specify whether the effect go all at once, word by word, or letter by letter. And you can indicate whether the effect happens automatically or whether PowerPoint waits for you to click the mouse or press Enter to initiate the animation.

Custom animation lets you create four basic types of animation effects for slide objects:

- ✔ **Entrance effect:** This is how an object enters the slide. If you don't specify an entrance effect, the object starts in whatever position that you placed it on the slide. If you want to be more creative, though, you can have objects appear via any of the 52 different entrance effects, such as Appear, Blinds, Fade, Descend, Boomerang, Bounce, Sling, and many others.

- ✔ **Emphasis effect:** This effect lets you draw attention to an object that is already on the slide. PowerPoint offers 31 different emphasis effects, including Change Fill Color, Change Font Size, Grow/Shrink, Spin, Teeter, Flicker, Color Blend, Blast, and many more.

- ✔ **Exit effect:** This is how an object leaves the slide. Most objects don't have exit effects, but if you want an object to leave, you can apply one of the 52 different effects — which are similar to the entrance effects — Disappear, Blinds, Peek Out, Ease Out, Spiral Out, and so on.

- ✔ **Motion path:** Motion paths are the most interesting types of custom animation. A motion path lets you create a track along which the object travels when animated. PowerPoint provides you with 64 predefined motion paths, such as circles, stars, teardrops, spirals, springs, and so on. If that's not enough, you can draw your own custom path to make an object travel anywhere on the slide you want it to go.

    If the motion path begins off the slide and ends somewhere on the slide, the motion path effect is similar to an entrance effect. If the path begins on the slide but ends off the slide, the motion path effect is like an exit effect. And if the path begins and ends on the slide, it is similar to an emphasis effect. In that case, when the animation starts, the object appears, travels along its path, and then zips off the slide.

    To draw a custom motion path, click the Add Effect button in the Custom Animation pane, choose Motion Paths Draw, then choose Draw Custom Path and select one of the motion path drawing tools from the menu that appears. The tools include straight lines, curves, freeform shapes, and scribbles. You can then draw your motion path using the tool you selected.

You can create more than one animation for a given object. For example, you can give an object an entrance effect, an emphasis effect, and an exit effect. That lets you bring the object on-screen, draw attention to it, and then have it leave. If you want, you can have several emphasis or motion path effects for a single object. You can also have more than one entrance and exit effect, but in most cases, one will do.

Each effect that you apply has one or more property settings that you can tweak to customize the effect. All the effects have a Speed setting that lets you set the speed for the animation. Some effects have an additional property setting that lets you control the range of an object's movement. (For example, the Spin effect has an Amount setting that governs how far the object spins.)

Adding an effect

To animate an object on a slide, follow these steps:

1. **In Normal View, call up the slide that contains the object you want to animate and then click the object to select it.**

   To animate text paragraphs, select the text placeholder that holds the text.

2. **Click the Animations tab on the Ribbon and then click Custom Animation in the Animations group.**

   The Custom Animation task pane appears, as shown in Figure 10-3. In this example, I want to animate a text box.

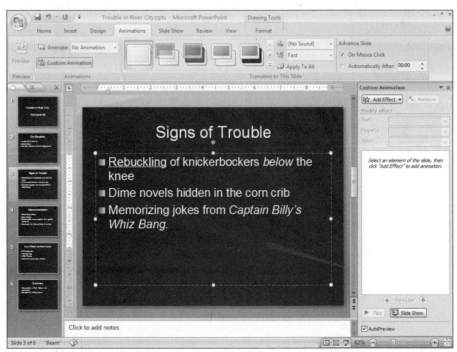

Figure 10-3: Animating an object.

3. **Click the Add Effect button and then select the type of effect you want to create from the menu that appears.**

   The menu lists the four types of effects: Entrance, Emphasis, Exit, and Motion Path. In this example, I choose Entrance so that I can create an entrance effect. A menu listing the effects appears.

4. Choose the specific effect that you want to apply. If the effect that you want isn't on the menu, choose More Effects.

An Add Effect dialog box listing all the effects for the type you chose appears. For example, Figure 10-4 shows the Add Entrance Effect dialog box that appears if you choose Add Effect⇨Entrance⇨More Effects.

The most commonly used effects for each type are listed right on the effect type menu. If the effect that you want to use appears on the menu, you can select it without calling up the Add Entrance Effect dialog box.

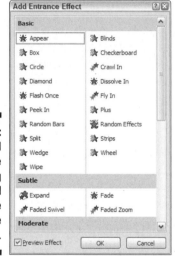

Figure 10-4:
The Add Entrance Effect dialog box lists all possible entrance effects.

5. Choose the effect that you want and then click OK.

The entrance effect you selected is added to the Custom Animation task pane, as shown in Figure 10-5. The effect's number (in this case, one) also appears on the slide next to the object the effect applies to. (Fear not; this number appears only on the slide when in Normal View, and only when the Custom Animation task pane is active. Your audience won't see the number when you show your presentation.)

6. (Optional) Adjust the property settings for the animation.

In Figure 10-5, the effect has two property settings: Direction and Speed. The Direction setting indicates which direction the smiley face should fly in from, and the Speed setting indicates how fast it should move.

Figure 10-5:
The Custom
Animation
task pane
lists the
animations
you create.

7. To preview the animation, click the Play button at the bottom of the Custom Animation task pane.

Or, if you prefer, just run the slide show to see how the animation looks. If nothing happens, click the mouse to start the animation.

If you add more than one effect to a slide, the effects are initiated one at a time by mouse clicks, in the order you create them. You can drag effects up or down in the custom animation list to change the order of the effects. For more information about changing the order or setting up automatic effects, see the section, "Timing your animations," later in this chapter.

If you want to change an effect — for example, use the Magnify entrance effect instead of the Fly In effect — select the effect in the Custom Animation task pane. The Add Effect button will change to a Change button, which you can then click to choose a new effect.

You can further tweak an effect by clicking the down arrow that appears next to the effect in the custom animation list and then choosing Effect Options. This brings up a dialog box similar to the one shown in Figure 10-6. This dialog box has settings that let you add a sound to the animation, change the color of the object after the animation completes, and specify how you want text animated (All at Once, One Word at a Time, or One Letter at a Time). Depending on the type of effect, additional controls might appear in this dialog box.

Figure 10-6:
The settings dialog box for an animation effect.

More about animating text

The most common reason for animating text is to draw attention to your text one paragraph at a time while you show your presentation. One way to do this is to create an entrance effect for the text placeholder and then adjust the effect settings so that the entrance effect is applied one paragraph at a time. When you do that, your slide initially appears empty except for the title. Click once, and the first paragraph appears. Talk about that paragraph for a while and then click again to bring up the second paragraph. You can keep talking and clicking until all the paragraphs have appeared. When you click again, PowerPoint calls up the next slide.

Another approach is to use an emphasis effect instead of an entrance effect. This allows all the paragraphs to display initially on the slide. When you click the mouse, the emphasis effect is applied to the first paragraph — it changes colors, increases in size, spins, whatever. Each time you click, the emphasis effect is applied to the next paragraph in sequence.

Either way, you must first add the effect for the text placeholder, and then call up the Effect Settings dialog box by clicking the down arrow next to the effect in the custom animation list and then choosing Effect Settings. This summons the settings dialog box for the text object. Click the Text Animation tab to see the animation settings, as shown in Figure 10-7.

The Group Text setting controls how paragraphs appear when you click the mouse during the show, based on the paragraph's outline level. If you have only one outline level on the slide, grouping By 1st Level Paragraphs will do. If you have two or more levels, leaving grouping text By 1st Level Paragraphs causes each paragraph to be animated along with any paragraphs that are subordinate to it. If you'd rather animate the second-level paragraphs separately, group your text By 2nd Level Paragraphs instead.

Figure 10-7:
Animating
text.

The other controls on this tab let you animate each paragraph automatically after a certain time interval or display the paragraphs in reverse order. (David Letterman, if you're reading this, you can use this feature when you present your Top Ten lists.)

Timing your animations

Most animations are initiated by mouse clicks. However, you can set up several animations to activate automatically — in sequence or all at the same time. To do so, you must use PowerPoint's animation timing features.

The first trick to controlling animation timing is to get the effects listed in the custom animation list in the correct order. Effects are added to the list in the order you create them. If you plan carefully, you might be able to create the effects in the same order that you want to animate them. More likely, you'll need to change the order of the effects. Fortunately, you can do that easily enough by dragging the effects up or down in the Custom Animation task pane.

After you get the effects in the right order, choose an option from the Start drop-down list that's near the top of the Custom Animation task pane to set the Start setting for each effect. This setting has three options:

  ✔ **On Click:** Starts the effect when you click the mouse or press Enter

  ✔ **With Previous:** Starts the effect when the effect immediately above it starts

   Use this option to animate two or more objects simultaneously.

  ✔ **After Previous:** Starts the effect as soon as the preceding effect finishes

Starting with the first effect in the list, click each effect to select it and then choose the Start setting for the effect. If all the effects except the first are set to With Previous or After Previous, the entire slide's animations run automatically once you start the first effect by clicking the mouse.

For example, Figure 10-8 shows a slide with three polygons drawn to resemble pieces of a puzzle. You can animate this puzzle so that the three pieces come together at the same time.

If you want to find out how to draw the shapes that are animated in this illustration, you can look ahead to Chapter 13.

Figure 10-8:
An animated puzzle.

Follow these steps to set up an animated puzzle like the one shown in Figure 10-8:

1. **Add a Fly In entrance effect for the top-left piece with the following settings:**

   - *Start:* On Click

   - *Direction:* From Top-Left

   - *Speed:* Medium

2. **Add a Fly In entrance effect for the top-right piece with the following settings:**

   - *Start:* With Previous

   - *Direction:* From Top-Right

   - *Speed:* Medium

3. Add a Fly In entrance effect for the bottom piece with the following settings:

- *Start:* With Previous

- *Direction:* From Bottom

- *Speed:* Medium

For even more control over an effect's timings, click the down arrow to the right of the effect and then choose Timing. A dialog box similar to the one in Figure 10-9 appears. Here's the lowdown on the timing settings:

- ✔ **Start:** This is the same as the Start setting in the Custom Animation task pane.

- ✔ **Delay:** This lets you delay the start of the animation by a specified number of seconds.

- ✔ **Speed:** This is the same as the Speed setting in the Custom Animation task pane.

- ✔ **Repeat:** This lets you repeat the effect so the object is animated several times in succession.

- ✔ **Rewind when done playing:** Certain effects leave the object in a different condition than the object was when you started. For example, the object might change color or size or move to a new position on the slide. If you select the Rewind When Done Playing option, the object is restored to its original condition when the animation finishes.

Figure 10-9:
Establishing
the timing
settings.

Making Text Jiggle

One of my favorite cute little animations is to make text — especially a short heading — jiggle. Not a lot, but just a little. The effect works best if the text has a funny typeface, such as Cosmic or Jokerman. By using a very small motion path and setting the timing options to repeat until the end of the slide, you can make the text jiggle just a little bit the entire time the slide is on-screen:

1. **Type the text that you want to jiggle and use the Font drop-down list to choose an appropriately silly typeface.**

2. **Use the Zoom control at the bottom-right corner of the screen to zoom in to 400%.**

   You want to zoom way in so you can draw a very small motion path.

3. **Choose Slide Show⇨Custom Animation to call up the Custom Animation task pane.**

4. **Click Add Effect and then choose Motion Paths⇨Draw Custom Path⇨ Scribble.**

   The cursor changes to a little pencil.

5. **Draw a tightly knit scribble pattern right in the center of the text.**

   Just wiggle the pencil cursor back and forth and up and down in an area of just a few pixels. Go back and forth quite a few times to make the jiggle effect appear to be random.

6. **Zoom back out to normal size.**

7. **In the Custom Animation task pane, click the arrow next to the animation you just created and then choose Timing.**

   This brings up the dialog box that lets you set the timing options.

8. **Change the speed to Very Fast and the Repeat drop-down to Until End of Slide. Then click OK.**

9. **Run the slide show to check the effect.**

You might have to try this several times before you get an effect you like. Don't be afraid to experiment!

Chapter 11

Masters of the Universe Meet the Templates of Doom

*W*ant to add a bit of text to every slide in your presentation? Or maybe add your name and phone number at the bottom of your audience handouts? Or place a picture of Rush Limbaugh at the extreme right side of each page of your speaker notes?

Masters are the surefire way to add something to every slide. No need to toil separately at each slide. Add something to the Master, and it shows up automatically on every slide. Remove it from the Master and — poof! — it disappears from every slide. Very convenient.

Masters govern all aspects of a slide's appearance: background color, objects that appear on every slide, text that appears on all slides, and more.

Working with Masters

In PowerPoint, a Master governs the appearance of all the slides or pages in a presentation. Each presentation has at least three Masters:

✔ **Slide Master:** Dictates the format of your slides

You work with this Master most often when you tweak your slides to cosmetic perfection.

✔ **Handout Master:** Controls the look of printed handouts

✔ **Notes Master:** Determines the characteristics of printed speaker notes

Each Master specifies the appearance of text (font, size, and color, for example), slide background color, animation effects, and any additional text or other objects that you want to appear on each slide or page.

In addition, each Master can contain one or more *layouts* that provide different arrangements of text and other elements on the slide. For example, a typical Slide Master might contain a Title layout and several Text layouts for various types of body text slides.

One interesting — and often useful — aspect of Slide Masters is that any elements you add to the Master itself are also included in each layout that's associated with the Master. For example, if you set the background color for the Slide Master, that color is used for each layout. Likewise, if you add a big blue rectangle in the top-left corner of the Slide Master, that rectangle is visible in the top-left corner of each layout.

However, you can also add elements to an individual layout. Then, the element is present only for that layout. For example, you may want to add additional graphical elements to the Title layout. Then, those elements appear only on slides that use the Title layout.

Here are a few other points to ponder while you lie awake at night thinking about Slide Masters:

✔ Masters aren't optional. Every presentation has them. You can, however, override the formatting of objects contained in the Master for a particular slide. This capability enables you to vary the appearance of slides when necessary.

✔ PowerPoint allows you to create more than one Slide Master in a single presentation, so you can mix two or more slide designs in your presentations. That's why I say a presentation has *at least* three Masters. If you have more than one Slide Master, a presentation will have more than three Masters altogether. Note, however, that you can still have only one Handout or Notes Master in each presentation. For more information about using more than one Slide Master, see the section, "Yes, You Can Serve Two Masters," at the end of this chapter.

✔ If you've used previous versions of PowerPoint, you might be wondering what happened to the Title Master. In the old days, there was actually a separate Master for title slides. However, in PowerPoint 2007, title slides don't have their own Masters. Instead, the format of title slides is controlled by a Title Slide layout that belongs to a particular Slide Master.

Modifying the Slide Master

If you don't like the layout of your slides, call up the Slide Master and do something about it, as shown in these steps:

1. **Call up Slide Master View by opening the View tab on the Ribbon and then clicking the Slide Master button, found in the Presentation Views group.**

   Alternatively, you can hold down the Shift key and then click the Normal View button near the bottom right of the screen.

2. **Behold the Slide Master in all its splendor.**

   Figure 11-1 shows a typical Slide Master. You can see the placeholders for the slide title and body text. Although none are visible in this example, the Master can also contain background colors and other elements that are present on each slide.

   The Slide Master includes placeholders for three objects that appear at the bottom of each slide: the Date area, Footer area, and Number area. These special areas are described later in this chapter under the heading, "Using Headers and Footers."

   A thumbnail of each Slide Master as well as the layouts for each Master are shown on the left side of the screen.

3. **Make any formatting changes that you want.**

   Select the text you want to apply a new style to and make your formatting changes. If you want all the slide titles to be in italics, for example, select the title text and then press Ctrl+I or click the Italic button on the Formatting toolbar.

   Make sure the Slide Master itself is selected — not one of its layouts. That way, any changes you make apply to all the layouts associated with the Slide Master.

4. **(Optional) To add elements that are specific to one of the layouts, select the layout and then add your changes.**

   For example, you may want to add additional graphical elements or select different fonts for your title slides. To do that, select the Title Slide layout and make your changes.

5. **Click the Normal View button near the bottom right of the window to return to Normal View.**

   You're done!

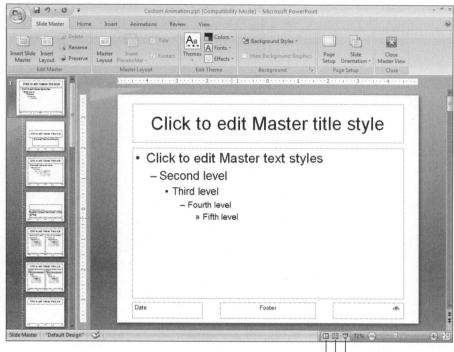

Figure 11-1:
Slide
Master
View.

Normal View

Slide Sorter

Slide View

Notice that the body object contains paragraphs for five outline levels formatted with different point sizes, indentations, and bullet styles. If you want to change the way an outline level is formatted, this is the place to do so.

You can type all you want in the title or object area placeholders, but the text that you type doesn't appear on the slides. The text that appears in these placeholders is provided only so that you can see the effect of the formatting changes you apply. (To insert text that appears on each slide, see the upcoming section, "Adding recurring text or other elements.")

You can edit any other object on the Master by clicking it. Unlike the title and object area placeholders, any text that you type in other Slide Master objects appears exactly as you type it on each slide.

Working with the Slide Master and Edit Master tabs

When you switch to Slide Master View, an entirely new tab appears on the Ribbon. This new tab — appropriately called the Slide Master tab — is pictured in Figure 11-2.

Figure 11-2: The Slide Master tab.

Throughout this chapter, I show you how to use many of the controls in this tab. For now, here's a quick overview of each group on this tab and the controls found in them:

- ✔ **Edit Master:** The controls in this group let you edit the Slide Master. You can use the Insert Slide Master button to create a new Slide Master, or you can use the Insert Layout button to add a new layout to an existing Master. You can also use the Delete and Rename buttons to delete or rename Masters or layouts. For information about the Preserve button, see the section "Preserving your masters," later in this chapter.

- ✔ **Master Layout:** The controls in this group let you edit a layout by adding or removing placeholders, the title, and footer elements.

- ✔ **Edit Theme:** The controls in this group let you apply a theme to a Master or a layout. For more information about themes, flip to Chapter 9.

- ✔ **Background:** The controls in this group let you set the background for a Master or a layout. Refer to Chapter 9 for more information.

- ✔ **Page Setup:** The control in this group lets you change the orientation for a page. (Unfortunately, PowerPoint doesn't allow you to have Masters with different orientations in a single presentation. When you change the orientation of a Slide Master or a layout, the orientation of all Masters and layouts in the presentation is changed.)

- ✔ **Close:** This group contains a Close button that returns you to Normal View.

Adding recurring text or other elements

To add recurring text to each slide, follow this procedure:

1. **Call up the Slide Master (by clicking Slide Master in the Presentation Views group of the Views tab) if it's not displayed already.**

2. **Add a text box to the Slide Master by selecting the Insert tab on the Ribbon and then clicking the Text Box button (found in the Text group).**

   Click where you want to add the text.

3. **Type the text that you want to appear on each slide.**

   For example, **Call 1-800-555-NERD today! Don't delay! Operators are standing by!**

4. **Format the text however you want.**

   For example, if you want bold, press Ctrl+B or click the Bold button on the Formatting toolbar. (See Chapter 8 for more on text formatting.)

5. **Click the Normal View button to return to your presentation.**

   Now's the time to gloat over your work. Lasso some co-workers and show 'em how proud you are that you added some text that appears on each slide in your presentation.

You can add other types of objects to the Slide Master, too. You can add clip art, pictures, or even a video or sound clip. Anything that you can add to an individual slide can be added to the Slide Master.

After you place an object on the Slide Master, you can grab it with the mouse and move it or resize it in any way you want. The object appears in the same location and size on each slide.

To delete an object from the Slide Master, click it and press Delete. To delete a text object, you must first click the object and then click again on the object frame. Then press Delete.

Applying themes to your Masters

You can use the Edit Theme group in the Slide Master tab on the Ribbon to change the theme applied to a Slide Master. *Note:* All the layouts that belong to a given Master use the same theme. So, it doesn't matter whether the Slide Master itself or one of its layouts is selected when you change the theme; either way, the entire Slide Master is changed.

To change the theme for a Slide Master, follow these steps:

1. **Choose View⇨Presentation Views⇨Slide Master or Shift+click the Normal View button at the bottom right of the PowerPoint window to summon the Slide Master.**

2. **Use the Themes drop-down list on the Slide Master tab to select the theme you want to apply to the Slide Master.**

3. **(Optional) Use the Colors, Fonts, and Effects controls to modify the color scheme, fonts, and effects used for the theme.**

   Treat yourself to a bag of Cheetos if it works the first time. If it doesn't work, have a bag of Cheetos anyway. Then rub all that orange gunk that sticks to your fingers on the computer screen. That will apply the Cheetos Orange color scheme to your Slide Master — at least temporarily.

PowerPoint themes are hefty enough that I have devoted an entire chapter to them. Go to Chapter 9 if you need to know how they work.

If you want to adjust the slide background, use the Background Styles control. Chapter 9 walks you through this feature.

Adding new layouts

If you don't like the standard layouts that come with PowerPoint's built-in Slide Master, you can add an additional layout and customize it any way you want. To add your own layout, just follow these steps:

1. **Switch to Slide Master View by choosing View⇨ Presentation Views⇨ Slide Master or Shift+click the Normal View button near the bottom right of the window.**

2. **On the Slide Master tab on the Ribbon, click Insert Layout in the Edit Master group.**

   A new, blank layout is inserted in the current Slide Master.

3. **Use the Insert Placeholder drop-down list in the Master Layout group on the Slide Master tab on the Ribbon to insert whatever placeholders you want to add to the new layout.**

   This control reveals a list of placeholder types you can insert. The options are Content, Text, Picture, Chart, Table, Diagram, Media, and Clip Art.

4. **Play with the layout until you get it just right.**

   You can move and resize the placeholders to your heart's content, and you can apply any formatting or other options you want for the layout.

5. **When you're happy, click the Close button to switch back to Normal View.**

Adjusting the Handout and Notes Masters

Like the Slide Master, the Handout and Notes Masters contain formatting information that's applied automatically to your presentation. This section tells you how you can modify these Masters.

Changing the Handout Master

Follow these simple steps to change the Handout Master:

1. **Choose View⇨Presentation Views⇨Handout Master or hold down the Shift key while clicking the Slide Sorter View button.**

   The Handout Master rears its ugly head, as shown in Figure 11-3. Notice that it includes a special Handout Master tab on the Ribbon.

2. **Mess around with it.**

Figure 11-3: The Handout Master.

The Handout Master shows the arrangement of handouts for slides printed two, three, four, six, or nine per page, plus the arrangement for printing outlines. You can switch among these different handout layouts by using the Slides-Per-Page control in the Page Setup group on the Handout Master tab.

Unfortunately, you can't move, resize, or delete the slide and outline placeholders that appear in the Handout Master. You *can,* however, add or change elements that you want to appear on each handout page, such as your name and phone number, a page number, and maybe a good lawyer joke.

3. **Click Close on the Handout Master tab on the Ribbon.**

   PowerPoint returns to Normal View.

4. **Print a handout to see whether your changes worked.**

   Handout Master elements are invisible until you print them, so you should print at least one handout page to check your work.

When you print handout pages, the slides are formatted according to the Slide Master. You can't change the appearance of the slides from the Handout Master.

Changing the Notes Master

Notes pages consist of a reduced image of the slide, plus any notes that you type to go along with the slide. For more information about creating and using notes pages, see Chapter 5.

When printed, notes pages are formatted according to the Notes Master. To change the Notes Master, follow these steps:

1. **Choose View⇨Presentation Views⇨Notes Master.**

   The Notes Master comes to life, as shown in Figure 11-4.

2. **Indulge yourself.**

   The Notes Master contains two main placeholders — one for your notes text and the other for the slide. You can move or change the size of either of these objects, and you can change the format of the text in the notes placeholder. You also can add or change elements that you want to appear on each handout page. Also notice the convenient placement of the header, footer, date, and page number blocks.

3. **Click Close Notes Master tab.**

   PowerPoint returns to Normal View.

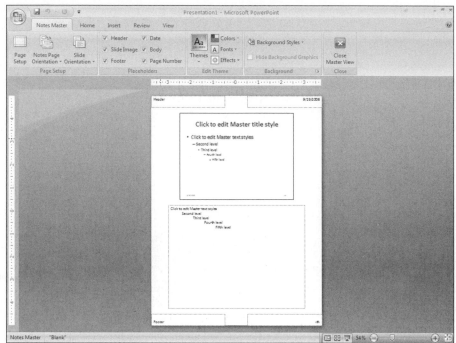

Figure 11-4:
The Notes
Master.

4. **Print your notes to see whether your changes worked.**

At the very least, add page numbers to your speaker notes. That way, if you drop a stack of notes pages, you can use the page numbers to quickly sort them back into order.

If public speaking gives you severe stomach cramps, add the text "Just picture them naked" to the Notes Master. It works every time for me.

Using Masters

You don't have to do anything special to apply the formats from a Master to your slide; all slides automatically pick up the Master format unless you specify otherwise. So this section really should be titled "Not Using Masters" because it talks about how to *not* use the formats provided by Masters.

Overriding the Master text style

To override the text style specified by a Slide Master, simply format the text however you want while you're working in Normal View. The formatting changes you make apply only to the selected text. The Slide Masters aren't affected.

The only way to change one of the Masters is to do it directly by switching to the appropriate Master View. Thus, any formatting changes you make while in Slide View affect only that slide.

If you change the layout or formatting of text elements on a slide (for example, if you move the title placeholder or change the title font) and then decide that you liked it better the way it was, you can quickly reapply the text style from the Slide Master. Right-click the slide in the Slide Preview pane (on the left side of the screen) and then choose Reset Slide from the menu that appears.

Hiding background objects

Slide Masters enable you to add background objects that appear on every slide in your presentation. You can, however, hide the background objects for selected slides. You can also change the background color or effect used for an individual slide. These steps show you how:

1. **Display the slide that you want to show with a plain background.**

2. **Click the Design tab on the Ribbon and then select the Hide Background Graphics check box found in the Background group.**

Hiding background objects or changing the background color or effect applies only to the current slide. Other slides are unaffected.

If you want to remove some but not all the background objects from a single slide, try this trick:

1. **Hide the background graphics from the slide.**

   To hide a background object, choose Design➪Background➪Hide Background Objects.

2. **Call up the Slide Master by choosing View➪Presentation Views➪Slide Master.**

3. **Hold down the Shift key and then click each of the background objects that you want to appear.**

4. **Press Ctrl+C to copy these objects to the Clipboard.**

5. **Return to Normal View by clicking the Normal button at the bottom of the screen.**

6. **Press Ctrl+V to paste the objects from the Clipboard.**

7. **Click the Design tab on the Ribbon and then click the Sent to Back button (in the Arrange group) if the background objects obscure other slide objects or text.**

Note that if you paste objects in this way, those objects are no longer tied to the Slide Master. Thus, if you later change the objects on the Slide Master, the change won't be reflected on the slides with the pasted copies of the objects.

Using Headers and Footers

Headers and footers provide a convenient way to place repeating text at the top or bottom of each slide, handout, or notes page. You can add the time and date, slide number or page number, or any other information that you want to appear on each slide or page, such as your name or the title of your presentation.

The PowerPoint Slide Masters include three placeholders for such information:

- ✔ The **Date area** can be used to display a date and time.
- ✔ The **Number area** can be used to display the slide number.
- ✔ The **Footer area** can be used to display any text that you want to see on each slide.

In addition, Handout and Notes Masters include a fourth placeholder, the *Header area,* which provides an additional area for text that you want to see on each page.

Although the Date, Number, and Footer areas normally appear at the bottom of the slide in the Slide Masters, you can move them to the top by switching to Slide View or Slide Master View and then dragging the placeholders to the top of the slide.

Adding a date, number, or footer to slides

To add a date, slide number, or footer to your slides, follow these steps:

1. **Click the Insert tab on the Ribbon and then click the Header and Footer button (found in the Text group).**

   The Header and Footer dialog box appears, as shown in Figure 11-5. (If necessary, click the Slide tab so that you see the slide footer options as shown in the figure.)

Figure 11-5:
The Header and Footer dialog box.

2. **To display the date, select the Date and Time check box. Then select the date format that you want in the list box beneath the Update Automatically radio button.**

   Alternatively, you can select the Fixed radio button and then type any text that you want in the Fixed text box. The text that you type appears in the Date area of the Slide Master.

   If you're the sort of bloke who begins a presentation with *G'day mates!*, you might want to change the Language and Calendar Type settings.

3. **To display slide numbers, select the Slide Number check box.**

4. **To display a footer on each slide, select the Footer check box and then type the text that you want to appear on each slide in the Footer text box.**

   For example, you may type your name, your company name, a subliminal message, or the name of your presentation.

5. **If you want the date, number, and footer to appear on every slide except for the title slide, select the Don't Show on Title Slide check box.**

6. **Click Apply to All.**

If you're going to give a presentation on a certain date in the future (for example, at a sales conference or a trade show), type the date that you'll be giving the presentation directly into the Fixed text box. You can use the same technique to postdate presentations that you never really gave but need to supply to your legal counsel to back up your alibi.

If you want to change the Footer areas for just one slide, click Apply instead of Apply to All. This option comes in handy for those occasional slides that contain a graphic or a block of text that crowds up against the footer areas. You can easily suppress the footer information for that slide to make room for the large graphic or text.

Adding a header or footer to notes or handouts pages

To add header and footer information to notes or handouts pages, follow the steps described in the preceding section, "Adding a date, number, or footer to slides," except click the Notes and Handouts tab after the Header and Footer dialog box appears. Clicking this tab displays a dialog box that's similar to the Header and Footer dialog box for Slide, except that it gives you an additional option to add a header that appears at the top of each page. After you indicate how you want to print the Date, Header, Number, and Footer areas, click the Apply to All button.

Editing the header and footer placeholders directly

If you want, you can edit the text that appears in the header and footer placeholders directly. First, display the appropriate Master — Slide, Handout, or Notes. Then click the date, number, footer, or header placeholder and start typing.

You may notice that the placeholders include special codes for the options that you indicated in the Header and Footer dialog box. For example, the date placeholder may contain the text *<date,time>* if you indicated that the date should be displayed. You can type text before or after these codes, but you should leave the codes themselves alone.

Yes, You Can Serve Two Masters

In spite of the Biblical edict, Microsoft has endowed PowerPoint with the ability to have more than one Slide Master. This feature lets you set up two or more Slide Masters and then choose which Master you want to use for each slide in your presentation.

The following sections explain how to use the multiple Masters feature.

Creating a new Slide Master

To add a new Master to a presentation, follow these steps:

1. **Switch to Slide Master View.**

   From the View tab on the Ribbon, click the Slide Master button (found in the Presentation Views group). Or if you prefer, hold down the Shift key and click the Normal View button near the lower-right corner of the screen.

2. **In the Slide Master tab on the Ribbon, click the Insert Slide Master button in the Edit Master group.**

   A new Slide Master appears, as shown in Figure 11-6. Notice that a thumbnail for the new Slide Master is added to the list of thumbnails on the left side of the screen, and that the new Slide Master uses Power-Point's default settings (white background, black text, and so forth).

Figure 11-6:
Creating a
new Slide
Master.

3. **Modify the new Slide Master to your liking.**

   You can make any formatting changes you want: Change the background color and text styles, add additional background objects, and so on.

4. **Click Close on the Slide Master tab on the Ribbon to return to Normal View.**

   You can now begin using the new Master that you created. (See the section, "Applying Masters," later in this chapter for more information.)

Another way to create a new Slide Master is to duplicate one of your presentation's existing Slide Masters. When you do that, the new Slide Master inherits the formatting of the original one. This can save you a lot of work, especially if you want to create a new Slide Master that varies from an existing one in only a minor way, such as having a different background color.

To duplicate a Slide Master, click the Master that you want to duplicate in the thumbnails on the left of the screen and then press Ctrl+D.

To delete a Slide Master, click the Master that you want to delete. Then click the Delete Master button in the Slide Master tab on the Ribbon (located in the Edit Master group). Or, just press Delete.

Applying Masters

If you have created multiple Masters for a presentation, you can select which Master to use for each slide in your presentation. To apply a Master to one or more slides, follow these steps:

1. **Select the slide or slides to which you want to apply the alternate Slide Master.**

   The easiest way to do this is to click the slide that you want in the thumbnails area on the left of the screen. To select more than one slide, hold down the Ctrl key and click each slide that you want to select.

2. **Click the Home tab on the Ribbon and then click the Layout button (in the Slides group).**

   This action summons the gallery, as shown in Figure 11-7. Here, you can see all the layouts for all the Slide Masters contained in the presentation.

3. **Select the Slide Master layout you want to apply to the slides you selected.**

   The Slide Master is applied to the selected slides.

Figure 11-7:
Choosing a
layout.

Preserving your Masters

PowerPoint has a bad habit of deleting Slide Masters when they're no longer used in your presentation. For example, if you create a new Slide Master and then apply it to all the slides in your presentation, PowerPoint assumes that you no longer need the original Slide Master. So, the original is deleted. Poof! Your presentation is now one pickle short of a full jar.

You can prevent this from happening with the Preserve Master option for your Slide Masters. Any new Slide Masters that you create automatically gets the Preserve Master option, so they won't be deleted. However, the Slide Masters that your presentations start off with don't have the Preserve Master option, so you may want to set it yourself.

To preserve a Master, switch to Slide Master view, click the thumbnail for the Master that you want to preserve, and then click the Preserve button on the Slide Master tab on the Ribbon (found in the Edit Master group). A little push-pin icon appears next to the Master's thumbnail to show that the Master will be preserved.

Don't click the Preserve button indiscriminately! If you click it for a Master that already has the Preserve Master setting, Preserve Master is removed for that Master. Then the Master is subject to premature deletion.

Restoring Lost Placeholders

If you've played around with your Masters too much, you may inadvertently delete a layout placeholder that you wish you could get back. For example, suppose that you delete the footer placeholder from a Master and now you want it back. No problem! Just follow these steps:

1. **Switch to Slide Master View.**

2. **Call up the Master with the missing placeholder.**

3. **In the Slide Master tab on the Ribbon, click the Master Layout button (in the Master Layout group).**

   This calls up the Master Layout dialog box, as shown in Figure 11-8.

Figure 11-8:
The Master
Layout
dialog box.

The Master Layout dialog box is one of the strangest dialog boxes you encounter. If you summon it for a Master that still has all its placeholders, all the check boxes on the Master Layout dialog box are grayed out. So, all you can do is look at the controls, grunt, scratch your head, and then click OK to dismiss the seemingly useless dialog box. However, if you *have* deleted one or more placeholders, the check boxes for the missing placeholders are available.

4. **Select the check boxes for the placeholders that you want to restore.**

5. **Click OK.**

   The missing placeholders reappear.

Working with Templates

If you had to create every presentation from scratch, starting with a blank slide, you would probably put PowerPoint back in its box and use it as a bookend. Creating a presentation is easy, but creating one that looks good is a different story. Making a good-looking presentation is tough even for the artistically inclined. For left-brained, nonartistic types, it's next to impossible.

Thank heavens for templates. A *template* is simply a PowerPoint presentation file with predefined Slide Masters and boilerplate text. Templates jump-start the process of creating good-looking presentations. You can create your own templates, but fortunately PowerPoint comes with more than 70 templates designed by professional artists who understand color combinations, balance, and all that other artsy stuff. Have a croissant and celebrate.

Templates use the special file extension .potx, but you can also use ordinary PowerPoint presentation files (PPT) as templates. You can, therefore, use any of your own presentations as a template. If you make extensive changes to a presentation's Masters, you can use that presentation as a template for other presentations that you create. Or, you can save the presentation as a template by using the .potx file extension.

Because a template is a presentation, you can open it and change it if you want.

Creating a presentation based on a template

To create a new presentation based on a template, choose New from the Office menu to summon the New Presentation dialog box. Then, click Installed Templates in the Template Categories list to display a list of the templates that come with PowerPoint. See Figure 11-9.

To create a presentation based on one of these templates, simply click the template to select it and then click the Create button.

Another way to create a new presentation via a template is to click one of the categories listed under Microsoft Office Online. Then, you're presented with a frequently changing set of templates that are available for download from Microsoft's Office Web site.

Creating a new template

If none of the templates that come with PowerPoint appeals to you, you can easily create your own. All you have to do is create a presentation with the Masters and the color scheme set up just the way you want and then save it as a template. Here are a few points to remember about templates:

✔ If you want to make minor modifications to one of the supplied templates, open the template via the Open command. Then, make your changes and use the Save As command to save the template under a new name.

✔ You can also create your own presentation templates — complete with skeleton slides. Just create the template as a normal presentation and add however many slides that you want to include.

Part III
Embellishing Your Slides

The 5th Wave   By Rich Tennant

" Ooo-wait! That's perfect for the clinic's 'Your Procedure' presentation on the home page. Just stretch it out a little further...little more..."

In this part . . .

It is widely believed that Californians indulge in cosmetic surgery as often as they complain about utility rates. The chapters in this part are all about cosmetic surgery for your presentations. You discover how to perform such procedures as clip-art lifts, chart-o-suction, and media tucks. When you're done, your slides will look simply mahvelous.

Chapter 12

Inserting Pictures and Clip Art

. . . .

In This Chapter

▶ Using free pictures

▶ Finding a picture you like

▶ Moving, sizing, cropping, and stretching pictures

▶ Adding special effects such as borders, shadows, and reflections

▶ Even more picture options!

. . . .

Face it: Most of us weren't born with even an ounce of artistic ability. Some day (soon, hopefully), the genetic researchers combing through the billions and billions of genes strung out on those twisty DNA helixes will discover the Artist Gene. Then, in spite of protests from the da Vincis, Van Goghs, and Monets among us (who fear that their NEA grants will be threatened), doctors will splice the little gene into our DNA strands so that we can all be artists. Of course, this procedure won't be without its side effects: Some will develop an insatiable craving for croissants, and others will inexplicably develop French accents and whack off their ears. But artists we shall be.

Until then, we have to rely on clip art, pictures we've found on the Internet, or pictures that we scanned into the computer with a scanner or took with a digital camera.

Exploring the Many Types of Pictures

The world is awash with many different picture file formats. Fortunately, PowerPoint works with almost all these formats. The following sections describe the two basic types of pictures that you can work with in PowerPoint: bitmap pictures and vector drawings.

Bitmap pictures

A *bitmap picture* is a collection of small dots that compose an image. Bitmap pictures are most often used for photographs and for icons and other buttons used on Web pages. You can create your own bitmap pictures with a scanner, a digital camera, or a picture-drawing program such as Adobe Photoshop. You can even create crude bitmap pictures with Microsoft Paint, which is the free painting program that comes with Windows.

The dots that make up a bitmap picture are called *pixels.* The number of pixels in a given picture depends on two factors: the picture's resolution and its size. *Resolution* refers to the number of pixels per inch. A typical computer monitor displays 72 pixels per inch, though many monitors can display at higher resolutions. At 72 pixels per inch, a 1-inch square picture requires 5,184 pixels (72 x 72). Photographs that will be printed on an inkjet or laser printer usually have a much higher resolution, often 300 pixels per inch or more. At 300 pixels per inch, a 4-x-6-inch photograph requires more than two million pixels.

The amount of color information stored for the picture — also referred to as the picture's *color depth* — affects how many bytes of computer memory the picture requires. The color depth determines how many different colors the picture can contain. Most pictures have one of two color depths: 256 colors or 16.7 million colors. Most simple charts, diagrams, cartoons, and other types of clip art look fine at 256 colors. Photographs usually use 16.7 million colors.

Pictures with 16.7 million colors are also known as *TrueColor* pictures or *24-bit color* pictures.

A 4-x-6-inch photograph, which has more than two million pixels, requires about 2MB to store with 256 colors. With TrueColor, the size of the picture jumps to a whopping 6.4MB. Fortunately, bitmap pictures can be compressed to reduce their size without noticeably distorting the image. Depending on the actual contents of the picture, a 6MB picture might be reduced to 250KB or less.

Bitmap picture files usually have filename extensions such as `.bmp`, `.gif`, `.jpg`, `.png`, or `.pcx`. Table 12-1 lists the bitmap file formats that PowerPoint supports.

If you have a choice in the matter, I recommend you use JPEG format images for photographs that you want to include in PowerPoint presentations because JPEG's built-in compression saves hard drive space.

Table 12-1	PowerPoint's Bitmap Picture File Formats
Format	*What It Is*
BMP	Garden variety Windows bitmap file, used by Windows Paint and many other programs
GIF	Graphics Interchange Format, a format commonly used for small Internet pictures
JPEG	JPEG, a common format for photographs that includes built-in compression
PCD	Kodak Photo CD format
PCT	Macintosh PICT files
PCX	A variant type of bitmap file
PNG	Portable Network Graphics file, an image format designed for Internet graphics
TGA	Targa files
TIFF	Tagged Image Format file, another bitmap program most often used for high-quality photographs

Victor, give me a vector

Besides bitmap pictures, you can also use vector drawing with PowerPoint. A *vector drawing* is a picture file that contains a detailed definition of each shape that makes up the image. Vector drawings are usually created with high-powered drawing programs such as Adobe Illustrator.

PowerPoint supports all the most popular vector drawing formats, as described in Table 12-2.

Table 12-2	PowerPoint's Vector File Formats
Format	*What It Is*
CDR	Format for CorelDRAW!, a popular, upper-crust drawing program
CGM	Computer Graphics Metafiles
DRW	Format for Micrografx Designer or Micrografx Draw, two popular ooh-aah drawing programs

(continued)

Table 12-2 *(continued)*	
Format	**What It Is**
EMF	An Enhanced Windows MetaFile picture
EPS	Encapsulated PostScript, a format used by some high-end drawing programs
WMF	Windows MetaFile, a format that many programs recognize (note that WMF files can hold bitmap as well as vector data)
WPG	A WordPerfect drawing

Using Clip Art

Are you sitting down? Whether you buy PowerPoint by itself or get it as a part of Microsoft Office, you also get a collection of thousands of pictures, sound clips, and motion clips that you can pop directly into your presentations.

PowerPoint lets you access clip art through a special Clip Art task pane that lets you search for clip art by keyword. The Clip Art task pane makes it easy to find just the right picture to embellish your presentation.

The first time you access the clip art, a dialog box appears, offering to search your entire hard drive and create a catalog of all the pictures it contains. I suggest you accept this offer so that you can use it to access your own picture files in addition to the clip art files that come with PowerPoint.

In addition to pictures, PowerPoint can work sound and video clips. For more information about using sound and video, see Chapter 16.

Don't overdo the pictures. One surefire way to guarantee an amateurish look to your presentation is to load it down with three clip art pictures on every slide that all chime or go *zip* or *boing*. Judicious use is much more effective.

Dropping in some clip art

The following steps explain how to drop clip art into your presentation:

1. **Move to the slide on which you want to plaster the clip art.**

   If you want the same clip art picture to appear on every slide, move to Slide Master View.

2. On the Ribbon, choose Insert➪Illustrations➪Clip Art.

After a brief moment's hesitation, the Clip Art task pane pops up in all its splendor, as shown in Figure 12-1.

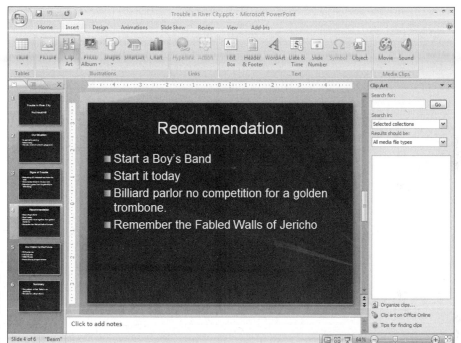

Figure 12-1:
The Clip Art
task pane.

3. Type a keyword in the Search Text box and then click the Search button.

For example, to search for pictures of trombones, type **Trombone** in the Search text box and then click Search.

PowerPoint searches through the Clip Organizer to locate the clip art you're looking for, and then it displays thumbnails of the pictures it finds in the Clip Art task pane.

4. Click the picture that you want to use.

The picture is inserted on the current slide, as shown in Figure 12-2. Notice that a special Ribbon Format tab with tools for working with pictures has appeared. This Format tab appears whenever you select a picture object.

5. If you're finished inserting pictures, click the Clip Art task pane's Close button (the X in the upper-right corner of the task pane).

The task pane vanishes.

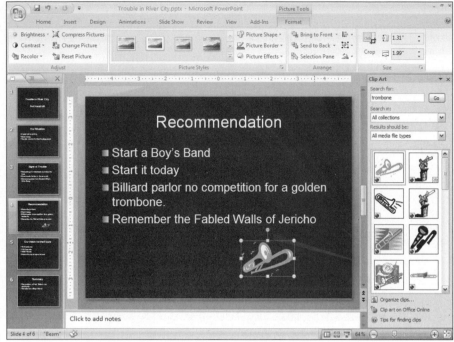

You'll probably want to move the picture and change its size. To find out how, see the following section.

If you find a clip art picture you like, you can find other pictures that are drawn in a similar style by right-clicking the picture in the Clip Art task pane (or by clicking the down-arrow on the right side of the picture) and then choosing Find Similar Style.

Moving, sizing, and stretching clip art

Because PowerPoint chooses an arbitrary position on the slide to insert clip art, you undoubtedly want to move the clip art to a more convenient location. You probably also want to change the size of the clip art if it's too big or too small for your slide.

Follow these steps to force your inserted clip art into full compliance:

1. **Click the picture and drag it wherever you want.**

   You don't have to worry about clicking exactly the edge of the picture or one of its lines; just click anywhere in the picture and drag it around.

2. **Notice the eight handles. Drag one of them to resize the picture.**

You can click and drag any of these handles to adjust the size of the picture. When you click one of the corner handles, you can change the height and width of the picture at the same time. When you drag one of the edge handles (top, bottom, left, or right) to change the size of the picture in just one dimension, you distort the picture's outlook as you go.

When you resize a picture, the picture changes its position on the slide. As a result, you can count on moving it after you resize it. If you hold down the Ctrl key while dragging a handle, however, the picture becomes anchored at its center point as you resize it. Therefore, its position is unchanged, and you probably don't have to move it.

Stretching a clip art picture by dragging one of the edge handles can dramatically change the picture's appearance. For example, you can stretch an object vertically to make it look tall and thin or horizontally to make it look short and fat.

Getting clip art from the Internet

As if the vast collection of clip art that comes with Office and PowerPoint isn't enough, Microsoft also maintains a clip library on the Internet that you can use. Assuming you have a working Internet connection, you can access this additional clip art library by clicking Clip Art on Office Online at the bottom of the Clip Art task pane. This opens a separate Internet Explorer window, which you can then use to search for additional clip art images. See Figure 12-3.

If you find a clip art image that you want, you can mark it for later download. Then, after you've found all the images you want to download, you can choose an option that allows you to download the images directly into Clip Organizer. You can then call up the images by using the Clip Art task pane as described earlier in this chapter, in the section "Dropping in some clip art."

Inserting Pictures from a File

If you happen to already have an image file on your computer that you want to insert into a presentation, PowerPoint lets you insert the file. These steps show you how:

1. **Move to the slide on which you want to splash a picture.**

2. **Open the Insert tab on the Ribbon and then click the Picture button in the Illustrations group.**

   This summons the Insert Picture dialog box, shown in Figure 12-4.

Figure 12-3:
Getting clip art from the Internet.

3. **Dig through the bottom of your hard drive until you find the file that you want.**

   The picture you want might be anywhere. Fortunately, the Insert Picture dialog box has all the controls you need to search high and low until you find the file. Just click the icons at the left side of the box or click the Look In text box, and you're halfway there.

4. **Click the file and then click Insert.**

   You're done! Figure 12-5 shows how a picture appears when it has been inserted on a slide.

As you can see in Figure 12-5, PowerPoint scales your pictures so they fill as much of the slide as possible. You need to resize the picture if you want it to be smaller. Just select the picture and then drag one of the size handles in the corner of the picture.

You also can paste a picture directly into PowerPoint by way of the Clipboard. Anything that you can copy to the Clipboard you can paste into PowerPoint. For example, you can doodle a sketch in Paintbrush, copy it, and then zap over to PowerPoint and paste it. *Voila* — instant picture!

Figure 12-4:
The Insert
Picture
dialog box.

Figure 12-5:
Stay, boy.
Good boy!

Cropping a Picture

Sometimes you want to cut off the edges of a picture so that you can include just part of the picture in your presentation. For example, you might have a picture of two people, only one of whom you like. You can use PowerPoint's cropping feature to cut off the other person. (Note that you can crop bitmap images, but not vector pictures.)

To crop a picture, select the picture and click the Crop button located near the right side of the Format tab on the Ribbon, in the group labeled Size. The selection handles change to special crop marks. You can then drag the crop marks around to cut off part of the picture. When you're satisfied, just click outside of the picture. Figure 12-6 shows the picture that was inserted in Figure 12-5 after it has been cropped and resized.

Figure 12-6:
A picture that has been cropped.

If you decide later that you don't like the cropping, you can right-click the picture and choose Format Picture from the menu that appears. Then click the Reset button.

Adding Style to Your Pictures

PowerPoint enables you to draw attention to your pictures by adding stylistic features such as borders, shadows, and reflections. Figure 12-7 shows a slide with several copies of a picture, each with a different style applied.

Figure 12-7:
Pictures
with style.

To add a style effect to a picture, select the picture and open the Picture Tools tab on the Ribbon. Then, simply select the picture style you want to apply.

PowerPoint comes with 28 predefined picture styles, shown in the gallery pictured in Figure 12-8. Each of these styles is simply a combination of three types of formatting you can apply to pictures: Shape, Border, and Effects. If you want, you can apply these formats individually as described in the following sections.

Note that if you use one of these predefined picture styles, the picture will be updated automatically if you later change the presentation's theme. As a result, you should use one of the predefined styles whenever possible.

Figure 12-8:
The Picture
Style
gallery.

Applying a picture shape

A *picture shape* is a shape that is used to crop a picture. For example, if you choose a circle as the shape, the picture is cropped to a circle. Figure 12-9 shows six pictures of my dog with various shapes applied to it.

Figure 12-9:
Pictures
with
different
types of
shapes
applied.

To apply a shape to a picture, follow these steps:

1. **Select the picture you want to apply the shape to and then click the Format tab on the Ribbon.**

2. **Open the Insert tab on the Ribbon and then click the Picture Shape button in the Picture Styles group.**

   This summons the Picture Shape gallery, as shown in Figure 12-10.

Figure 12-10:
The Picture Shape gallery.

3. **Click the shape you want to apply to the picture.**

   The picture is cropped by the shape you select.

4. **If the shape has a yellow adjustment handle, drag it to adjust the shape.**

   Many of the shapes have handles that let you adjust one or more aspects of the shape. The location of this handle depends on the shape. If the shape you selected has one or more of these handles, you can further refine your picture by dragging the handle until you're satisfied with the result.

Applying a picture border

You can apply a border to a picture by choosing Format➪Picture Styles➪ Picture Border on the Ribbon. This reveals the Picture Border menu, which lets you choose the border color, weight (the width of the border lines), and the pattern of dashes you want to use.

Note that if you have applied a shape to the picture, the border is applied to the shape.

Applying picture effects

The Picture Effects button in the Picture Styles group (located on the Format tab) lets you apply several interesting types of effects to your pictures. When you click this button, a menu with the following effect options is displayed:

- **Shadow:** Applies a shadow to the picture. You can select one of several predefined shadow effects or call up a dialog box that lets you customize the shadow.

- **Reflection:** Creates a reflected image of the picture beneath the original picture.

- **Glow:** Adds a glowing effect around the edges of the picture.

- **Soft Edges:** Softens the edges of the picture.

- **3-D Rotation:** Rotates the picture in a way that creates a three-dimensional effect.

The best way to figure out how to use these effects is to experiment with them to see how they work.

More Things You Can Do with Pictures

The Picture Tools group on the Format tab includes several additional controls that let you manipulate pictures in fun ways. These tools are described in the following list:

- **Brightness:** Lets you change the image brightness.
- **Contrast:** Lets you change the image contrast.

✓ **Recolor:** Changes the color tone of the picture. You can also use this control to set a transparent background color for the image.

✓ **Compress Pictures:** Instructs PowerPoint to compress the images so that they take up less disk space. In most cases, this does not noticeably diminish the quality of the pictures.

✓ **Change Picture:** Lets you pick a different picture.

✓ **Reset Picture:** Removes any formatting you've applied to the picture, including sizing, cropping, shapes, borders, effects, colorizations, and so on.

Chapter 13

Drawing on Your Slides

Chim-chiminey, chim-chiminey, chim-chim cheroo, I draws what I likes and I likes what I drew. . . .

*A*rt time! Get your crayons and glue and don an old paint shirt. You're going to cut out some simple shapes and paste them on your PowerPoint slides so that people either think that you're a wonderful artist or scoff at you for not using clip art.

This chapter covers the drawing features of PowerPoint 2007. One of the best things about PowerPoint is the cool drawing tools. Once upon a time, PowerPoint had but rudimentary drawing tools — the equivalent of a box of crayons — but PowerPoint now has powerful drawing tools that are sufficient for all but the most sophisticated aspiring artists.

Some General Drawing Tips

Before getting into the specifics of using each PowerPoint drawing tool, the following sections describe a handful of general tips for drawing pictures.

Zooming in

When you work with the PowerPoint drawing tools, you might want to increase the zoom factor so that you can draw more accurately. I often work at 200, 300, or even 400 percent when I'm drawing. To change the zoom factor, use the zoom slider located in the bottom-right corner of the screen.

Before you change the zoom factor to edit an object, select the object that you want to edit. This way, PowerPoint zooms in on that area of the slide. If you don't select an object before you zoom in, you might need to scroll around to find the right location.

Displaying the ruler

If you want to be precise about lining up objects on the slide, make sure that the ruler is on. If you can't see the ruler on-screen, open the View tab in the Ribbon and select the Ruler check box (found in the Show/Hide group). Figure 13-1 shows how PowerPoint looks when the ruler is activated. (You can also see the zoom slider in the bottom right-corner of this figure.)

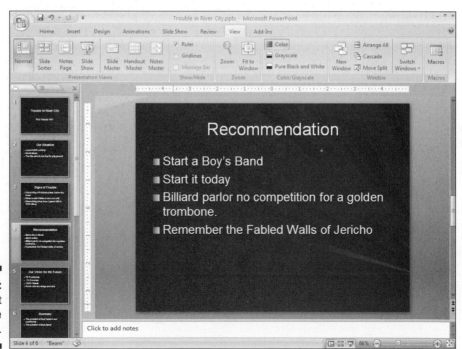

Figure 13-1:
PowerPoint with the rulers on.

When you work with drawing objects, PowerPoint formats the ruler so that zero is at the middle of the slide. When you edit a text object, the ruler changes to a text ruler that measures from the margins and indicates tab positions.

Sticking to the color scheme

You can assign individual colors to each object that you draw, but the purpose of the PowerPoint color schemes (described in Chapter 9) is to talk you out of doing that. If possible, let solid objects default to the color scheme's fill color or, if you must change the fill color, change it to one of the alternative colors provided by the scheme. The beauty of doing this is that if you change the color scheme later, the fill color for objects changes to reflect the new fill color. Once you switch to a color that's not in the theme, however, the object ignores any subsequent changes to the theme.

Saving frequently

Drawing is tedious work. You don't want to spend two hours working on a particularly important drawing only to lose it all just because a comet strikes your building or an errant Scud lands in your backyard. You can prevent catastrophic loss from incidents such as these by pressing Ctrl+S or by frequently clicking the Save button as you work. And always wear protective eyewear.

Don't forget Ctrl+Z

In my opinion, Ctrl+Z — the ubiquitous Undo command — is the most important keyboard shortcut in any Windows program, and PowerPoint is no exception. Remember that you're never more than one keystroke away from erasing a boo-boo. If you do something silly — like forgetting to group a complex picture before trying to move it — you can always press Ctrl+Z to undo your last action. Ctrl+Z is my favorite and most frequently used PowerPoint key combination. (For left-handed mouse users, Alt+Backspace does the same thing.) And if you aren't ready to climb shrieking on a chair at the first sign of a mouse, try clicking the handy Undo button on the Quick Access toolbar.

Drawing Simple Objects

To draw an object on a slide, first call up the Insert tab on the Ribbon. Then click the Shapes button (located in the Illustrations group) to reveal a gallery of shapes you can choose from, as shown in Figure 13-2. Finally, select the shape you want to draw from the Shapes gallery, shown in Figure 13-2.

Figure 13-2:
The Shapes
gallery.

You find detailed instructions for drawing with the more important tools in the following sections. Before I get to that, though, I want to give you some pointers to keep in mind:

- ✔ **Choosing a location:** Before you draw an object, move to the slide on which you want to draw the object. If you want the object to appear on every slide in the presentation, display the Slide Master by choosing View➪Presentation Views➪Slide Master or by Shift+clicking the Normal View button.

- ✔ **Fixing a mistake:** If you make a mistake while drawing a shape, the Undo command on the Quick Access Toolbar can usually correct the mistake for you.

- ✔ **Holding down the Shift key:** If you hold down the Shift key while drawing a shape, PowerPoint forces the shape to be "regular." That is, rectangles are squares, ellipses are circles, and lines are constrained to horizontal or vertical, or 45-degree diagonals.

Drawing straight lines

You can use the Line button to draw straight lines on your slides. Here's the procedure:

1. **Click the Line button in the Shapes group on the Insert tab.**

2. **Point the cursor to where you want the line to start.**

3. **Click and drag the cursor to where you want the line to end.**

4. **Release the mouse button when you reach your destination.**

After you've drawn the shape, the Ribbon displays the Drawing Tools tab, as shown in Figure 13-3. You can then use the controls in the Shape Styles group to change the fill, outline, and effects applied to the line.

Figure 13-3:
The
Drawing
Tools tab.

After you've drawn a line, you can adjust it by clicking it and then dragging the handles that appear on each end of the line.

Remember that you can force a line to be perfectly horizontal or vertical by holding down the Shift key while you draw. If you hold the Shift key and drag diagonally while you draw the line, the line will be constrained to perfect 45-degree angles.

Drawing rectangles, squares, ovals, and circles

To draw a rectangle, follow these steps:

1. **On the Insert tab, click the Shape buttons (in the Illustrations group), then click the Rectangle button.**

2. **Point the cursor to where you want one corner of the rectangle to be positioned.**

3. **Click and drag to where you want the opposite corner of the rectangle to be positioned.**

4. **Release the mouse button.**

The steps for drawing an oval are the same as the steps for drawing a rectangle except that you click the Oval button rather than the Rectangle button. To draw a square or perfectly round circle, select the Oval button or the Rectangle button but hold down the Shift key while you draw.

You can adjust the size or shape of a rectangle or circle by clicking it and dragging any of its love handles.

Creating Other Shapes

Rectangles and circles aren't the only two shapes that PowerPoint can draw automatically. The Shapes galley includes many other types of shapes you can draw, such as pentagons, stars, and flowchart symbols.

The Shapes gallery (refer to Figure 13-2) organizes shapes into the following categories:

- ✔ **Recently Used Shapes:** The top section of the gallery lists the 24 shapes you've used most recently. The shapes found in this section change each time you draw a new shape.

- ✔ **Lines:** Straight lines, curved lines, lines with arrowheads, scribbly lines, and free-form shapes that can become polygons if you want. The free-form shape is useful enough to merit its own section, "Drawing a polygon or free-form shape," which immediately follows this section.

- ✔ **Rectangles:** Basic rectangular shapes, including not just a regular rectangle but also rectangles with corners lopped off.

- ✔ **Basic Shapes:** Squares, rectangles, triangles, crosses, happy faces, lightning bolts, hearts, clouds, and more.

- ✔ **Block Arrows:** Fat arrows pointing in various directions.

- ✔ **Equation Shapes:** Shapes for drawing simple math equations.

- ✔ **Flowchart:** Various flowcharting symbols.

- ✔ **Stars and Banners:** Shapes that add sparkle to your presentations.

- ✔ **Callouts:** Text boxes and speech bubbles like those used in comic strips.

- ✔ **Action Buttons:** Buttons that you can add to your slides and click during a slide show to go directly to another slide or to run a macro.

Drawing a shape

The following steps explain how to draw a shape:

1. **Click the Shapes button in the Illustrations group of the Insert tab.**

   The Shapes gallery appears.

2. **Select the shape you want to insert.**

   When you select one of the shapes, the Shapes gallery disappears and PowerPoint is poised to draw the shape you selected.

3. **Click the slide where you want the shape to appear and then drag the shape to the desired size.**

   Hold down the Shift key while drawing the Shape to create an evenly proportioned shape.

   When you release the mouse button, the Shape object takes on the current fill color and line style.

4. **(Optional) Start typing if you want the shape to contain text.**

   After you've typed your text, you can use PowerPoint's formatting features to change its typeface, size, color, and so on. For more information, refer to Chapter 8.

Some shapes — especially the stars and banners — cry out for text. Figure 13-4 shows how you can use a star shape to add a jazzy burst to a slide.

You can change an object's shape at any time. First, select the shape. Then, open the Drawing Tools tab on the Ribbon, look in the Insert Shapes group, click the Edit Shape button, and choose Change Shape from the menu that appears.

 Many shape buttons have an extra handle shaped like a yellow diamond that enables you to adjust some aspect of the object's shape. For example, the block arrows have a handle that enables you to increase or decrease the size of the arrowhead. The location of these handles varies depending on the shape you're working with. Figure 13-5 shows how you can use these extra handles to vary the shapes produced by six different shapes. For each of the six shapes, the first object shows how the shape is initially drawn; the other two objects drawn with each shape show how you can change the shape by dragging the extra handle. (Note that the yellow handles aren't shown in this figure. When you select a shape that has one of these adjustment handles, the handles will appear.)

Figure 13-4:
Use a star
shape to
make your
presentation
look like a
late-night
infomercial.

Figure 13-5:
You can
create
interesting
variations
by grabbing
the extra
handles on
these
shapes.

Drawing a polygon or free-form shape

Mr. Arnold, my seventh-grade math teacher, taught me that a *polygon* is a shape that has many sides and has nothing to do with having more than one spouse (one is certainly enough for most people). Triangles, squares, and rectangles are polygons, but so are hexagons and pentagons, and any unusual shapes whose sides all consist of straight lines. Politicians are continually inventing new polygons when they revise the boundaries of congressional districts.

One of the most useful shapes in the Shapes gallery is the Freeform Shape tool. It's designed to create polygons, but with a twist: Not all the sides have to be straight lines. The Freeform Shape tool lets you build a shape whose sides are a mixture of straight lines and free-form curves. Figure 13-6 shows three examples of shapes that I created with the Freeform Shape tool.

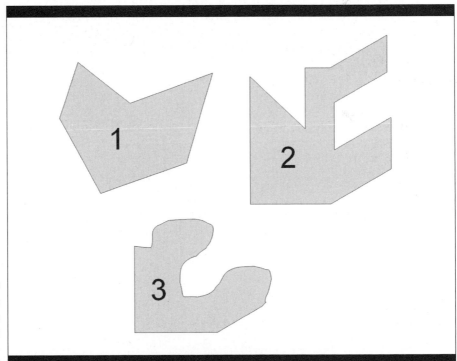

Figure 13-6:
Three
free-form
shapes.

Follow these steps to create a polygon or free-form shape:

1. **Select the Freeform shape (shown in the margin) from the Shapes gallery.**

You can find the Shapes gallery in the Shapes group on the Insert tab. When you select the Freeform shape tool, the cursor changes to a cross-hair pointer.

2. **Click where you want to position the first corner of the object.**

3. **Click where you want to position the second corner of the object.**

4. **Keep clicking wherever you want to position a corner.**

5. **(Optional) To draw a free-form side on the shape, hold down the mouse button when you click a corner and then drag to draw the free-form shape. When you get to the end of the free-form side, release the mouse button.**

   You can then click again to add more corners. Shape 3 in Figure 13-6 has one free-form side.

6. **To finish the shape, click near the first corner — the one that you created in Step 3.**

   You don't have to be exact: If you click anywhere near the first corner that you put down, PowerPoint assumes that the shape is finished.

You're finished! The object assumes the line and fill color from the slide's color scheme.

You can reshape a polygon or free-form shape by double-clicking it and then dragging any of the love handles that appear on the corners.

If you hold down the Shift key while you draw a polygon, the sides are constrained to 45-degree angles. Shape 2 in Figure 13-6 was drawn in this manner. How about a constitutional amendment requiring Congress to use the Shift key when it redraws congressional boundaries?

You also can use the Freeform Shape tool to draw a multisegmented line, called an *open shape*. To draw an open shape, you can follow the steps in this section, except that you skip Step 6. Instead, double-click or press Esc when the line is done.

Drawing a curved line or shape

Another useful tool is the Curve Shape tool, which lets you draw curved lines or shapes. Figure 13-7 shows several examples of curved lines and shapes drawn with the Curve Shape tool.

Figure 13-7:
Examples of
curved lines
and shapes.

Here is the procedure for drawing a curved line or shape:

1. **Select the Curve shape tool from the Shapes gallery.**

   You'll find the Shapes gallery in the Shapes group on the Insert tab.
   When you select this tool, the cursor changes to a cross-hair pointer.

2. **Click where you want the curved line or shape to begin.**

3. **Click where you want the first turn in the curve to appear.**

   The straight line turns to a curved line, bent around the point where you
   clicked. As you move the mouse, the bend of the curve changes.

4. **Click to add turns to the curve.**

   Each time you click, a new bend is added to the line. Keep clicking until
   the line is as twisty as you want.

5. **To finish a line, double-click where you want the end of the curved
   line to appear. To create a closed shape, double-click over the starting
   point, where you clicked in Step 3.**

Creating a text box

A text box is a special type of shape that is designed to place text on your slides. To create a text box, call up the Insert tab, select the Text Box button in the Text group, and then click where you want one corner of the text box to appear and drag to where you want the opposite corner, just like you're drawing a rectangle. When you release the mouse button, you can type text.

You can format the text that you type in the text box by highlighting the text and using the usual PowerPoint text formatting features, most of which are found on the Home tab. For more information about formatting text, see Chapter 8.

You can format the text box itself by using Shape Fill, Shape Outline, Shape Effects, and other tools available on the Drawing Tools tab, as described in the next section. By default, text boxes have no fill or line color, so the box itself is invisible on the slide — only the text is visible.

Most shapes also function as text boxes. If you want to add text to a shape, just click the shape and start typing. The text appears centered over the shape. (The only shapes that don't accept text are lines and connectors.)

Styling Your Shapes

The center section of the Drawing Tools tab is called Shape Styles. It lets you control various stylistic features of your shapes. For example, you can set a fill color, set the outline, and add effects such as shadows or reflections.

You can set these styles individually, or you can choose one of the preselected shape styles that appears in the Shape Styles group. Note that the styles that appear in the Shape Styles group vary depending on the type of shape you've selected. For example, if you select a line, various predefined line styles are displayed. But if you select a rectangle, the styles appropriate for rectangles are displayed.

Setting the shape fill

The Shape Fill control (in the Shape Styles group of the Drawing Tools tab) lets you control how shapes are filled. The simplest type of fill is a solid color. But you can also use a picture, a gradient fill, or a pattern to fill the shape.

Working with shape fills is similar to working with background and theme colors. For more information on backgrounds and themes, check out Chapter 9.

Setting the shape outline

The Shape Outline control (in the Shape Styles group of the Drawing Tools tab) lets you change the style of line objects or the border for solid shape objects. You can change the following settings for the outline:

- **Color:** Sets the color used for the outline.
- **Weight:** Sets the thickness of the line.
- **Dashes:** The dashing pattern used for the lines that outline the object. The default uses a solid line, but different patterns are available to create dashed lines.
- **Arrows:** Lines can have an arrowhead at either or both ends. Arrowheads are used mostly on line and arc objects.

For maximum control over the outline style, select the More command from the menu that appears when you click the Fill, Outline, or Effects buttons. This brings up the Format Shape dialog box shown in Figure 13-8. From this dialog box, you can control all aspects of a line's style: its color, width, dash pattern, and end style (various arrowheads can be applied).

Figure 13-8:
Formatting
the outline.

Applying shape effects

The Shape Effects button on the Drawing Tools tab on the Ribbon lets you apply several interesting types of effects to your shapes. When you click this button, a menu with the following effect options is displayed:

✔ **Shadow:** Applies a shadow to the picture. You can select one of several predefined shadow effects, or you can call up a dialog box that lets you customize the shadow.

✔ **Reflection:** Creates a reflected image of the picture beneath the original picture.

✔ **Glow:** Adds a glowing effect around the edges of the picture.

✔ **Soft Edges:** Softens the edges of the picture.

✔ **Bevel:** Creates a beveled effect.

✔ **3-D Rotation:** Rotates the picture in a way that creates a three-dimensional effect.

The best way to discover how to use these effects is to experiment with them to see how they work.

Flipping and Rotating Objects

To *flip* an object means to create a mirror image of it. To *rotate* an object means to turn it about its center. PowerPoint lets you flip objects horizontally or vertically, rotate objects in 90-degree increments, or freely rotate an object to any angle.

Rotation works for text boxes and Shape text. Thus, you can use rotation to create vertical text or text skewed to any angle you want. However, flipping an object doesn't affect the object's text.

Flipping an object

PowerPoint enables you to flip an object vertically or horizontally to create a mirror image of the object. To flip an object, follow these steps:

1. **Choose the object that you want to flip.**

2. **Open the Drawing Tools tab, click the Rotate button on the Arrange group, and then choose Flip Horizontal or Flip Vertical.**

Rotating an object 90 degrees

You can rotate an object in 90-degree increments by following these steps:

1. **Choose the object that you want to rotate.**

2. **Open the Drawing Tools tab, click the choose Rotate button on the Arrange group, and then choose Rotate Right or Rotate Left.**

3. **To rotate the object 180 degrees, click the appropriate Rotate button again.**

Using the rotate handle

Remember how all the bad guys' hideouts were slanted in the old *Batman* TV show? The rotate handle lets you give your drawings that same kind of slant. With the rotate handle, you can rotate an object to any arbitrary angle just by dragging it with the mouse.

The rotate handle is the green handle that appears when you select an object that can be rotated. The rotate handle appears above the object, connected to the object by a line, as shown in Figure 13-9. You can rotate an object to any angle simply by dragging the rotate handle.

Figure 13-9:
The rotate handle lets you rotate an object to any arbitrary angle.

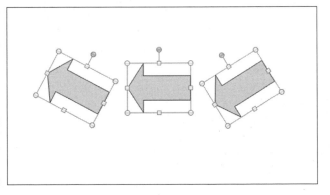

The following steps show you how to use the rotate handle:

1. **Click the object that you want to rotate.**

2. **Drag the rotate handle in the direction that you want to rotate the object.**

   As you drag, an outline of the object rotates around. When you get the object's outline to the angle you want, release the mouse button, and the object is redrawn at the new angle.

To restrict the rotation angle to 15-degree increments, hold the Shift key while dragging around the rotation handle.

Drawing a Complicated Picture

When you add more than one object to a slide, you might run into several problems. What happens when the objects overlap? How do you line up objects so that they don't look like they were thrown at the slide from a moving car? And how do you keep together objects that belong together?

The following sections show you how to use PowerPoint features to handle overlapped objects and how to align and group objects.

Changing layers

Whenever you have more than one object on a slide, the potential exists for objects to overlap one another. Like most drawing programs, PowerPoint handles this problem by layering objects like a stack of plates. The first object that you draw is at the bottom of the stack; the second object is on top of the first; the third is atop the second object; and so on. If two objects overlap, the one that's at the highest layer wins; objects below it are partially covered. (Note that PowerPoint's layers aren't nearly as powerful as layers in programs like Adobe Illustrator or AutoCAD. All they really do is set the stacking order when objects are placed on top of one another.)

So far, so good — but what if you don't remember to draw the objects in the correct order? What if you draw a shape that you want to tuck behind a shape that you've already drawn, or what if you want to bring an existing shape to the top of the pecking order? No problem. PowerPoint enables you to change the stacking order by moving objects toward the front or back so that they overlap just the way you want.

The Drawing Tools tab provides two controls that let you move an object forward or backward in the layer order:

✔ **Bring to Front:** Brings the chosen object to the top of the stack. Note that this button has a down arrow next to it. If you click this down arrow, you reveal a menu with two subcommands: Bring to Front and Bring Forward. The Bring Forward command moves the object just one step closer to the top of the heap, whereas the Bring to Front command moves the object all the way to the top.

✔ **Send to Back:** Sends the chosen object to the back of the stack. Again, this button has a down arrow next to it. You can click this down arrow to access the Send Backward subcommand, which sends the object one level down in the layer order.

Layering problems are most obvious when objects have a fill color. If an object has no fill color, objects behind it are allowed to show through. In this case, the layering doesn't matter much.

To bring an object to the top of another, you might have to use the Bring Forward command several times. The reason is that even though the two objects appear to be adjacent, other objects might occupy the layers between them.

Line 'em up

Nothing looks more amateurish than objects dropped randomly on a slide with no apparent concern for how they line up with each other. The Drawing Tools tab includes an Align button that brings up a menu with the following commands:

✔ Align Left

✔ Align Center

✔ Align Right

✔ Align Top

✔ Align Middle

✔ Align Bottom

✔ Distribute Horizontally

✔ Distribute Vertically

The first three commands align items horizontally; the last three align items vertically.

You can also distribute several items so that they are spaced evenly. Select the items that you want to distribute, click the Draw button, choose Align or Distribute, and then choose Distribute Horizontally or Distribute Vertically. PowerPoint then adjusts the spacing of the objects that appear between the two outermost objects selected.

Using the grids and guides

To help you create well-ordered slides, PowerPoint lets you display a grid of evenly spaced lines over the slide. These lines aren't actually a part of the slide, so your audience won't see them when you give your presentation. They exist simply to make the task of lining things up a bit easier.

In addition to the grid, PowerPoint also lets you use guides. The guides are two lines — one horizontal, the other vertical — that appear on-screen. Although the gridlines are fixed in their location on your slides, you can move the guides around as you want. Any object that comes within a pixel's breadth of one of these guidelines snaps to it. Like the grid, the guides don't show up when you give your presentation. They appear only when you're editing your slides. Guides are a great way to line up objects in a neat row.

To display the grid or guides, click the Align button in the Drawing Tools tab and then choose Grid Settings. This summons the Grid and Guides dialog box, shown in Figure 13-10.

Figure 13-10:
The Grid and Guides dialog box.

To activate the grid, select the Snap Objects to Grid check box and then adjust the grid spacing to whatever setting you want. If you want to actually see the grid on-screen, select the Display Grid on Screen check box.

To fire up the guides, select the Display Drawing Guides on Screen check box. After the guides are visible, you can move them around the slide by clicking and dragging them.

Group therapy

A *group* is a collection of objects that PowerPoint treats as though it were one object. Using groups properly is one key to putting simple shapes together to make complex pictures without becoming so frustrated that you have to join a therapy group. ("Hello, my name is Doug, and PowerPoint drives me crazy.")

To create a group, follow these steps:

1. **Choose all objects that you want to include in the group.**

   You can do this by holding down the Shift key and clicking each of the items, or by clicking and dragging the resulting rectangle around all the items.

2. **Right click one of the selected objects and then choose Group➪Group from the menu that appears.**

You can also find the Group command on the Drawing Tools tab, but it's much easier to find by right-clicking.

To take a group apart so that PowerPoint treats the objects as individuals again, follow these steps:

1. **Right click the group you want to break up.**

2. **Choose Group➪Ungroup.**

If you create a group and then ungroup it so that you can work on its elements individually, you can easily regroup the objects. These steps show you how:

1. **Right click one of the objects that was in the original group.**

2. **Choose Group➪Regroup.**

   PowerPoint remembers which objects were in the group and automatically includes them.

PowerPoint enables you to create groups of groups. This capability is useful for complex pictures because it enables you to work on one part of the picture, group it, and then work on the next part of the picture without worrying about accidentally disturbing the part that you've already grouped. After you have several such groups, select them and group them. You can create groups of groups of groups and so on, *ad nauseam.*

Chapter 14

Charting for Fun and Profit

· ·

In This Chapter

▶ Adding a chart to your presentation

▶ Getting data from other programs

▶ Moving and resizing your chart

▶ Embellishing your chart with titles, legends, and other stuff

· ·

*O*ne of the best ways to prove a point is with numbers, and one of the best ways to present numbers is in a chart. With PowerPoint, adding a chart to your presentation is easy. And getting the chart to look the way you want is usually easy, too. It takes a little bit of pointing and clicking, but it works. This chapter shows you how.

Understanding Charts

If you've never attempted to add a chart to a slide, the process can be a little confusing. A *chart* is simply a series of numbers rendered as a graph. You can supply the numbers yourself, or you can copy them from a separate file, such as an Excel spreadsheet. You can create all kinds of different charts, ranging from simple bar charts and pie charts to exotic doughnut charts and radar charts. Very cool, but a little confusing to the uninitiated.

The following list details some of the jargon that you have to contend with when you're working with charts:

✔ **Graph or chart:** Same thing. These terms are used interchangeably. A graph or chart is nothing more than a bunch of numbers turned into a picture. After all, a picture is worth a thousand numbers.

✔ **Microsoft Graph:** A program that was used in earlier versions of PowerPoint to create charts. Microsoft Graph isn't used anymore. For more information, refer to the sidebar, "Whatever happened to Microsoft Graph?"

✔ **Chart type:** PowerPoint supports several chart types: bar charts, column charts, pie charts, line charts, scatter charts, area charts, radar charts, Dunkin' Donut charts, and others. You can even create cone charts that look like something that fell off a Fembot in an Austin Powers movie. Different types of charts are better suited to displaying different types of data.

✔ **Chart Layout:** A predefined combination of chart elements such as headings and legends that lets you easily create a common type of chart.

✔ **Chart Style:** A predefined combination of formatting elements that controls the visual appearance of a chart.

✔ **Datasheet:** Supplies the underlying data for a chart. After all, a chart is nothing more than a bunch of numbers made into a picture. Those numbers come from the datasheet. In previous versions of PowerPoint, the datasheet was a mini-spreadsheet that resembled Excel. For PowerPoint 2007, Microsoft finally decided to give up on the mini-spreadsheet. Now, the datasheet is actually an Excel spreadsheet. Thus, when you create a chart, PowerPoint automatically starts Excel (if it isn't already running) and uses Excel to hold the numbers in the datasheet.

✔ **Series:** A collection of related numbers. For example, a chart of quarterly sales by region might have a series for each region. Each series has four sales totals, one for each quarter. Each series is usually represented by a row on the datasheet, but you can change the datasheet so that each column represents a series. Most chart types can plot more than one series. Pie charts can plot only one series at a time, however. The name of each series can be displayed in a legend.

✔ **Axes:** The lines on the edges of a chart. The *X-axis* is the line along the bottom of the chart; the *Y-axis* is the line along the left edge of the chart. The X-axis usually indicates categories. Actual data values are plotted along the Y-axis. Microsoft Graph automatically provides labels for the X- and Y-axes, but you can change them.

✔ **Legend:** A box used to identify the various series plotted on the chart. PowerPoint can create a legend automatically if you want one.

The most interesting thing to know about charting in PowerPoint 2007 is that it is closely integrated with Excel 2007. When you insert a chart in PowerPoint, Excel is automatically started, and the data that you chart is placed in an Excel workbook. However, that Excel workbook isn't stored as a separate document. Instead, the chart and the datasheet workbook are stored within the PowerPoint document.

Whatever happened to Microsoft Graph?

If you've worked with previous versions of PowerPoint, you might have been frustrated by the fact that charts were created by an external program called Microsoft Graph. In PowerPoint 2007, Microsoft has finally eliminated the separate Graph program. Instead, PowerPoint now relies on Microsoft Excel 2007 to create its charts.

Why the change? Microsoft did a little research and found out that half of all the charts inserted into PowerPoint presentations were actually created in Excel anyway. The main reason people did that was that the data to be charted typically existed already in an Excel workbook. Rather than copy the data into PowerPoint and then create a chart, it was actually easier to create the chart in Excel and copy it into PowerPoint.

Microsoft Graph still exists, but PowerPoint uses it only in two cases:

✔ **When you open a presentation that contains a chart created with a previous version:** In this case, PowerPoint uses Microsoft Graph to display the graph.

✔ **When Excel 2007 is not present on your computer:** In this case, PowerPoint reverts to the old way of doing charts.

Incidentally, Word 2007 uses Excel to create its charts, too. So with Office 2007, charting is now identical whether you use Excel, Word, or PowerPoint.

Adding a Chart to Your Presentation

To add a chart to your presentation, you have several options:

✔ Create a new slide by using a layout that includes a Content placeholder (an object that reserves space for content on the slide). Then click the Chart icon in the Content placeholder to create the chart.

✔ Use the Insert tab to insert a chart into any slide.

✔ Create the chart separately in Excel 2007 and then paste the chart into PowerPoint. This is the most common method if the chart is based on data that's already stored in an Excel workbook.

Adding a new slide with a chart

The following procedure shows how to insert a new slide that contains a chart:

1. **Move to the slide that you want the new slide to follow.**

2. **Click the Home tab and then click the Add Slide button in the Slides group.**

   This action reveals a list of slide layouts.

3. Click one of the slide layouts that includes a Content placeholder.

Several slide types include a Content placeholder. When you click the one you want, a slide with the selected layout is added to your presentation, as shown in Figure 14-1. (In this case, I chose the "Title and Content" layout.)

Figure 14-1:
A slide with a content placeholder.

As you can see, the Content placeholder includes six little icons for inserting different types of content:

• **Table:** Inserts a table, as described in Chapter 17.

• **Chart:** Inserts a chart.

• **Clip Art:** Inserts a clip art picture.

• **Picture:** Inserts a picture, as described in Chapter 12.

• **Smart Art:** Inserts a smart art graphic, as described in Chapter 15.

• **Media:** Inserts a movie, as described in Chapter 16.

4. Click the Chart icon in the middle of the Content placeholder.

The Chart icon is the one in the middle of the top row of icons. Clicking this icon summons the Create Chart dialog box shown in Figure 14-2.

Figure 14-2:
The Create Chart dialog box.

5. Select the type of chart you want to create.

You can select any of the following chart types:

- **Column:** Data is shown as vertical columns. The columns can be displayed side by side or stacked, and you can pick various shapes for the columns including simple bars, 3-D blocks, cylinders, cones, and pyramids.

- **Line:** The data is shown as individual points linked by various types of lines.

- **Pie:** The data is shown as slices in a circular pie.

- **Bar:** The same as a column chart, except the columns are laid out horizontally instead of vertically.

- **Area:** Similar to a line chart, except that the areas beneath the lines are shaded.

- **X Y (Scatter):** Plots individual points using two values to represent the X, Y coordinates.

- **Surface:** Similar to a line chart but represents the data as a three-dimensional surface.

- **Stock:** Plots high/low/close values.

- **Doughnut:** Similar to a pie chart, but with a hole in the middle.

- **Bubble:** Similar to a scatter chart but uses a third value to determine the size of the bubble.

- **Radar:** Plots data relative to a central point rather than X, Y axes.

6. **Click OK.**

PowerPoint whirs and grinds for a moment and then inserts the chart into the slide, as shown in Figure 14-3. The reason for all the commotion is that to insert the chart, PowerPoint must find out whether Excel is already running. If not, PowerPoint launches Excel and rearranges your screen so that PowerPoint and Excel are displayed side by side, as you can see in the figure.

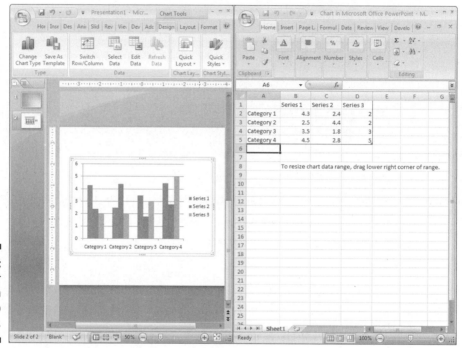

Figure 14-3:
A chart after it has been inserted into PowerPoint.

If Excel happens to be running already when you insert the chart, it won't be tiled alongside PowerPoint as shown in Figure 14-3. Instead, it remains where it is — most likely maximized in its own full-screen window. You can press Alt+Tab to switch back and forth between PowerPoint and Excel.

7. **Change the sample data to something more realistic.**

The data for the chart is shown in Excel, tiled alongside PowerPoint, as you can see back in Figure 14-3. You need to change this worksheet to provide the data you want to chart. Notice that the chart changes to reflect the new data as soon as you return to PowerPoint (by clicking anywhere in the PowerPoint window).

For more information, turn to the section "Working with Chart Data," later in this chapter.

8. **Customize the chart any way you want.**

For example, you can change the chart layout or style, as described later in this chapter. Figure 14-4 shows a finished chart.

Figure 14-4:
A slide with
a finished
chart.

Adding a chart to an existing slide

If you prefer, you can add a chart to an existing slide by following these steps:

1. **Move to the slide on which you want to place the chart.**

2. **Activate the Insert tab on the Ribbon. Click Chart in the Illustrations group.**

   This summons the Create Chart dialog box, shown earlier in Figure 14-2.

3. **Select the type of chart you want to create and then click OK.**

   PowerPoint launches Excel (if it isn't already running) and inserts a chart based on sample data.

   See the section "Changing the Chart Type!" later in this chapter for more information about chart types.

4. **Change the sample data to something more realistic.**

   For more information about working with chart data, check out the section "Working with Chart Data," later in this chapter.

5. **Finish the chart by setting the chart layout and style.**

   For more information, see the sections "Changing the Chart Layout" and "Changing the Chart Style," later in this chapter.

6. **Rearrange everything.**

The chart undoubtedly falls on top of something else already on the slide. You probably need to resize the chart by selecting it and then dragging it by the love handles. You can move the chart like any other object: Just click and drag it to a new location. You might also need to move, resize, or delete other objects to make room for the chart or change the layer order of the chart or other surrounding objects. You'll find information about these manipulations in Chapter 13.

Pasting a chart from Excel

If the data you want to chart already exists in an Excel workbook, the easiest way to chart it in PowerPoint is to first create the chart in Excel. Then copy the chart to the clipboard, switch over to PowerPoint, and paste the chart to the appropriate slide. When you do so, the chart appears in PowerPoint exactly as it did in Excel.

When you paste an Excel chart into PowerPoint, a smart tag appears next to the chart. You can click this smart tag to reveal a menu with the following choices:

- **Excel Chart (entire workbook):** This option creates a copy of the Excel data and stores it as a workbook object within your PowerPoint file. This effectively severs the chart in the PowerPoint presentation from the original workbook, so any changes you make to the data in the original workbook are not reflected in the PowerPoint chart.

- **Chart (linked to Excel data):** This copies the chart into the PowerPoint presentation but creates a link to the data in the original Excel workbook. Then any changes you make to the data in the original Excel workbook will be reflected in the chart.

- **Paste as Picture:** Converts the chart to a collection of PowerPoint shape objects, with no linkage to the original Excel chart or data.

- **Keep Source Formatting:** This option keeps all of the formatting you applied in the original Excel chart. Thus, the PowerPoint chart looks exactly like the Excel chart.

- **Use Destination Theme:** This option reformats the chart according to the Presentation Theme used in the PowerPoint presentation. You get a chart that is formatted consistently with the rest of your presentation.

Changing the Chart Type

PowerPoint enables you to create 14 basic types of charts. Each type conveys information with a different emphasis. Sales data plotted in a column chart might emphasize the relative performance of different regions, for example, and the same data plotted as a line chart might emphasize an increase or decrease in sales over time. The type of chart that's best for your data depends on the nature of the data and which aspects of it you want to emphasize.

Fortunately, PowerPoint doesn't force you to decide the final chart type up front. You can easily change the chart type at any time without changing the chart data. These steps show you how:

1. **Click the chart to select it.**

   When you select a chart, a set of three tabs called the Chart Tools is added to the ribbon.

2. **Click the Design tab.**

   Figure 14-5 shows the Chart Tools.

Figure 14-5:
The Chart
Tools on the
Ribbon.

3. **Click the Change Chart Type button.**

   PowerPoint displays a gallery of chart types.

4. **Click the chart type that you want.**

5. **Click OK, and you're done.**

Working with Chart Data

The data that provides the numbers plotted in a PowerPoint chart is stored in an Excel workbook. Depending on how you created the chart, this Excel workbook can either be a separate workbook document or be embedded within your PowerPoint document. Either way, you can work with Excel whenever you want to modify the chart data.

To change the data on which a chart is based, select the chart. A set of three tabs called the Chart Tools is automatically added to the Ribbon when you select the chart. Next, choose the Design tab. This tab includes a group called Data, which provides four controls. These controls let you perform various tricks on the data, as described in the following sections.

Switching rows and columns

The first control in the Data group is called Switch Row/Column. It changes the orientation of your chart in a way that can be difficult to describe but easy to visualize. Look back at the chart in Figure 14-4. It is based on the following data:

	River City	Pixley	Hootersville
Instruments	20.4	50.6	45.9
Music	27.4	38.6	46.9
Uniforms	90	34.6	45

As shown earlier in Figure 14-4, the rows are used to determine the data categories. Thus, the chart displays the data for Instruments, Music, and Uniforms along the horizontal axis.

If you click the Switch Row/Column button, the chart changes, as shown in Figure 14-6. Here, the chart categorizes the data by city, so sales for River City, Pixley, and Hootersville are shown along the horizontal axis.

Figure 14-6: Swapping the row/column orientation of a chart.

Changing the data selection

The Edit Data Source button in the Data group of the Design tab lets you change the selection of data that your chart is based on. When you click this button, you're escorted over to Excel, and the dialog box shown in Figure 14-7 is displayed.

Figure 14-7:
The Edit
Data Source
dialog box.

This dialog box lets you do three basic tasks:

- **Change the range.** You can change the range of data that's used for the chart by using the Chart Data Range text box.

- **Switch row/column.** You can switch rows and columns by clicking the Switch Row/Column button. This has the same effect as clicking the Switch Row/Column button back in PowerPoint.

- **Modify ranges and series.** You can play with the individual ranges that contain the data for each series. You can add a new series, edit the range used for an existing series, delete a series, or change the order in which the series are presented.

Editing the source data

To change the actual data values on which a chart is based, click the Source Data button in the Data group of the Design tab. This action launches Excel to display the chart data. You can then make any changes you want. When you return to PowerPoint (by clicking anywhere in the PowerPoint window), the chart will be updated to reflect your changes.

Refreshing a chart

If a chart is linked to a separate Excel workbook, you can update the chart to reflect any changes that have been made to the underlying data. To do so, follow these steps:

1. **Click the chart to select it.**

   The Ribbon expands to include three Chart Tools tabs. (Refer to Figure 14-5.)

2. **Click the Design tab on the Ribbon.**

3. **Click the Refresh button in the Data group.**

   The chart is updated with the data from the underlying Excel workbook.

Changing the Chart Layout

A *chart layout* is a predefined combination of chart elements such as legends, titles, and so on. Microsoft studied thousands of charts and talked to chart experts to come up with galleries of the most common layouts for each chart type. For example, Figure 14-8 shows the Layout gallery for column charts.

Figure 14-8: The Chart Layout gallery for column charts.

To change the layout for a chart, follow these steps:

1. **Click the chart to select it.**

   The Ribbon expands to include three Chart Tools tabs. (Refer to Figure 14-5.)

2. **Click the Layout tab on the Ribbon.**

3. **Click the Quick Layout button.**

   This brings up the Chart Layout Gallery, which was shown in Figure 14-8.

4. **Click the layout you want to use.**

   The layout you select is applied to the chart.

Changing the Chart Style

A *chart style* is a pre-defined combination of formatting elements such as colors and shape effects. Microsoft provides a large assortment of chart styles to choose from. For example, Figure 14-9 shows the Chart Style gallery for column charts.

Figure 14-9:
The Chart Style gallery for column charts.

To change the style for a chart, follow these steps:

1. **Click the chart to select it.**

   The Ribbon expands to include the three Chart Tools tabs. (Refer to Figure 14-5.)

2. **Click the Design tab.**

3. **Select the style you want to use from the Chart Styles group.**

   The Chart Styles group displays the most commonly used styles for the chart type.

   If the style you want to use isn't visible in this group, you can click the More button to display a gallery of all available styles. (The More button is the down-arrow button at the bottom of the scroll bar that appears at the right side of the Chart Styles group.)

Embellishing Your Chart

PowerPoint enables you to embellish a chart in many ways: You can add titles, labels, legends, and who knows what else. The easiest way to add these elements is by selecting a chart layout, as described in the section "Changing the Chart Layout." However, you can create your own unique chart layout by adding these elements individually.

To do that, select the chart to reveal the Chart Tools tabs, then select the Layout tab. Figure 14-10 shows how this tab appears.

Figure 14-10:
The Layout
tab.

The Shapes group on this tab lets you insert a picture, shape, or text box. For more information about working with these elements, refer to Chapter 13.

The Labels group on the Layout tab lets you add various types of labels to your chart:

- **Chart titles:** A chart title describes the chart's contents. It normally appears at the top of the chart, but you can drag it to any location.

- **Axis titles:** These titles describe the meaning of each chart axis. Most charts use two axes titles: the Primary Horizontal Axis Title and the Primary Vertical Axis Title.

- **Legends:** A *legend* identifies the data series that appear in the chart. When you click the Legend button, a menu with several choices for the placement of the legend appears. You can also choose More Legend Options to display the Format Legend dialog box, shown in Figure 14-11. From this dialog box, you can set the position of the legend as well as control various formatting options for the legend, such as the fill and border style. (Note that you can also drag the legend to move it to another location in the chart.)

  PowerPoint enables you to create a legend, but you're on your own if you need a myth or fable.

- **Data Labels:** Lets you add labels to the data points on the chart. For maximum control over the data labels, choose More Data Label Options to display the dialog box shown in Figure 14-12.

Figure 14-11:
The Format
Legend
dialog box.

Figure 14-12:
The Format
Data Labels
dialog box.

For most slide types, data labels add unnecessary clutter without adding much useful information. Use labels only if you think that you must back up your chart with exact numbers.

✔ **Data Table:** The *data table* is a table that shows the data used to create a chart. Most charts do not include a data table, but you can add one if you think your audience will benefit from seeing the raw numbers. For example, Figure 14-13 shows a chart with a data table.

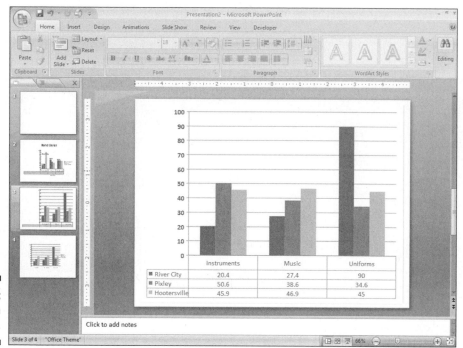

Figure 14-13: A chart with a data table.

The Axes group on the Layout tab includes just two controls:

✔ **Axes:** Sometimes an axe is what you'd like to use to fix your computer. But in this case, *axes* refer to the X- and Y-axes on which chart data is plotted. The *X-axis* is the horizontal axis of the chart, and the *Y-axis* is the vertical axis. For 3-D charts, a third axis — *Z* — is also used. The Axes control lets you show or hide the labels used for each chart axis.

✔ **Gridlines:** *Gridlines* are light lines drawn behind a chart to make it easier to judge the position of each dot, bar, or line plotted by the chart. You can turn gridlines on or off via the Gridlines button.

The Background group on the Layout tab includes the following useful controls for formatting various parts of the chart background:

- ✔ **Plot area:** This button lets you format the background of the main area of the chart.

- ✔ **Chart wall:** For chart formats that have a walls, this button lets you control the format of the wall.

- ✔ **Chart floor:** For chart formats that have a floor, this button lets you control the floor's format.

- ✔ **3-D View:** For charts that have a 3-D format, this button lets you control the rotation and other aspects of the 3-D display.

Chapter 15

Working with SmartArt

. . . .

. . . .

*Y*ou'll hear nothing but yawns from the back row if your presentation consists of slide after slide of text and bulleted lists with an occasional bit of clip art thrown in for good measure. Mercifully, PowerPoint is well equipped to add all sorts of embellishments to your slides. This chapter shows you how to work with one of the coolest ways to embellish your slides: adding special diagrams called *SmartArt.*

Understanding SmartArt

PowerPoint includes a nifty little feature called SmartArt, which lets you add several different types of useful diagrams to your slides. With SmartArt, you can create List, Process, Cycle, Hierarchy, Relationship, Matrix, and Pyramid diagrams.

The idea behind SmartArt diagrams is to represent bullet lists as a diagram of interconnected shapes. Although many different types of SmartArt diagrams are available, they all work the same way. The only real difference among the various SmartArt diagram types is how they graphically represent the bullets. For example, consider the following bullet list:

✔ Arrive

✔ Work

✔ Lunch

✔ More work

✔ Leave

Figure 15-1 shows this list represented by two different types of SmartArt. All I did to create both of these SmartArt diagrams was select the text, right-click, and choose Convert to SmartArt. The only difference between the two is the type of SmartArt diagram I selected.

Note that many of the SmartArt diagram types can display two or more outline levels in your bullet list. For example, suppose you have this list:

- Arrive
    - Stop for coffee on the way
    - Try not to be late
- Work
    - Coffee break at 10:00
    - Look smart!
- Lunch
    - Best part of the day!
- More work
    - Coffee break at 2:00
    - Try to stay awake at 4:00
- Leave
    - Leave early today?

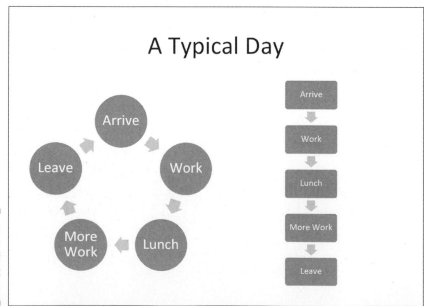

Figure 15-1:
Two examples of SmartArt diagrams.

Figure 15-2 shows how this list appears when formatted as a horizontal process chart. As you can see, the second-level bullets are incorporated as text within the diagram.

Figure 15-2:
How
second-
level text is
displayed in
a horizontal
process
chart.

One of the most useful aspects of SmartArt is that you can easily change from one type of diagram to another. Thus, if you decide that a diagram doesn't convey the message you intend, you can try changing the diagram type to see whether the message is clearer.

Creating a SmartArt Diagram

The easiest way to create a SmartArt diagram is to create a new slide and enter the bullet list as if you were going to display the list as normal text and then convert the text to SmartArt. Just follow these steps:

1. **Create a new slide with the Title and Content layout.**

2. **Type your bullet list.**

   Use one or two levels of bullets, but try to keep the list as short and concise as you can.

3. **Right-click anywhere in the list and choose Convert to SmartArt.**

   A menu of SmartArt diagram types appears, as shown in Figure 15-3.

4. **Select the SmartArt type you want to use.**

   If the SmartArt type doesn't appear in the menu, you can click More SmartArt Graphics to display the Choose a SmartArt Graphic dialog box, as shown in Figure 15-4. As you can see, this dialog box lets you choose from about a million different SmartArt diagram types. PowerPoint offers seven basic categories of SmartArt diagram; these diagram types are pictured and described in Table 15-1.

Figure 15-3:
Converting
text to
SmartArt.

Figure 15-4:
The Choose
a SmartArt
Graphic
dialog box.

5. Click OK.

The diagram is created.

6. Modify the diagram however you see fit.

For more information, see the section "Tweaking a SmartArt Diagram,"
later in this chapter.

7. You're done!

Well, you're never really done. You can keep tweaking your diagram until the end of time to get it perfect. But at some point, you have to say, "enough is enough," and call it finished.

Table 15-1	**Types of Diagrams You Can Create**	
Icon	**Diagram Type**	**Description**
List	List	Shows a simple list. Some of the list diagrams show information that doesn't have any particular organization; others display information in a way that implies a sequential progression, such as steps in a task.
Process	Process	Shows a process in which steps flow in a sequential fashion.
Cycle	Cycle	Shows a process that repeats in a continuous cycle.
Hierarchy	Hierarchy	Shows hierarchical relationships, such as organization charts.
Relationship	Relationship	Shows how items are conceptually related to one another. Included in this group are various types of radial and Venn diagrams.
Matrix	Matrix	Shows four items arranged into quadrants.
Pyramid	Pyramid	Shows how elements build upon one another to form a foundation.

Tweaking a SmartArt Diagram

After you've created a SmartArt diagram, you can adjust its appearance in many ways. The easiest is to change the Quick Style that's applied to the diagram. A Quick Style is simply a collection of formatting elements such as colors and shape effects that are assigned to the various elements of a SmartArt diagram.

Microsoft provides a large assortment of Quick Styles to choose from. For example, Figure 15-5 shows the style gallery for Pyramid diagrams.

Figure 15-5:
The Quick
Style Gallery
for pyramid
diagrams.

To change the quick style for a SmartArt diagram, follow these steps:

1. **Click the diagram to select it.**

   This adds the SmartArt tools to the Ribbon.

2. **Click the Design tab.**

   Figure 15-6 depicts the SmartArt Tools tab.

Figure 15-6:
The
SmartArt
Tools
Design tab.

3. **Select the style you want to use from the Quick Styles group.**

   The Quick Styles group displays the most commonly used styles for the diagram type. If the style you want to use isn't visible in this group, you can click the More button to display a gallery of all available styles.

Note that the SmartArt Tools Design tab also includes controls that let you modify the SmartArt diagram by adding additional shapes or bullet items or changing the chart type. You can also reset the diagram to its original appearance by clicking the Reset Graphic button found in the Reset group.

Editing the SmartArt Text

When you create a SmartArt diagram from an existing bullet list, the bullet text is replaced by the diagram. This raises an important question: After you've converted the text to SmartArt, what do you do if you need to modify the text?

To modify SmartArt text, simply select the SmartArt diagram. Then click the little double-arrow icon that appears on the left edge of the diagram's selection box. This reveals a fly-out window called the Text pane, in which you can edit the bullet points. See Figure 15-7.

Flowcharts, anyone?

One type of diagram that people often want to create with PowerPoint is a flowchart. Although SmartArt doesn't have an option for creating flowcharts, you can easily create flowcharts by using PowerPoint's AutoShapes. For example, take a look at the following flowchart, which I created with just a few minutes' work.

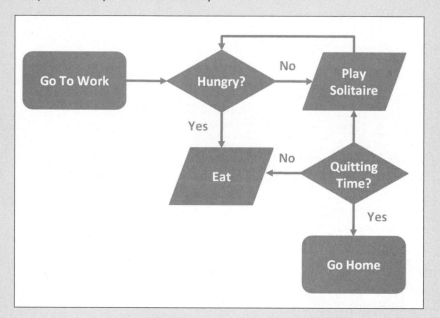

To create a flowchart like this, follow these basic steps:

1. **Draw each flowchart shape by using basic shape objects as described in Chapter 13.**

   Use the shapes in the Flowchart section of the Shapes gallery to create the shapes for the flowchart, and use arrows to connect the shapes.

2. **Enter text into each flowchart shape by clicking the shape and typing.**

   If necessary, adjust the text font and size.

3. **Adjust the alignment of your shapes.**

   Here's where the flowcharting AutoShapes really shine: The connectors stay attached to the shapes even when you move the shapes around! Pretty slick, eh?

Working with Organization Charts

Organization charts — you know, those box-and-line charts that show who reports to whom, where the buck stops, and who got the lateral arabesque — are an essential part of many presentations.

The hierarchical SmartArt diagrams are ideal for creating organization charts. You can create diagrams that show bosses, subordinates, co-workers, and assistants. You can easily rearrange the chain of command and add new boxes or delete boxes. Figure 15-8 shows a finished organization chart.

The bullet list I used to create this chart looked like this before I converted it to SmartArt:

✔ Doc
- Sneezy
- Grumpy
  - Sleepy
  - Happy
- Bashful

Notice that Dopey isn't in this list. That's because Dopey is in a special kind of box on the chart, called an *Assistant.* You find out how to add Assistant boxes later in this chapter.

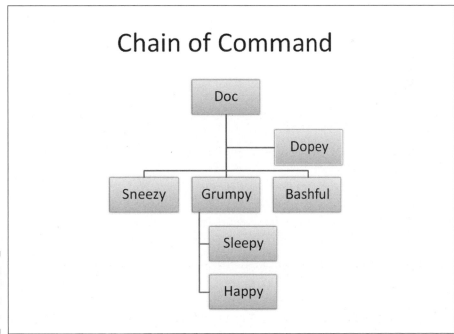

Figure 15-8:
A finished organization chart.

Keep in mind that organization charts are useful for more than showing employee relationships. You also can use them to show any kind of hierarchical structure. For example, back when I wrote computer programs for a living, I used organization charts to plan the structure of my computer programs. They're also great for recording family genealogies, although they don't have any way to indicate that Aunt Milly hasn't spoken to Aunt Beatrice in 30 years.

Previous versions of PowerPoint used a clumsy program called Microsoft Organization Chart to handle organization charts. The new SmartArt feature is easier to use, though it isn't quite as adept at creating complicated charts as the old program was.

Adding boxes to a chart

You can add a box to an organization chart by calling up the Text pane and editing the text. Refer to the section "Editing the SmartArt Text," earlier in this chapter, for tips on how to do that.

Alternatively, you can use the controls in the SmartArt Tools tab on the Ribbon to add boxes. One nice feature that these controls provide is the ability to add an *Assistant,* which is a box that appears outside of the hierarchical chain of command. Here are the steps:

1. **Click the box you want the new box to be below or next to.**

2. **Open the SmartArt Tools tab on the Ribbon.**

3. **Click the Add Shape button to reveal a menu of choices. Then select one of the following options:**

   • *Add Shape Before:* Inserts a new box at the same level as the selected box, immediately to its left.

   • *Add Shape After:* Inserts a new box at the same level as the selected box, immediately to its right.

   • *Add Shape Above:* Inserts a new box above the selected box.

   • *Add Shape Below:* Inserts a new box beneath the selected box.

   • *Add Assistant:* Inserts a new box beneath the selected box, but the new box is connected with a special elbow connector to indicate that the box is an Assistant, and not a subordinate.

4. **Click the new box and then type whatever text you want to appear in the box.**

5. **If necessary, drag the box to adjust its location.**

Deleting chart boxes

To delete a box from an organization chart, select the box and press Delete. PowerPoint automatically adjusts the chart to compensate for the lost box.

When you delete a box from an organization chart, you should observe a moment of somber silence — or throw a party. It all depends on whose name was in the box, I suppose.

Changing the chart layout

PowerPoint lets you choose from four methods of arranging subordinates in an organization chart branch:

- **Standard:** Subordinate shapes are placed at the same level beneath the superior shape.

- **Both Hanging:** Subordinates are placed two per level beneath the superior with the connecting line between them.

- **Left Hanging:** Subordinates are stacked vertically beneath the superior, to the left of the connecting line.

- **Right Hanging:** Subordinates are stacked vertically beneath the superior, to the right of the connecting line.

Figure 15-9 shows an organization chart that uses all four of these layouts. Sneezy, Grumpy, and Bashful use Standard layout. Sleepy and Happy use Both Hanging layout. Groucho, Harpo, and Chico use Left Hanging layout, and Manny, Moe, and Jack use Right Hanging layout.

To change the layout of a branch of your chart, first click the shape at the top of the branch click the SmartArt Tools Design tab on the Ribbon. Then click the Org Chart button in the Create Graphic group and choose the layout type you want to use.

Figure 15-9:
An
organization
chart that
uses all four
layout types.

Chapter 16

Lights! Camera! Action! (Adding Sound and Video)

*O*ne of the cool things about PowerPoint is that it lets you create slides that contain not only text and pictures but also sounds and even movies. You can add sound effects such as screeching brakes or breaking glass to liven up dull presentations. You can even add your own applause, making your presentation like a TV sitcom or game show. You can also add a musical background to your presentation.

Additionally, you can insert a film clip from *The African Queen* or a picture of the space shuttle launching if you think that will help keep people awake. This chapter shows you how to add those special effects.

This chapter is short because you can't do as much with sound and video in PowerPoint as you can with, say, a professional multimedia-authoring program such as Macromedia Director. Still, PowerPoint allows you to paste sound and video elements into your slide show, thus giving you the power to craft some impressive high-tech presentations.

Getting Ready to Add Sound to a Slide

A sterile *beep* used to be the only sound you could get from your computer. Nowadays, you can make your computer talk almost as well as the computers in the *Star Trek* movies, or you can give your computer a sophomoric sense of audible distaste. At last, the computer can be as obnoxious as the user!

As with all good things, there's a catch. Nearly all computers in operation these days have the ability to play sounds. However, not all of them are hooked up to speakers so that you can actually hear the sounds. If you can't hear sounds from your computer, it's probably because it doesn't have speakers, the speakers aren't connected, or the volume is turned down.

Investigating sound files

Computer sounds are stored in *sound files,* which come in two basic varieties:

- ✔ **Wave files:** Wave files contain digitized recordings of real sounds. These sounds can be sound effects, such as cars screeching, guns firing, or drums rolling; music; or even quotes from movies or your favorite TV shows. (Imagine Darth Vadar saying to your audience, "I find your lack of faith disturbing.")

  Wave files come in several formats:

  - *WAV:* The basic format for wave files is the standard Windows WAV format. Both Windows and PowerPoint come with a collection of WAV files that provide simple sound effects such as swooshes, blips, applause, and drum rolls.

  - *MP3* and *WMA:* For longer sound clips, such as complete songs, the popular formats to use include MP3, a compressed format that is popular for sounds obtained from the Internet, and WMA, a newer audio format developed by Microsoft for newer versions of Windows. You can tell the format of a sound file by the filename's extension (.mp3 or .wma). (There's an improved version of MP3 out called MP4, but it isn't used much yet.)

- ✔ **MIDI files:** MIDI files contain music stored in a form that the sound card's synthesizer can play. Windows comes with several MIDI files, and you can download many more from the Internet. MIDI files have the file extension .mid.

To insert a sound into a PowerPoint presentation, all you have to do is paste one of these sound files into a slide. Then when you run the presentation in Slide Show View, you can have the sounds play automatically during slide transitions, or you can play them manually by clicking the Sound button.

You're more likely to use wave files than MIDI files in a PowerPoint presentation. MIDI files are great for playing music, but the wave files enable you to add truly obnoxious sounds to a presentation.

MP3 and the Internet

MP3 files are a compressed form of wave files that allow entire songs to be squeezed into a reasonable amount of hard drive space. For example, the Steppenwolf song, "Wild Thing," weighs in at just under 2.5MB in an MP3 file. The same file in WAV format requires a whopping 26MB — more than ten times the space.

Napster, the online file exchange system that let users swap MP3 files, popularized the MP3 format. Of course, this file swapping bothered the music industry, which sued because it said users were illegally trading copyrighted music without paying for it, which of course they were and we (oops, I mean they) all knew it.

There are plenty of sources for MP3 files on the Internet, including the newly resurrected Napster and iTunes. You can legally download music from these sources, and you can still find plenty of online sources to trade music under the table. Another popular way to obtain MP3 files is to rip them from a music CD. You can find software to do that by using a search engine (such as `www.google.com`) for "CD rip."

Keep in mind, however, that the legality of using copyrighted music in your PowerPoint presentations is questionable. So if you use hot MP3 files you got from the Internet or ripped from a CD, don't blame me if one day you wake up and find your house surrounded by federal agents and CNN news crews, who refer to you as a "dangerous copyright abuser" and your house as a "compound." They'll probably even interview your ninth-grade English teacher, who will tell the nation that all you could talk about when you were a troubled teen was stealing Aerosmith music from the Internet and using it in illegal PowerPoint presentations.

Fortunately, the national shortage of sound files ended years ago. PowerPoint comes with a handful of useful sound files, including drum rolls, breaking glass, gunshots, and typewriter sounds. Windows comes with some useful sounds, too. If you have access to the Web, you have a virtually unlimited supply of sounds at your disposal. Pop into any of the popular search engines (such as `www.yahoo.com` or `www.google.com`) and perform a general search, such as "WAV file collection," or a specific search, such as "Star Trek sounds."

Sound files consume large amounts of hard drive space. Even just a few seconds of sound can take 100K or more. It might not seem like much space, but it adds up.

Inserting a sound object

In this section, I explain how to insert a sound object onto a slide. You can configure the sound object to play automatically whenever you display the slide, or you can set it up so that it will play only when you click the sound object's icon. Note that if you want the sound to play automatically and the sound is a

WAV file, it's easier to add it to the slide transition (as described in Chapter 10) than to add it as a separate object. It you want to control when the sound plays or if the sound file is in a format other than WAV, follow these steps:

1. **Move to the slide to which you want to add the sound.**

2. **Open the Insert tab on the Ribbon and then click the Sound button located on the right side of the tab.**

    The Insert Sound dialog box appears, as shown in Figure 16-1.

Figure 16-1:
The Insert
Sound
dialog box.

3. **Select the sound file that you want to insert.**

    You might have to rummage about your hard drive to find the folder that contains your sound files. (Use Start⇨Search to search for files.)

4. **Click OK.**

    A dialog box appears, asking whether you want the sound to play automatically when you display the sound, or play only when you click the sound's icon.

5. **Click either the Automatically or When Clicked buttons.**

    Either way, the sound clip is added to your slide and represented by a little speaker icon.

You can also insert one of the many sounds that come with PowerPoint or that are available online on the Microsoft Web site. To do so, click the down-arrow on the Sound button and then choose Sound From Clip Organizer. This summons the Clip Art task pane (see Figure 16-2), which features a list of sound files that are available for your use. Scroll through the list to find the sound you want and then double-click the sound to add it to your file. (To hear a preview of the sound before you insert it, right-click the sound and choose the Preview/Properties command.)

Figure 16-2:
Inserting a
sound from
the Media
Gallery.

Here are a few other random thoughts on adding sounds to your slides:

✔ To play a sound while working in Normal View, double-click the sound icon. However, to play the sound during a slide show, click only once.

✔ If the sound file is smaller than 100KB, PowerPoint copies the sound file into your presentation file. However, if the sound file is larger than 100KB, PowerPoint just adds a link to the sound file so that your presentation won't become bloated with large sound files. If you use large sound files and then copy your presentation to another computer, be sure to copy the large sound files as well. (You can change the 100KB threshold by selecting a sound object and then opening the Sound Tools tab on the Ribbon. There you can find a control named Max Sound File Size that lets you set the maximum size of sound files to embed.)

✔ Remember that you can also play WAV files as a part of the slide transition. For more information, see Chapter 10.

✔ If you change your mind and decide you don't want any sounds, you can easily remove them. To remove a sound, click the sound's icon (which resembles a speaker) and press Delete.

✔ You can hide the sound icon while the sound is playing during a slide show by selecting the sound, opening the Sound Tools tab on the Ribbon, and then selecting the Hide During Show check box.

Playing a Sound Over Several Slides

Sometimes, you have a sound file that you want to have played while you display several slides. You might even have a sound that you want to loop endlessly until your presentation ends. Unfortunately, PowerPoint has a nasty habit of stopping a sound when you move to the next slide.

You can alter this behavior in two ways. First, if you want a sound to play from the current slide all the way to the end of the show, simply select the sound, call up the Sound Tools tab on the Ribbon, and set the Play Sound option to Play Across Slides.

If you want more control over how the sound is played, follow these steps:

1. **Select the sound icon.**

2. **Choose the Animations tab on the Ribbon and then click Custom Animation in the Animations group.**

   Yes, this is actually a Custom Animation feature. When you click Custom Animation, the Custom Animation task pane appears to the right of the slide, as shown in Figure 16-3.

Figure 16-3:
The Custom Animation task pane for a sound.

3. Click the down arrow next to the sound item and then choose Effect Options from the menu that appears.

This action summons the Play Sound dialog box, shown in Figure 16-4.

Figure 16-4:
The Play
Sound
dialog box.

4. Select the After option (in the Stop Playing section) and then set the number of slides you want the sound to play for.

When you count the slides, start counting with the slide the sound is on. For example, suppose you have a presentation with 10 slides. You insert a sound on slide 3, and you want the sound to play while slides 3, 4, 5, and 6 are displayed but to stop when slide 7 is displayed. In this case, set the number of slides to 4.

5. Click OK.

That's it!

If the sound file is not long enough to last through all the slides you want it to play over, right-click the sound icon, choose Effects Options to call up the Play Sound dialog box (shown earlier in Figure 16-4), and click the Timing tab, shown in Figure 16-5. Then set the Repeat option to the number of times you want the sound to repeat. If you aren't sure, set the number of repeats to 9999. That way, the sound will repeat almost indefinitely.

Nothing stops you from including more than one sound on a slide if you want. For example, you can add background music and a sound effect such as applause or the sound of a train wreck.

Figure 16-5:
The Timing
tab of the
Play Sound
dialog box.

Playing a Track from a CD

Besides sound files, PowerPoint can also tell your CD player to play tracks from a regular audio CD. To use this feature, follow these steps:

1. **Get a CD that has music you want to play during your presentation, and make note of the track you want to play.**

   You won't be able to see the names of the tracks in PowerPoint, so you need to know which track number you want.

2. **Insert the CD in your computer's CD drive.**

3. **On the Insert tab, click the down arrow next to the Sound button and then choose Play CD Audio Track.**

   This brings up the dialog box shown in Figure 16-6.

Figure 16-6:
The Insert
CD Audio
dialog box.

4. **Select the starting and ending track numbers.**

   To play just one track, set both the starting and ending track numbers to the track you want to play. Set these options to different numbers to play more than one track.

5. **Set the other sound options however you want.**

   You can adjust the sound's volume, specify whether you want an icon to appear on the slide, and tell PowerPoint whether you want the sound icon to appear while the sound is playing.

6. **Click OK.**

   A dialog box appears, asking whether you want the sound to play automatically when the slide is displayed.

7. **Click Yes or No.**

   That's all there is to it! Now the CD plays when you show the presentation.

 Don't forget you have to have the CD in your computer's CD drive when you show the presentation!

Recording a Narration

PowerPoint includes a nifty feature that lets you record your own voice to use as a narration for the slide show. As you record your narration, PowerPoint stores the narration you record for each file separately so that when you play back your presentation with the narration, the slides are automatically synchronized with the narrations you recorded. PowerPoint can also store timings for each slide so that when you replay the presentation, PowerPoint automatically advances each slide along with the narration.

To record a narration, go to the first slide of your presentation and then follow these steps:

1. **Open the Slide Show tab and then click the Record Narration button in the Set Up group.**

   The Record Narration dialog box, shown in Figure 16-7, appears. Notice that this dialog box helpfully informs you how much hard drive space you have available on your computer and calculates the maximum length of the narration that you can record, based on the amount of free hard drive space. In this example, I have 8,480MB of free hard drive space, enough to record 13,442 minutes of narration . . . about 224 hours.

2. **Set the microphone level.**

   To do so, click the Set Microphone Level button. This brings up the Microphone Check dialog box, shown in Figure 16-8. Talk into the microphone, reading the text displayed in the dialog box. As you speak, PowerPoint adjusts your microphone sensitivity to an acceptable range. When you're finished, click OK.

   The Microphone Check dialog box doesn't really care what you say, as long as you talk.

Figure 16-8:
Setting the
microphone
level.

3. **Click OK to begin the slide show.**

   The first slide of your presentation is displayed.

4. **Speak your narration into the microphone. Press Enter each time you want to advance to a new slide.**

   Or if you have set up builds or other animations, press Enter to advance through the builds and animations.

   When you reach the end of the slide show, PowerPoint displays the dialog box shown in Figure 16-9.

5. **Click Save if you want PowerPoint to automatically advance your slides in sequence with your narration. To advance slides manually, click Don't Save.**

   You're taken to PowerPoint's Slide Sorter View, where the timing for each slide is displayed along with the slides.

Figure 16-9:
The
narration is
recorded.
Do you want
to save the
slide
timings?

6. **Press F5 or click the Slide Show button to begin the slide show so you can see whether your narration works.**

   The slide show begins. The narration will play through your computer's speakers, and the slides will advance automatically along with the narration if you clicked Save in Step 5.

Here are some additional things to keep in mind about narrations:

✔ As you record the narration, leave a little gap between each slide. PowerPoint records the narration for each slide as a separate sound file and then attaches the sound to the slide. Unfortunately, you get cut off if you talk right through the slide transitions.

✔ The narration cancels out any other sounds you placed on the slides.

✔ You can record or rerecord a narration for just one slide by calling up that slide in Normal View and then choosing Slide Show⇨Set Up⇨Record Narration. PowerPoint asks whether you want to begin recording at the current slide or the first slide: Click the Current Slide button. When you're finished recording the slide's narration, press Esc to stop the show.

✔ To delete a narration, click the speaker icon in the corner of the slide and press Delete. To delete the narration for an entire presentation, delete the speaker icon from every slide.

Adding Video to Your Slides

Welcome to the MTV era of computing. If your computer has the chutzpah, you can add small video clips to your presentations and play them at will. I'm not sure why you would want to, but hey, who needs a reason?

Adding a movie motion clip to a slide is similar to adding a sound clip. A crucial difference exists, however, between motion clips and sound bites: Video is meant to be *seen* (and sometimes *heard*). An inserted motion clip should be given ample space on your slide.

If you think sound files are big, wait till you see how big motion clips are. Ha! They consume hard drive space the way an elephant consumes veggies. (The whole multimedia revolution is really a conspiracy started by hard drive manufacturers.)

The following steps show you how to add a video clip to a slide:

1. **Find a good movie.**

   The hardest part about using video in a PowerPoint presentation is finding a video file that's worth showing. Many good sources offer video clips. PowerPoint comes with movies in the Media Gallery, and Microsoft has additional movies that you can download from the online Media Gallery. You can also find a wide variety of video clips available for download on the Web.

2. **Move to the slide on which you want to insert the movie.**

   Hopefully, you left a big blank space on the slide to put the movie in. If not, rearrange the existing slide objects to make room for the movie.

3. **Open the Insert tab on the Ribbon and then click Movie in the Media Clips group.**

   The Insert Movie dialog box appears, shown in Figure 16-10.

Figure 16-10:
Inserting a
video.

4. **Select the movie that you want to insert.**

   You might need to scroll the list to find the movie you're looking for or navigate your way to a different folder.

5. Click OK.

A dialog box appears, asking whether you want to play the movie automatically when the slide comes up or wait for you to click the movie before playing it. (If you select a simple type of movie called an animated GIF, PowerPoint skips this step.)

6. Click Automatically or When Clicked.

The movie is inserted on the slide, as shown in Figure 16-11.

7. Resize the movie if you want and drag it to a new location on the slide.

When you resize the movie, try to do it by using one of the corner handles. If you drag one of the side handles, you distort the image.

To play the movie while you're working on the presentation in Normal View, double-click the movie. During a Slide Show, a single click does the trick, unless you set the movie to play automatically. In that case, the movie runs as soon as you display the slide.

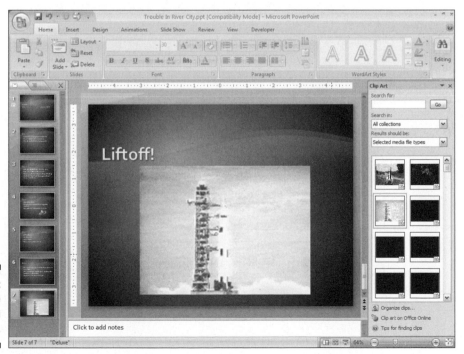

Figure 16-11:
A movie
inserted on
a slide.

You can also insert a movie from the Clip Organizer by clicking the down arrow next to the Movie button in the Media Clips group and then choosing Movie From Clip Organizer. This calls up the Clip Art task pane to display movies that you can access from the Clip Organizer. If you find a movie you're interested in, click the arrow next to the movie and choose Preview/Properties. This calls up the dialog box shown in Figure 16-12, from which you can preview the movie. If you like it, close the Preview/Properties dialog box and then click the movie in the Clip Art task pane to insert it onto the slide.

Figure 16-12: The Preview/ Properties dialog box.

Chapter 17

More Things to Insert on Your Slides

The Insert tab on the Ribbon is chock-full of goodies you can insert into your presentations. The most important of these goodies have already been covered in other chapters: shapes (Chapter 13), new slides (Chapter 2), pictures and clip art (Chapter 12), SmartArt (Chapter 15), and movies and sounds (Chapter 16).

But you can insert a lot more, including tables, WordArt, hyperlinks, and actions. This chapter covers these items.

Inserting Tables

Tables are a great way to present lots of information in an orderly fashion. For example, if you want to create a slide that shows how many people like or hate various computer presentation programs, a table is the way to go. Or if you're considering purchasing some new computer equipment and want to list the prices for five different computer configurations from three different vendors, a table is the best way.

Creating a table in a Content placeholder

Basic tables are simple to create in PowerPoint. The easiest way to create a slide that contains a table is to use the Title and Content slide layout. Just follow these steps:

1. **Open the Home tab on the Ribbon and then click the New Slide button in the Slides group to add a slide with the Title and Content layout.**

   A new slide is created.

2. **Click the Table icon in the center of the Content placeholder.**

   The Insert Table dialog box appears, as shown in Figure 17-1.

Figure 17-1:
The Insert
Table
dialog box.

3. **Set the number of rows and columns you want for the table and then click OK.**

   The table appears, as shown in Figure 17-2.

Figure 17-2:
An empty
table,
waiting for
data.

4. **Type information into the table's cells.**

   You can click any cell in the table and start typing. Or you can move from cell to cell by pressing the Tab key or the arrow keys.

5. **Play with the formatting if you want.**

   You can use Table Tools on the Ribbon, described later in this section, to control the formatting for the table.

6. **Stop and smell the roses.**

   When you're done, you're done. Admire your work.

Figure 17-3 shows an example of a finished table.

Inserting a table on a slide

You can use the Table button on the Insert tab to insert a table on an existing slide. When you click this button, a grid-like menu appears that enables you to select the size of the table you want to create, as shown in Figure 17-4. You can use this technique to create a table as large as ten columns and eight rows.

Figure 17-3: A finished table.

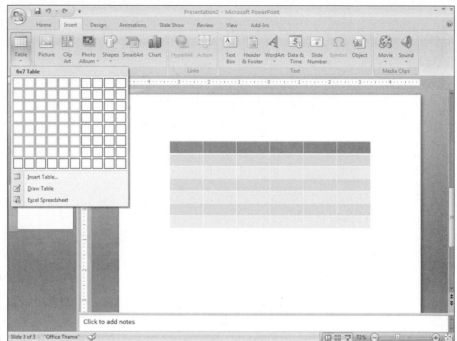

Figure 17-4:
Inserting a
table.

Drawing a table

A third way to create a table is to use the Draw Table command. The Draw Table command lets you draw complicated tables on-screen using a simple set of drawing tools. This command is ideal for creating tables that are not a simple grid of rows and columns, but rather a complex conglomeration in which some cells span more than one row and others span more than one column.

Here's the procedure for creating a table by using the Draw Table tool:

1. **On the Insert tab on the Ribbon, click the Table button in the Tables group and then choose Draw Table from the menu that appears.**

   PowerPoint changes the cursor to a little pencil.

2. **Draw the overall shape of the table by dragging the mouse to create a rectangular boundary for the table.**

   When you release the mouse button, a table with a single cell is created, as shown in Figure 17-5. Notice also in this figure that Table Tools is displayed on the Ribbon.

3. **Carve the table into smaller cells.**

   To do that, just drag lines across the table. For example, to split the table into two rows, point the cursor somewhere along the left edge of the table and then click and drag a line across the table to the right edge. When you release the mouse button, the table splits into two rows.

You can continue to carve the table into smaller and smaller cells. For each slice, point the cursor at one edge of where you want the new cell to begin and click and drag to the other edge.

4. **If you want to change the line size or style drawn for a particular segment, use the Pen Style and Pen Weight drop-down controls in the Draw Borders group (under Table Tools on the Ribbon).**

You can change the style of a line you've already drawn by tracing over the line with a new style.

5. **If you make a mistake while drawing the table cells, click the Eraser (the one that looks like an eraser) button in the Draw Borders group and erase the mistaken line segment.**

Click the Draw Table button if you want to draw additional segments after using the Erase tool.

6. **When you're done, click outside of the table to finish drawing the table.**

Figure 17-6 shows a table carved up into several cells, with various types of line style and line weights.

Figure 17-5: Drawing a table.

Figure 17-6:
A finished
table.

Applying style to a table

After you've created a table, you can set its style by using the controls under Table Tools on the Ribbon. The easiest way to format a table is by applying one of PowerPoint's predefined table styles.

Before you apply a style, however, use the check boxes that appear at the left side of the Design tab under Table Tools on the Ribbon. These check boxes determine whether PowerPoint uses special formatting for certain parts of the table:

- ✓ **Header Row:** Indicates whether the style should format the first row differently than the other rows in the table

- ✓ **Total Row:** Indicates whether the style should format the last row differently than the other rows in the table

- ✓ **Banded Rows:** Indicates whether alternating rows should be formatted differently

- ✓ **First Column:** Indicates whether the style should format the first column differently than the other column in the table

- ✓ **Last Column:** Indicates whether the style should format the last column differently than the other columns in the table

> ✔ **Banded Columns:** Indicates whether alternating columns should be formatted differently

After you've set the Quick Style options, you can apply a Table Style to the table by clicking the style you want to apply (refer to Figure 17-5). If the style doesn't appear in the Table Styles group under Table Tools on the Ribbon, click the More button to reveal the Table Styles gallery, shown in Figure 17-7. This displays all the built-in styles provided with PowerPoint.

Figure 17-7:
The Table Styles gallery.

In addition to using one of the preselected table styles, you can format each cell and line in your table by using the following controls under Table Tools:

> ✔ **Shading:** Sets the background color for the selected cells
> ✔ **Borders:** Lets you control which edges of the selected cells have borders
> ✔ **Table Effects:** Applies shadow and reflection effects to the selected cells

Working with the Layout tab

When you select a table, a special Layout tab is available, as shown in Figure 17-8. The controls on this tab let you adjust the layout of your table in various ways. Table 17-1 lists the function of each of these controls.

Figure 17-8:
The Layout
tab under
Table Tools.

Table 17-1		The Layout Tab
Control	**Name**	**What It Does**
Select ▾	Select	Activates the Selection cursor so you can select cells
Show Gridlines	Show Gridlines	Shows or hides table gridlines
Delete	Delete	Deletes a row or column
Insert Above	Insert Above	Inserts a new row above the current row
Insert Below	Insert Below	Inserts a new row below the current row
Insert Left	Insert Left	Inserts a new column to the left of the current column
Insert Right	Insert Right	Inserts a new column to the right of the current column
Merge Cells	Merge Cells	Merges adjacent cells to create one large cell
Split Cells	Split Cells	Splits a merged cell into separate cells
0.4"	Height	Sets the row height
3"	Width	Sets the column width
Distribute Rows	Distribute Rows	Adjusts the height of the selected rows to distribute the rows evenly

Control	Name	What It Does
Distribute Columns	Distribute Columns	Adjusts the width of the selected columns to distribute the columns evenly
	Align Left	Left-aligns the text
	Center	Centers the text
	Align Right	Right-aligns the text
	Align Top	Vertically aligns the text with the top of the cell
	Align Middle	Vertically aligns the text with the middle of the cell
	Align Bottom	Vertically aligns the text with the bottom of the cell
Text Direction	Text Direction	Changes the direction of text in a cell
Margins	Margins	Sets the table margins
Table Size	Table Size	Sets the overall size of the table
Arrange	Arrange	Brings up a menu that lets you send the table to the front or back of the slide and change the table's alignment.

Inserting WordArt

In Chapter 8, you discover how to apply WordArt formatting to any bit of text in PowerPoint 2007. WordArt also appears on the Insert tab on the Ribbon, which provides a convenient way to insert a text box with text that is already formatted with WordArt formatting.

To insert WordArt, follow these steps:

1. **Move to the slide on which you want to insert WordArt.**

2. **Click the Insert tab on the Ribbon and then click the WordArt button in the Text group.**

   A gallery of WordArt styles is displayed, as shown in Figure 17-9.

Figure 17-9: The WordArt gallery.

3. **Select the WordArt style you want to use.**

   The WordArt text box is inserted on the slide, as shown in Figure 17-10.

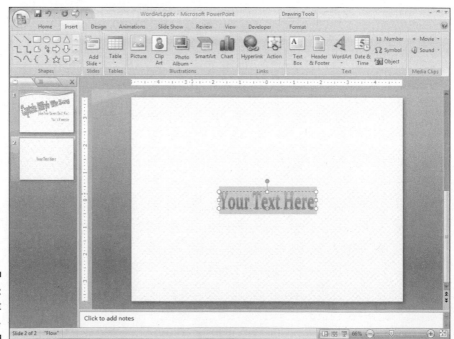

Figure 17-10: A WordArt text box.

4. **Click the WordArt text box and then type the text you want to use.**

5. **Apply any other WordArt formatting you want.**

   For more information about WordArt formatting, refer to Chapter 8.

Using Hyperlinks

In PowerPoint, a *hyperlink* is simply a bit of text or a graphic image that you can click when viewing a slide to summon another slide, another presentation, or perhaps some other type of document, such as a Word document or an Excel spreadsheet. The hyperlink may also lead to a page on the World Wide Web.

For example, suppose that you have a slide that contains a chart of sales trends. You can place a hyperlink on the slide that, if clicked during a slide show, summons another slide presenting the same data in the form of a table. That slide can in turn contain a hyperlink that, when clicked, summons an Excel spreadsheet that contains the detailed data on which the chart is based.

Another common use for hyperlinks is to create a table of contents for your presentation. You can create a slide — usually the first or second slide in the presentation — that contains links to other slides in the presentation. The table of contents slide may include a link to every slide in the presentation, but more likely, it contains links to selected slides. For example, if a presentation contains several sections of slides, the table of contents slide may contain links to the first slide in each section.

Hyperlinks are not limited to slides in the current presentation. Hyperlinks can lead to other presentations. When you use this kind of hyperlink, a person viewing the slide show clicks the hyperlink, and PowerPoint automatically loads the indicated presentation. The hyperlink can lead to the first slide in the presentation, or it can lead to a specific slide within the presentation.

A common use for this type of hyperlink is to create a menu of presentations that can be viewed. For example, suppose that you have created the following four presentations:

- The Detrimental Effects of Pool

- Case Studies in Communities Destroyed by Pool Halls

- Marching Bands through the Ages

- Understanding the Think System

You can easily create a slide listing all four presentations and containing hyperlinks to them. The person viewing the slide show simply clicks a hyperlink, and off he or she goes to the appropriate presentation.

Here are a few additional thoughts to ponder concerning hyperlinks:

- ✔ **Hyperlinks aren't limited to PowerPoint presentations.** In PowerPoint, you can create a hyperlink that leads to other types of Microsoft Office documents, such as Word documents or Excel spreadsheets. When the person viewing the slide show clicks one of these hyperlinks, PowerPoint automatically runs Word or Excel to open the document or spreadsheet.

- ✔ **A hyperlink can also lead to a page on the World Wide Web.** When the user clicks the hyperlink, PowerPoint runs Internet Explorer to connect to the Internet and displays the Web page.

  For more information about browsing the World Wide Web, see my book *Internet Explorer 6 For Windows For Dummies,* published by Wiley Publishing, Inc.

- ✔ **Hyperlinks work only when the presentation is shown in Slide Show View.** You can click a hyperlink all you want while in Slide View, Outline View, or Slide Sorter View, and the only thing that happens is that your finger gets tired. Links are active only when viewing the slide show.

Creating a hyperlink to another slide

Adding a hyperlink to a presentation is easy. Just follow these steps:

1. **Select the text or graphic object that you want to make into a hyperlink.**

   The most common type of hyperlink is based on a word or two of text in a slide's body text area.

2. **Choose Insert➪Links➪Hyperlink.**

   Alternatively, click the Insert Hyperlink button found on the standard toolbar or use the keyboard shortcut Ctrl+K. One way or the other, the Insert Hyperlink dialog box, shown in Figure 17-11, is summoned.

Figure 17-11: The Insert Hyperlink dialog box.

The dialog box has four icons on the left side, as follows:

- **Existing File or Web Page:** This means you can link to another file in another application, or to a Web page on the Internet.

- **Place in This Document:** This means you can link one part of your PowerPoint presentation to another part.

- **Create New Document:** This is just what it says it is. You can, however, choose now or another time to edit the new document by clicking the appropriate button.

- **E-mail Address:** Use this to link to an e-mail address. This feature is useful in an intranet or Internet setting because this link allows the reader to write e-mail to the e-mail address that you link to.

3. **Click the Place in This Document icon on the left side of the dialog box.**

   A list of the slides in the current presentation appears in the dialog box.

4. **Click the slide that you want the hyperlink to lead to and then click OK.**

   The Insert Hyperlink dialog box vanishes, and the hyperlink is created.

If you selected text in Step 1, the text changes color and is underlined. If you selected a graphical object, the picture isn't highlighted in any way to indicate that they are hyperlinks. However, the cursor always changes to a pointing hand whenever it passes over a hyperlink, thus providing a visual clue that the user has found a hyperlink.

Creating a hyperlink to another presentation

Creating a hyperlink that opens another presentation is much like the procedure described in the preceding section, "Creating a hyperlink to another slide," but with a couple important differences:

1. **Select the text or graphical object that you want to make into a hyperlink.**

2. **Click the Hyperlink button in the Links group on the Insert tab.**

   The Insert Hyperlink dialog box appears.

3. **Click the Existing File or Web Page icon in the list of icons on the left side of the dialog box.**

4. **Click Current Folder.**

5. **Select the file that you want to link to.**

   You might have to rummage about your hard drive to find the presentation.

6. **Click OK.**

The presentation that you link to doesn't have to be in the same folder or even on the same drive as the current presentation. In fact, you can link to a presentation that resides on a network file server, if you want.

You can also link to a specific slide within another presentation by clicking the Bookmark button in the Insert Hyperlink dialog box. This brings up another dialog box listing the slides in the selected presentation. Choose the slide you want to link to; then click OK to return to the Insert Hyperlink dialog box.

If you want to create a hyperlink to an existing Web page, just type the address of the Web page in your outline or on your slide and a hyperlink automatically appears. You can select any page of a Web site as long as you know the URL for that specific page.

When you follow a link to another presentation, PowerPoint automatically opens the other presentation. This means that you now have both presentations open. When you're finished viewing the second presentation, close it to return to the original presentation.

To remove a hyperlink, right-click the hyperlink that you want to zap and then choose Remove Hyperlink from the menu that appears. To change a hyperlink, right-click it and choose Edit Hyperlink.

Adding Action Buttons

An *action button* is a special type of AutoShape that places a button on the slide. When the user clicks the button during a slide show, PowerPoint takes whatever action you have designated for the button. A well-planned arrangement of action buttons scattered throughout a presentation can make it easy for someone to view the presentation in any order he or she wants.

The following sections describe how action buttons work and show you how to add them to your presentations.

Assigning button actions

When you create an action button, you assign a shape for the button (you have 12 shapes to choose from; the shapes are described a bit later in this section) and an action to be taken when the user clicks the button or merely points the cursor at it. The action for a button can be any of the following:

- ✔ **Activate a hyperlink:** This is the most common button action. It causes a different slide in the current presentation, a different presentation altogether, a non-PowerPoint document, or even an Internet Web page to appear.

- ✔ **Run a program:** For example, you can set up a button that runs Microsoft Word or Excel.

- ✔ **Run a macro:** PowerPoint lets you create *macros,* which are programs written in a powerful programming language called Visual Basic for Applications.

- ✔ **Play a sound:** This is just one way to add sound to a PowerPoint presentation. For more ways, refer to Chapter 16.

Choosing button shapes

PowerPoint provides a selection of built-in shapes for action buttons. Table 17-2 lists the action button shapes that you can place in your presentation and indicates what type of action is associated with each type.

Table 17-2		Action Buttons
Button Image	*Name*	*What Button Does*
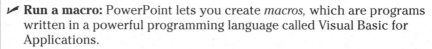	Back or Previous	Displays the previous slide in the presentation
	Forward or Next	Displays the next slide in the presentation
	Beginning	Displays the first slide in the presentation
	End	Displays the last slide in the presentation
	Home	Displays the first slide in the presentation.
	Information	No default action for this button type.

(continued)

Table 17-2 *(continued)*

Button Image	Name	What Button Does
	Return	Displays the most recently viewed slide
	Movie	No default action for this button type
	Document	No default action for this button type
	Sound	No default action for this button type
	Help	No default action for this button type
	Custom	No default action for this button type

Creating a button

To add a button to a slide, follow these steps:

1. **Move to the slide on which you want to place a button.**

2. **Open the Insert tab on the Ribbon and click the More button in the Shapes group to reveal the Shapes gallery.**

3. **Click the button for the action button shape that you want to create.**

   The action buttons are found at the very bottom of the Shapes gallery.

4. **Draw the button on the slide.**

   Start by pointing to the spot where you want the upper-left corner of the button to appear. Then click and drag to where you want the lower-right corner of the button to appear.

   When you release the mouse button, the Action Settings dialog box appears, as shown in Figure 17-12.

5. **If you want, change the action settings for the action button.**

   In most cases, the default setting for the action button that you chose is appropriate for what you want the button to do. For example, the action setting for a Forward or Next button is Hyperlink to Next Slide. If you want the slide to hyperlink to some other location, change the Hyperlink To setting.

6. Click OK.

The Action Settings dialog box vanishes, and the button is created.

Figure 17-12:
The Action
Settings
dialog box.

Here are some additional thoughts concerning action buttons:

- **Change the look of a button:** You can format action buttons like any other shape object. That means you can use Drawing Tools on the Ribbon to apply fill colors, line styles, or shape effects such as bevels and 3-D rotations. For more information, refer to Chapter 13.

- **Move a button:** To move a button, just click it to select it. Then use the mouse to drag the button to a new location.

- **Change the action setting for a button:** You can change the action setting for a button by right-clicking the button and choosing the Action Settings command.

Creating a navigation toolbar

Grouping action buttons into a navigation toolbar makes a slide show easy to navigate. You can add a set of navigation buttons to the bottom of your Slide Master. Figure 17-13 shows a slide with navigation buttons in the lower-right corner. These buttons make getting around the show a snap. For this example, I use Beginning, Backward (Previous), Forward (Next), and Ending buttons, but you can include any buttons you want.

Summary

- Our community is imperiled by the presence of a Pool Table
- The only salvation from this dire situation is the formation of a Boy's Band
- Harold Hill is the man for the job.

Figure 17-13:
A slide with navigation buttons.

To create a navigation toolbar that appears on every slide, follow these steps:

1. Switch to Slide Master View.

From the View tab on the Ribbon, click the Slide Master button in the Presentation Views group. Or if you like shortcuts, hold down the Shift key and click the Normal View button at the lower-left corner of the PowerPoint window.

2. Create the action buttons that you want to include.

Follow the procedure described earlier in the section "Creating a button" to create each button. Make sure that all the buttons are the same size and line them up to create a tight cluster of buttons.

You can easily duplicate a button by holding down the Ctrl key while you drag the button to a new location. This technique makes it easy to create several similar buttons such as navigation buttons.

3. Return to Normal View.

Click the Normal View button or click the Normal button in the Presentation Views group on the View tab.

The buttons that you created appear on every slide in your presentation.

Part IV
Working with Others

"Roger! Check the sewing machine's connection to the PC. I'm getting PowerPoint slides embroidered across my curtains again."

In this part . . .

Remember, there is no I in PowerPoint. Well, I guess there is. But there's only one. That being said, many PowerPoint presentations are crafted by teams of people rather than by individuals. So, the chapters in this part focus on those features of PowerPoint that are designed with teamwork in mind. So get out there and collaborate!

Chapter 18

Using PowerPoint's Collaboration Tools

"*W*orks well with others" is more than standard fare for rookie resumes. It's also one of the PowerPoint mantras. Many presentations are designed not by and for a single presenter, but by a team of presenters. Fortunately, PowerPoint includes several simple tools that let you distribute your presentation to others and allow others to add comments to the presentation so you can get their feedback. This chapter shows you how to use those features.

Previous editions of PowerPoint included a feature that let you e-mail your presentations to others so they could review them and return them with their changes. Then you could combine the marked-up presentations returned from your colleagues and compare the changes.

It turned out that the feature didn't work all that well, and few people used it. Rather than fix the poorly implemented feature, Microsoft decided to just drop it for this release. Word and Excel still have excellent collaboration tools, but alas, PowerPoint has just the few simple collaboration tools presented in this chapter.

E-Mailing a Presentation

The first step in working on a team PowerPoint project is figuring out how to get a copy of the presentation to your teammates. If all your collaborators share a connection to a local network, you can do that by saving the presentation to a shared location on a network. You have to talk to your network administrator about getting a shared location set up for that purpose.

If your collaborators aren't all together on the same network, you can always e-mail copies of the presentation to your colleagues for their review. PowerPoint includes a built-in feature for doing that. Here are the steps:

1. **Open the presentation that you want to send out for review.**

    If the presentation is already open, choose Office⇨Save to save any changes you made since you opened it.

2. **Choose Office⇨Send⇨Email.**

    PowerPoint summons Outlook and creates a new message with the Subject line filled in ("Please review . . ."), the presentation attached to the message, and the message text set to "Please review the attached document." See Figure 18-1.

Figure 18-1:
Sending a presentation as an e-mail attachment.

3. **In the To field, add an e-mail address for each person to whom you want to send a review copy.**

    You can type the e-mail addresses directly into the To field, or you can click the To button to call up the Address Book. You can then use the Address Book to select your reviewers.

    If you want to send the presentation to more than one person, separate the e-mail addresses with semicolons.

4. **If you want, change the Subject field or message body.**

    You probably want to say something a little more cordial than the bland "Please review . . ." messages that PowerPoint creates automatically.

5. **Set any other Outlook options you want for the message.**

   You have a whole bevy of options to set for Outlook messages, such as high or low priority, signatures, stationery, read receipts, plain or HTML formatting, and more. But this isn't an Outlook book; I don't go into those options here.

6. **Click the Send button.**

   Your message is whisked away and will be delivered as soon as possible.

Using Comments

If you're reviewing a presentation, one of the best ways to communicate your thoughts to your colleagues is to insert *comments* into the presentation. A comment is a lot like a sticky note. (I'd call it a Post-It note, but then I'd have to remember the Word command to generate the little registered trademark symbol so the folks at 3M won't sue me. Oh, in case any 3M lawyers are reading: "Post-It is a registered trademark of the 3M corporation.")

The beauty of comments is that you can turn them on and off. Thus you can view the comments while you're editing your presentation, and you can turn them off when it's time for the show.

To add a comment to a presentation, follow these steps:

1. **Call up the slide to which you want to add a comment.**

2. **Open the Review tab on the Ribbon and then click the New Comment button.**

   A comment bubble appears on the slide. Your initials and a comment number appear in the small box next to the bubble.

3. **Type whatever you want in the comment bubble.**

   Offer some constructive criticism. Suggest an alternative approach. Or just comment on the weather. Figure 18-2 shows a completed comment.

Figure 18-2:
Creating a
comment.

MW4 | **Marcellus**   7/31/2006
Are you sure this is such a good idea? I mean, these are all such nice people here. Especially that Ethel Toffelmier!|

4. **Click anywhere outside the comment bubble to make it disappear.**

   Only the comment tag (the little box with the reviewer's initials and comment number) remains.

5. **If you want, move the comment tag.**

   You can move the comment closer to the slide item on which you're commenting by dragging the comment tag around the slide.

Here are some additional thoughts concerning working with comments:

✔ To change a comment, double-click the comment tag and then edit the text in the comment until you're satisfied.

✔ To delete a comment, click the comment to select it and then press Delete.

✔ To delete all of the comments on a particular slide, click the down arrow beneath the Delete button on the Review tab. Then choose Delete All Markup on the Current Slide.

✔ To delete all the comments in a presentation, click the down arrow beneath the Delete button and choose Delete All Markup in This Presentation.

✔ You can quickly scan through all the comments in a PowerPoint presentation by using the Previous and Next buttons on the Review tab on the Ribbon.

✔ You can use the Show Markup button on the Review tab to show or hide comments from a presentation.

Packaging Your Presentation on a CD

Often, you can find the need to share a PowerPoint presentation with someone who doesn't own a copy of PowerPoint. Fortunately, PowerPoint includes a Package for CD command that creates a CD that creates a CD with the presentation and a special program called the *PowerPoint Viewer* that can display the presentation on a computer that doesn't have PowerPoint installed.

Unfortunately, the PowerPoint Viewer program that's placed on the CD isn't able to display all the features of PowerPoint 2007 presentations with the same quality that PowerPoint 2007 displays them. As a result, your presentation will look slightly different when you view it with the PowerPoint Viewer.

To create a CD with your presentation, follow these steps:

1. **Open the presentation in PowerPoint and then choose File➪Publish➪Package For CD.**

   The Package For CD dialog box appears, as shown in Figure 18-3.

2. **Click Options.**

   This summons the Options dialog box, shown in Figure 18-4.

3. **Look over the options and change any that aren't set the way you want.**

   The following paragraphs describe each of the options that are available:

   - **Make a Self-Running Package:** Select this option to create a CD that will automatically play the presentation when the CD is inserted into a computer.

   - **Make a Package by Using Original File Formats:** Instructs the Package to CD Wizard to simply copy the presentation files to CD.

- **Linked Files:** Select this option to include any linked files, such as videos or large audio files.

- **Embedded TrueType Fonts:** Select this option to ensure that the fonts you use in your presentation will be available when you show the presentation on another computer.

- **Password to Open Each File:** Enter a password if the presentation contains top-secret information, such as the true whereabouts of Jimmy Hoffa.

- **Password to Modify Each File:** Enter a password if you want to prevent unauthorized people from changing the presentation.

- **Inspect Presentations for Inappropriate or Private Information:** Sorry, this option doesn't check your presentation for off-color jokes or naughty pictures. Instead, it checks for any personal information that might be embedded in your presentation.

4. **Click OK to return to the Package to CD dialog box.**

5. **If you want to add other presentations to the CD, click Add Files, select the files that you want to add, and then click Add.**

   You can put as many files as will fit on the CD. You can add other PowerPoint presentations or any other files you'd like to add to the CD, such as Word documents or text files.

6. **Click Copy to CD.**

   If you haven't already inserted a blank CD into the drive, you are prompted to insert one now.

7. **Insert a blank CD into your CD-RW drive and click Retry.**

   PowerPoint copies the files to the CD. This might take a few minutes, so now is a good time to catch a few z's. When the CD is finished, the drive spits it out and asks whether you want to make another copy.

8. **Remove the CD and then click Yes if you want to make another copy. Otherwise, click No and then click Close.**

   You're done!

The CD is set up so that the presentation should start running all by itself when you insert it into a computer. If it doesn't, open a My Computer window and then open the CD drive and double-click the `pptview.exe` link. A list of presentations on the CD appears. Double-click the one that you want to run, and off you go.

Chapter 19

Working with SharePoint

SharePoint Portal Server, also known as SPS, is a nifty feature that lets you set up Web sites where users can collaborate on documents. SPS sites let you do the following:

- ✔ Save documents in shared libraries so everyone in your group can access the documents.

- ✔ Have online discussions in which you comment on each other's work, argue about politics, and otherwise confer, consult, and cajole.

- ✔ Track the progress of your project, post announcements, assign tasks, and even schedule meetings.

- ✔ Take surveys to gauge the opinions of your team members.

- ✔ Control who can access the site.

In this chapter, you discover some of the basics of using an SPS site. Plus, you find out some of the spiffy ways in which PowerPoint 2007 integrates with SPS so that you can work with presentations stored on an SPS site without ever leaving PowerPoint.

Setting up an SPS Web site is a job for someone who's a bit of a computer guru and is well beyond the scope of this book. Whoever sets up your SPS Web site will give you the information you need to access it. In many cases, simply logging in to your computer network is sufficient to access the SharePoint site. But in some cases, you may need to provide the following information:

✔ The Internet address (URL) of the SPS site, such as `http://rivercity.` `SPS.conman.com`. I just made up this name as an example, so don't bother trying to go there.

✔ A username, such as `RCITY/Harold`.

✔ A password.

Creating a My Network Places Shortcut to Your SPS Site

You'll have a much easier time working with SPS sites if you first create a shortcut called a *network place* in your computer's My Network Places folder. This shortcut provides you with an easy way to answer when PowerPoint inevitably asks you for the location of your SPS site.

Creating a new network place is something you do totally outside of PowerPoint. Here are the steps:

1. **In Windows, click the Start button and then choose My Network Places.**

   This brings up the My Network Places window, shown in Figure 19-1.

Figure 19-1: My Network Places is the place to create a new network place.

2. **Click the Add a Network Place button in the Network Tasks pane on the left.**

   This starts the Add Network Place Wizard, shown in Figure 19-2.

Figure 19-2:
The Add
Network
Place
Wizard
helps you
create your
network
place.

3. Click Next to get the wizard started in the right direction.

The wizard responds by asking you what type of network place you want to create, as shown in Figure 19-3.

Isn't it fascinating that the Add Network Place Wizard divides the entire Internet into two parts: Microsoft's "MSN Communities" Web site and all other network locations? I guess that's the Microsoft World View.

Figure 19-3:
The
Microsoft
World View.

4. **Select Choose Another Network Location. Then click Next.**

The wizard displays the screen shown in Figure 19-4.

Figure 19-4:
Entering the
URL for your
network
place.

5. **Enter the URL of your SharePoint site and then click Next.**

For this step, you need help from your SharePoint system administrator, who can provide you with the URL for your SharePoint site. It will probably be something like `http://rivercity.SPS.conman.com`.

When you click Next, a login dialog box appears, asking for your credentials. It doesn't sing barbershop, but it needs your credentials nonetheless. (Please forgive my obscure reference to *The Music Man*. Humor me a little!)

6. **Enter your username and password, and select the Remember My Password check box if you don't want to have to re-enter your password every time you access the site. Then click OK.**

The screen shown in Figure 19-5 appears.

7. **Enter a descriptive name for your network place and click Next.**

This is the name that will appear in the My Network Places folder after the network place has been created.

When you click Next, the Add Network Place displays its final confirmation screen, shown in Figure 19-6.

Figure 19-5:
Entering a
description.

Figure 19-6:
Finishing the
wizard.

8. **Click Finish.**

Voila! The network place is created.

You can go on about your business; there's nothing else to see here.

Accessing a SharePoint Site

The easiest way to access a SharePoint Web site is to open a browser window and enter the URL of the SharePoint site in the address bar. You'll be taken to the home page of the site, as shown in Figure 19-7.

As you can see in this figure, the home page provides you with access to the many features available on the SharePoint site:

- ✔ **Announcements:** The home page can include announcements related to the project. Anyone with appropriate rights can add an announcement to the home page.

- ✔ **Calendar:** You can use the calendar to schedule upcoming events such as meetings, deadlines, or your birthday.

Figure 19-7:
A
SharePoint
site.

✓ **Links:** The home page may include links to related sites.

✓ **Documents:** The Documents section of the home page provides links to any *document libraries* available for the site. Most sites have a Shared Documents library, and some sites have additional libraries. For more information, see the section "Using a Document Library," later in this chapter.

✓ **Pictures:** The Pictures section lets you post pictures related to the project. (The SharePoint site shown in the figure doesn't have any pictures. I guess it's for a boring project.)

✓ **Lists:** The Lists section provides access to the calendar, a task list, and other lists the site administrator might create.

✓ **Surveys:** The site administrator can create surveys, which team members can fill out. You can find these surveys listed in the Surveys section of the home page.

✓ **Sites:** A SharePoint site can contain *subsites,* which are separate SharePoint sites contained within a main SharePoint site. Subsites are also listed as tabs near the top of the home page.

✓ **People and Groups:** This section is where site administrators grant access to additional team members and administer the rights of each team member.

✓ **Recycle Bin:** This is one of the best features of SharePoint! When you delete a file from a network share, the file is gone forever — there's no network recycle bin. However, SharePoint sites *do* have a recycle bin. So when you delete a file from a document library, you can recover the file from the recycle bin.

Using a Document Library

A *document library* is basically a file folder that resides on a SharePoint site. Most SharePoint sites have a document library called *Shared Documents,* and some sites have additional document libraries. Figure 19-8 shows a typical document library.

Working with a document library is similar to working with a file folder in Windows, but with additional features. Here are a few tips for working with document libraries:

✔ Just above the list of documents in the library is a row of pull-down menus. I suggest you click each of these menus to see what commands are available.

✔ A document library can contain folders just like a regular Windows folder. To create a folder, choose New Folder from the New pull-down menu.

✔ You can sort the list in order by any of the columns.

✔ You can upload a single file to a document library by choosing Upload Document from the Upload pull-down menu. This displays the page shown in Figure 19-9, which lets you browse for the file you want to upload.

✔ If you want to upload a bunch of files to the library, choose the Upload Multiple Documents command from the Upload pull-down menu. This displays the page shown in Figure 19-10, which lets you select multiple files to upload.

Figure 19-8:
A document
library.

Figure 19-9:
Uploading a
single file.

Figure 19-10:
Uploading
multiple
files.

✔ Choose Open with Windows Explorer to open a document library as a standard Windows folder, as shown in Figure 19-11. Then you can drag and drop files into or from the document library as if it were a local Windows folder.

✔ When you select a document in the document list portion of the library, the document name changes into a drop-down list that offers the following useful commands:

• **View Properties:** Displays the properties of the document.

• **Edit Properties:** Lets you change the document properties.

• **Manage Permissions:** Lets you specify who has access to the document.

• **Edit:** Lets you open the document for editing.

• **Delete:** Deletes the document.

• **Send To:** Lets you send the document to another location or an e-mail recipient.

• **Check Out:** Checks out the document. For more information, see the section "Checking Out a Document," later in this chapter.

• **Alert Me:** Another of SharePoint's cool features, this command lets you configure an e-mail alert that notifies you when the document has changed. Figure 19-12 shows the New Alert page that's displayed when you choose Alert Me. As you can see, you can specify the subject for the alert message, a list of recipients, the types of changes that generate the alert, and how often you should be alerted (immediately, daily, or weekly).

Figure 19-11:
Opening a document library as a Windows folder.

Figure 19-12:
Setting up
an alert.

Retrieving a presentation from a document library

You have two ways to open a presentation that resides in a document library. The first, as described earlier in this chapter, is to open the document library in a Web browser, locate the document you want to open, and choose the Edit command. This launches PowerPoint so you can edit the document.

The second is to open PowerPoint and then use the Office➪Open command to retrieve the document from the library. To do that, click My Network Places in the Look In list of the Open dialog box. (Technically, this list is called the *Office Places Bar.*) Then open the network place you created for the SharePoint site to list the document libraries available on the site. You can then navigate to the library that contains your document, as shown in Figure 19-13, and open your document in the usual way.

Figure 19-13:
Accessing a
SharePoint
site from
within
PowerPoint.

Adding a presentation to a document library

You can save a presentation to a document library directly from PowerPoint by following these steps:

1. Create a new presentation or open an existing presentation.

2. Choose File⇨Publish⇨Document Management Server.

This brings up a Save As dialog box that displays your Network Places.

3. Select the Network Places link to your SharePoint site.

If requested, enter your login credentials to access the SharePoint site.

4. Select the document library where you want to save the presentation.

5. If you haven't previously saved the presentation, type a name for the presentation file.

6. Click Save.

The presentation is uploaded to the SharePoint server and saved in the document library you selected in Step 4.

Checking out a document

Like any good library, SharePoint document libraries let you check out a presentation so that others can tell that you're using them. When you finish working with the presentation, you can check it back in. (Fortunately, the Check Out feature doesn't charge a fine for overdue items.)

Note that when you check out a presentation, PowerPoint makes a copy of the presentation on your local hard drive, in a folder named SharePoint Drafts within your My Documents folder.

To check out a presentation, open the presentation as usual. Then choose File⇨Server⇨Check Out. Note that the Server command appears on the File menu only when you have opened a document from a SharePoint server.

While you have the presentation checked out, other users can access a read-only copy of the presentation. But they can't save changes to the presentation or see any changes that you make until you check the presentation back in.

To check in a presentation, choose File⇨Servers⇨Check In. A dialog box appears. In this dialog box, you can type comments about the changes you made to the presentation. Then PowerPoint saves the presentation. The presentation remains open in PowerPoint, but because it is no longer checked out, other users can open the presentation and make changes to it.

You can also check out a document directly from the SharePoint site by opening the document library in a browser window, selecting the document, and choosing the Check Out command from the document's drop-down menu. This displays the dialog box shown in Figure 19-14, which notifies you that you are about to check out the file. Click OK to check out the file. You can then retrieve your checked-out copy of the file from `My Documents\ SharePoint Drafts`.

Figure 19-14: Checking out a file.

Microsoft Internet Explorer

You are about to check out:
Name: TOC PowerPoint 2007.doc
From: ...we.spbeta.iponet.net

☑ Use my local drafts folder

[OK]   [Cancel]

Some files can harm your computer. If this information looks suspicious, or you do not fully trust the source, do not open the file.

Here are a few additional thoughts concerning checking out presentation files:

- ✔ When you finish editing the presentation, you can check it in by choosing File⇨Server⇨Check In. When you do, any changes you've made to your local copy of the document are copied back to the server.

  PowerPoint asks you whether you want to keep the file checked out, which seems a little strange at first: Why would you check it in if you want to keep it checked out? The answer is that you might want to refresh the server copy of your presentation with changes you made but keep the file checked out so you can make additional changes.

  PowerPoint also asks you for comments that describe the changes you've made to the presentation.

- ✔ If you decide you don't want to commit any changes you made back to the server's copy of the presentation, you can discard your check-out. To do that from PowerPoint, choose File⇨Server⇨Discard Checkout. From a browser, open the document library and use the file's drop-down menu to choose Discard Checkout.

Chapter 20

Using a Slide Library and Other Ways to Reuse Slides

In This Chapter

▶ Stealing slides from another presentation

▶ Saving slides in a slide library

▶ Stealing slides from a slide library

*W*hat do you do when you're plodding along in PowerPoint and realize that the slide (or slides) you're trying to create probably already exist in some other presentation somewhere? You do what I do: You steal the slides from the other presentation. This chapter shows you how to do that.

Note that in the old days, the only way to steal slides from another presentation was to get on your horse and chase down the other presentation (that is, find the presentation on your hard drive), jump on board (open the presentation), and steal the slides at gunpoint (copy the slides you want to steal and paste them into the new presentation).

You can still steal slides that way — in fact, Microsoft has created a special command that makes it easy to steal slides directly from another presentation. But if you steal slides often and want to become a career criminal, the real way to do it is to set up a *slide library,* which is a central repository for slides. The slide library lives on a server, so anyone can access it, and it's managed by SharePoint so it has a bunch of nice SharePoint-like features.

Stealing Slides from Another Presentation

Stealing slides from another presentation isn't a serious crime. In fact, Microsoft provides a special command on the Insert tab on the Ribbon to let you do it. Here are the steps:

1. **Open the presentation you want to copy slides into.**

   Not the one you want to steal the slides from — the one you want to put the stolen slides into.

2. **Click the Insert tab on the Ribbon and then click the Add Slide button and choose Reuse Slides.**

   This step displays a Reuse Slides task pane, which appears on the right side of the screen as shown in Figure 20-1.

3. **Click the Open a PowerPoint File link in the Reuse Slides task pane.**

   This summons a Browse dialog box.

4. **Locate the presentation you want to steal slides from and then click Open.**

   The slides from the presentation you selected are displayed in the Reuse Slides task pane, as shown in Figure 20-2.

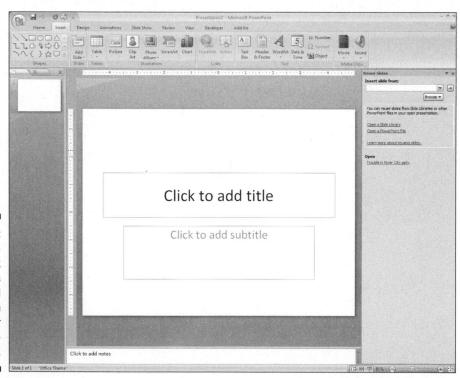

Figure 20-1:
The Reuse
Slides task
pane lets
you steal
slides from
other
presenta-
tions.

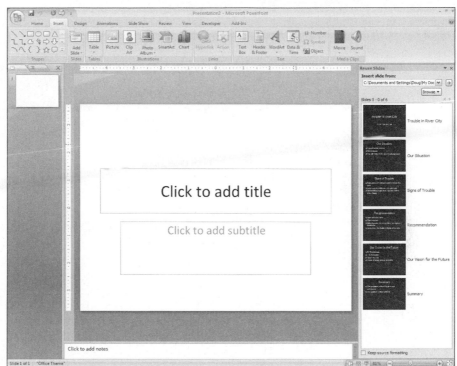

Figure 20-2:
Steal these
slides!

You are now privy to one of the coolest effects in PowerPoint: When you point at one of the slides in the Reuse Slides task pane, the slide magnifies to twice its original size so you can better see the contents of the slide.

5. **(Optional) Select the Keep Source Formatting check box if you want the slides to retain their original formatting.**

   Normally, you should keep this option deselected. With the option deselected, the slide assumes the theme of the presentation it is inserted into.

6. **Click the slides you want to steal.**

   Each slide you click is added to the presentation.

7. **When you're done, click the X at the top right of the Reuse Slides task pane to dismiss it.**

That's about all there is to stealing slides from other presentations.

Saving Slides in a Slide Library

A *slide library* is a special type of document library on a SharePoint server that's designed not to store whole documents, but individual slides. When you've saved slides in a slide library, you can easily insert them into a presentation. And as an added bonus, you can have PowerPoint check to see whether the slides have changed and automatically update them with the changes. Pretty cool, eh?

To save one or more slides to a slide library, you must first create the slide library. That's a task better left to a SharePoint system administrator, so you can skip that step here. Instead, assume that the slide library has already been created for you, and you've been provided with the URL (that is, the Web address) of the slide library and any login credentials you might need to access it.

Here are the steps for adding slides to a slide library:

1. **Open the presentation that contains the slides you want to add to the library.**

2. **Choose Publish⇨Publish Slides from the Office menu.**

   This brings up the dialog box shown in Figure 20-3.

Figure 20-3:
The Publish Slides dialog box.

3. **Select the slides you want to add to the library.**

   To select an individual slide, select the check box next to the slide thumbnail. To select all of the slides in the presentation, click the Select All button.

4. **Enter the URL of the slide library in the Publish To box.**

   Or if you prefer, you can click the Browse button to browse to the library.

5. **Click the Publish button.**

   The slides are copied to the slide library.

6. **Play a game of Solitaire.**

   Depending on the speed of your Internet connection and how many slides you selected, PowerPoint might take a while to publish the slides (probably not long enough for a game of Solitaire, but your boss doesn't have to know that).

7. **You're done!**

The slides have now been added to the library.

Stealing Slides from a Slide Library

You have two ways to steal slides from a slide library. The first is to do it from PowerPoint. Here are the steps:

1. **Open the presentation you want to copy slides into (*not* the one you want to steal the slides from).**

2. **Click the Insert tab on the Ribbon and then click the Add Slide button and choose Reuse Slides.**

   This displays a Reuse Slides task pane, shown earlier in Figure 20-1.

3. **Click the Open a Slide Library link in the Reuse Slides task pane.**

   This summons a Browse dialog box.

4. **Locate the Slide Library you want to steal slides from and then click Open.**

   The slides from the presentation you selected are displayed in the Reuse Slides task pane, in the same was as slides from a PowerPoint file are shown. Refer to Figure 20-2.

5. **(Optional) To keep the original formatting for the slides, select the Keep Source Formatting check box.**

   Normally, you should keep this option deselected.

6. **Click the slides you want to steal.**

Each slide you click is added to the presentation.

7. **When you're done, click the X at the top right of the Reuse Slides task pane to dismiss it.**

The second way to insert slides from a slide library is to use your Web browser to go directly to the slide library. Of course, you need to know the URL of the slide library to do that, and you need login credentials.

To insert a slide or slides from a slide library, follow these steps:

1. **If you want to insert slides into an existing presentation, open the presentation in PowerPoint.**

You can skip this step if you want to create an entirely new presentation from slides in a slide library.

2. **In a browser window, open the slide library that contains the slides you want to steal.**

Figure 20-4 shows a typical slide library.

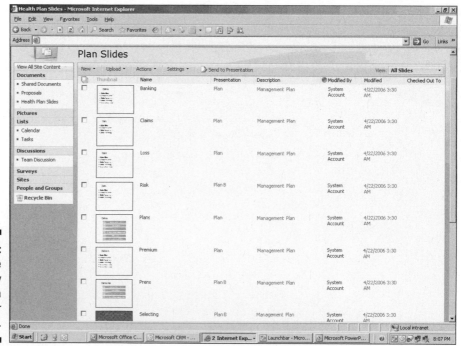

Figure 20-4:
A slide library viewed in a browser window.

3. **Select the check box next to each slide you want to insert.**

4. **Click the Send to Presentation button.**

   This brings up the Send Slides to PowerPoint dialog box shown in Figure 20-5.

Figure 20-5: The Send Slides to PowerPoint dialog box.

5. **To create a new PowerPoint presentation from the slide library, select the Send to a New Presentation option. Otherwise, select the presentation you want to insert the slides in from the drop-down list.**

6. **(Optional) To keep the original formatting for the slides, select the Keep Source Formatting check box.**

   Normally, you should keep this option deselected.

7. **If you want to receive an e-mail notice when any of the inserted slides have changed in the library, select the Tell Me When This Slide Changes check box.**

8. **Click Send.**

   The slides are inserted. You're done!

Chapter 21

Creating a Video Presentation with Microsoft Producer

*P*owerPoint is great for preparing presentations to give in person. But what about giving presentations when you can't be there? With digital video cameras practically being given away in cereal boxes these days, just about anyone can record a video of himself giving a presentation. Wouldn't it be great if you could easily combine the slides from a PowerPoint presentation with a video of you presenting it? Then anyone can watch the presentation later, when you can't be there. Microsoft Producer lets you do just that.

Producer is a great tool for collaboration amongst team members with different production skills. One person might be great at putting together PowerPoint presentations, another might be an excellent cinematographer, and a third might be a great presenter. Producer lets you combine these skills to create a polished presentation.

Introducing Microsoft Producer

Microsoft Producer is an add-on product to PowerPoint that lets you combine slides from existing PowerPoint presentations with media files (audio or video) to create presentations that you can view with a Web browser. You can view the resulting presentation on your computer, over a network, or even over the Internet. The audience members watching the presentation doesn't even have to own PowerPoint. As long as they have a Web browser and a current version of Microsoft's Media Player, they can view the presentation.

Figure 21-1 shows a typical Producer presentation being viewed in Internet Explorer. This presentation uses one of Producer's built-in templates, which places the video portion of the presentation at the top left of the page, a table of contents below the video, and the presentation's slides on the right.

Although Microsoft Producer doesn't come with PowerPoint, you can download it free of charge from Microsoft's Web site. Just point your browser to `www.microsoft.com/office/powerpoint/producer`. If that doesn't work (Microsoft has an annoying habit of reorganizing its Web site once in a while), go to a search service such as Google (`www.google.com`) and search for Microsoft Producer. After you find the page, follow the links to download the software and install it on your computer. Producer is a large download — about 40MB, so it might take awhile to download even with a high-speed Internet connection.

Although Producer can be used for more sophisticated video-editing tasks than simply playing a video alongside PowerPoint slides, this is a PowerPoint book, not a Microsoft Producer book. So in this chapter, I just show you how to create a simple presentation that combines PowerPoint slides with video. After you find out how to do that, you can experiment on your own with Producer's additional features.

Figure 21-1:
A Microsoft
Producer
presentation.

Creating a Producer Presentation

Before you fire up Producer to create a video presentation, you need to create the files that will compose the presentation. First, create the PowerPoint presentation with the slides that will be shown alongside the video. Then create the video itself. To do that, you need to write a script and then get hold of a digital video camera and record it. If possible, save the file in the same folder as the PowerPoint presentation. That way, you won't have to hunt for it later. Producer works with several popular video file formats, including ASF, AVI, MPG, and WMA.

The easiest way to create a new Producer presentation, especially while you're discovering how to use Producer, is to use the New Presentation Wizard. Producer offers to run the wizard when you first start Producer. If you want to run the wizard again later, you can start it by choosing File⇨ New Presentation Wizard.

Follow these steps to create a new presentation using the wizard:

1. **Start the wizard by choosing File⇨New Presentation Wizard.**

   Alternatively, you can start the wizard by selecting Use the New Presentation Wizard from the dialog box that appears when you start Producer. Either way, the wizard comes to life, as shown in Figure 21-2.

2. **Click Next.**

   The wizard asks you to choose from one of its many presentation templates, as shown in Figure 21-3. Scroll through the list and look at the templates. They provide various combinations of sizes and layouts for the slides, video, and other elements that compose a Producer presentation.

Figure 21-2:
The New Presentation Wizard.

3. Pick the template that seems most suited to your presentation and then click Next.

The wizard displays a selection of formatting options that let you choose fonts and colors, as shown in Figure 21-4. You can change these settings if you want to customize the appearance of your presentation.

4. **Change the font and colors for the presentation if you want and then click Next.**

   You are now asked to provide descriptive information for the presentation, such as the title, author, and a brief description, as shown in Figure 21-5. The information that you provide here is displayed on the start page, before your presentation plays.

Figure 21-5:
Providing
description
information.

5. **Type the title, author, and introductory text for your presentation and then click Next.**

   The wizard displays the page shown in Figure 21-6, which lets you specify which PowerPoint presentation to use.

Figure 21-6:
Picking a
presentation.

6. Click the Browse button to summon the Browse dialog box and then find your PowerPoint presentation. Click Open in the Browse dialog box to return to the wizard and then click Next.

This action brings up the next page of the wizard, which lets you import audio or video media files rather than PowerPoint presentations. See Figure 21-7.

Figure 21-7:
Adding audio and video.

7. Click the Browse button to summon the Browse dialog box. Find the video file that you want to include in the presentation. Click Open in the Browse dialog box to return to the wizard and then click Next.

The page shown in Figure 21-8 is displayed. This page asks whether you want to synchronize the slides in the PowerPoint presentation with the video.

Figure 21-8:
Do you want to synchronize?

8. **Click Yes to synchronize the slides and then click Next. When the final page of the wizard appears, click Finish to complete the wizard.**

   Producer grinds and whirs for a moment as it imports the files you specified in Steps 6 and 7 and builds the presentation. When it's all done, it clears its throat and displays the screen shown in Figure 21-9. This screen allows you to synchronize the slides with the video.

9. **Click the Play button (the big fat arrow beneath the video).**

   The video starts to play.

10. **Click Next Slide each time you want to advance to the next slide.**

    You have to pay attention during the video, which might be difficult because you're probably sick of the presentation by now. Each time you get to the point in the video where you want to advance to the next slide, click Next Slide. Producer keeps track of the time as you synchronize the slides, so when you play the presentation back, each slide advances at the right time.

11. **Click Finish when you're done.**

    Whew! You're now taken to the Producer screen, where you can continue to work on your presentation if you still have the energy.

Figure 21-9:
Get ready to
synchronize!

Editing a Presentation

After you create a presentation in Producer, you can tweak its fine points in order to get the presentation just right. Figure 21-5 shows the Producer window. I don't go into all the details of working with presentations in Producer, but I want to point out some of the highlights to get you going:

- ✔ **The Timeline area:** At the bottom of the window is an area called the *Timeline.* The Timeline shows the various *tracks* that make up the presentation. In this case, four tracks are present. At the top is the video portion of a MPEG file that I imported in the New Presentation Wizard. It's linked to the audio portion of the MPEG file, which is shown as a separate track in the timeline. The PowerPoint slides make up a third track, and the template used for those slides is the final track.

  You can adjust the timing of items in the Timeline by selecting them and then dragging their edges to make them longer or shorter. You can also rearrange items, such as individual slides in the Slides track, by dragging them to new locations.

- ✔ **The Media tab:** The middle section of the screen consists of three tabbed areas. This tab lists all the files that have been imported into the presentation. You can use this area to add or remove files. If you import a file into the presentation by choosing File➪Import, the file appears on the Media tab. You can then drag the item onto the Timeline to incorporate it into the presentation.

- ✔ **The Table of Contents tab:** The Table of Contents tab lets you edit the entries in the presentation's table of contents, which is displayed when the presentation runs. Producer creates the table of contents based on the contents of the PowerPoint presentation. Use the Table of Contents tab if you want to change the entries that Producer creates.

- ✔ **The Preview Presentation tab:** The Preview Presentation tab lets you preview your presentation, as shown in Figure 21-10.

Figure 21-10:
Working
with a
presentation
in Producer.

Saving and Publishing a Presentation

In Producer, saving a presentation is different from publishing a presentation. You want to save a presentation often as you work on the presentation. You can save a presentation by clicking the Save button on the Quick Access Toolbar or by choosing File⇨Save. Saving the presentation creates a Microsoft Producer file that you can open later and work on some more.

To actually show your presentation, you must first publish it by choosing File⇨Publish. This creates the HTML files that actually comprise the final presentation. To publish a presentation, follow these steps:

1. **Choose File⇨Publish Presentation.**

   This summons the Publish Wizard, shown in Figure 21-11.

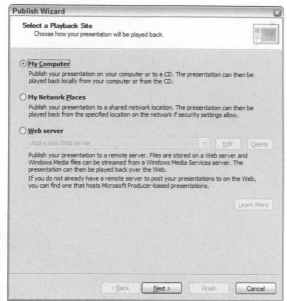

Figure 21-11:
The Publish
Wizard.

2. **Select the location where you want the presentation to be published.**

   The Publish Wizard gives you three options:

   - **My Computer:** This option publishes the presentation to your own computer, either to your computer's hard drive or to a CD drive if you have a CD burner.

   - **My Network Places:** This option publishes the presentation to a network server and lets other people view your presentation over a network.

   - **Web Server:** This option publishes the presentation to a Web server.

3. **Click Next.**

   You're taken to a page that lets you specify the location where you want the presentation to be published. The exact appearance of this page varies slightly depending on which option you specified in Step 2.

4. **Specify the location where you want the presentation published.**

   If you chose My Computer or My Network Places in Step 2, you can supply a filename for the presentation and browse your computer or network for the location where you want the presentation published. If you chose Web Server, you must supply the host address of the Web server you want to publish the presentation to, and you might be required to enter a username and password.

5. Click Next.

A page displaying the presentation's title, the presenter's name, and a description of the presentation appears. The wizard displays the information that you supplied when you created the presentation, but you can use this page to change the information if you want.

6. Click Next again.

Now the wizard displays a list of publishing profiles that are based on the user's connection speed. For users who will view the presentation from their own computer, either from the computer's hard drive or a CD, choose the first option: For Local Playback at 800 Kbps. The other options let you provide lower-quality video for users with slower connections.

Note that you can choose more than one of these profiles. If you do, the user is given the option of picking which one to use based on the speed of his or her connection. Keep in mind, however, that the faster connection speed profiles require more hard drive space.

7. Choose one or more profiles, then click Next.

The last page of the Publish Wizard appears. One more click is all you need. . . .

8. Click Finish and then take a nap.

Publishing a presentation is a time-consuming task. Even publishing a relatively short presentation to your local computer can take a few minutes. If you're publishing the presentation to a Web site, the process will take longer, depending on the speed of your Internet connection. The Publish Wizard displays progress bars to let you know how things are going. When it finishes, it asks whether you want to view the published presentation.

9. Click Yes to view the presentation or click No to skip it.

If you click Yes, a browser window opens so you can view the presentation. For more information, see the next section, "Viewing a Presentation."

Viewing a Presentation

To view a presentation, just open the HTML file that you created with the Publish Wizard in your Web browser. If you published the file to the Internet, fire up Internet Explorer or your favorite browser and type the address of the published presentation in the address bar. If you published the file to My Computer or My Network Places, open a My Computer or My Network Places window, locate the file, and double-click it.

The start page for a published presentation appears, as shown in Figure 21-12. To play the presentation, just click the Play link.

Figure 21-12:
Starting a
presentation.

Part V
The Part of Tens

The 5th Wave

By Rich Tennant

In this part . . .

PowerPoint is pretty good at slinging bullets, so I figured it would be fitting to end this book with a bevy of chapters that aren't much more than glorified bulleted lists. Each chapter in this part covers ten things (more or less) worth knowing about PowerPoint. Without further ado, here they are, direct from the home office in Fresno, California.

Chapter 22

Ten PowerPoint Commandments

And the hapless Windows user said, "But who am I to make this presentation? For I am not eloquent, but I am slow of speech and of tongue, and my colors clasheth, and my charts runneth over." And Microsoft answered, "Fear not, for unto you this day is given a program, which shall be called PowerPoint, and it shall make for you slides, which shall bring forth titles and bullets and, yea, even diagrams."

— Presentations 1:1

And so it came to pass that these ten PowerPoint commandments were passed down from generation to generation. Obey these commandments and it shall go well with you, with your flip chart, and with your overhead projector.

1. Thou Shalt Frequently Savest Thy Work

Every two or three minutes, press Ctrl+S. It takes only a second to save your file, and you never know when you'll be the victim of a rotating power outage (even if you don't live in California).

11. Thou Shalt Storeth Each Presentation in Its Proper Folder

Whenever you save a file, double-check the folder that you're saving it to. It's all too easy to save a presentation in the wrong folder and then spend hours searching for the file later. You'll wind up blaming the computer for losing your files.

III. Thou Shalt Not Abuseth Thy Program's Formatting Features

Yes, PowerPoint lets you set every word in a different font, use 92 different colors on a single slide, and fill every last pixel of empty space with clip art. If you want your slides to look like ransom notes, go ahead. Otherwise, keep things simple.

IV. Thou Shalt Not Stealeth Copyrighted Materials

Given a few minutes with Google or any other search engine, you can probably find just the right picture or snippet of clip art for any presentation need that might arise. But keep in mind that many of those pictures, clip art drawings, and media files are copyrighted. Don't use them if you don't have permission.

V. Thou Shalt Abideth by Thine Color Scheme, Auto-Layout, and Template

Microsoft hired a crew of out-of-work artists to pick the colors for the color schemes, arrange things with the slide layouts, and create beautifully crafted templates. Humor them. They like it when you use their stuff. Don't feel chained to the prepackaged designs, but don't stray far from them unless you have a good artistic eye.

VI. Thou Shalt Not Abuse Thine Audience with an Endless Array of Cute Animations

PowerPoint animations are cute, and sometimes quite useful. But if you do a goofy animation on every slide, pretty soon your audience will just think you're strange.

VII. Keep Thy Computer Gurus Happy

If you have a friend or co-worker who knows more about computers than you do, keep that person happy. Throw him or her an occasional Twinkie or a bag of Cheetos. Treat computer nerds as if they're human beings. After all, you want them to be your friends.

VIII. Thou Shalt Backeth Up Thy Files Day by Day

Yes, every day. One of these days, you'll come to work only to discover a pile of rubble where your desk used to be. A federal agent will pick up what's left of your computer's keyboard and laugh. But if you back up every day, you won't lose more than a day's work.

IX. Thou Shalt Fear No Evil, for Ctrl+Z Is Always with Thee

March ahead with boldness. Not sure what a button does? Click it! Click it twice if it makes you feel powerful! The worst that it can do is mess up your presentation. If that happens, you can press Ctrl+Z to set things back the way they should be.

If you really mess things up, just close the presentation without saving. Then open the previously saved version. After all, you did obey the first commandment, didn't you?

X. Thou Shalt Not Panic

You're the only one who knows you're nervous. You'll do just fine. Imagine the audience naked if that will help. (Unless, of course, you're making a presentation to a nudist club and they actually are naked, in which case try to imagine them with their clothes on.)

Chapter 23

Ten Tips for Creating Readable Slides

• •

*T*his chapter gives you a few random tips and pointers that will help you produce readable slides.

Try Reading the Slide from the Back of the Room

The number-one rule of creating readable slides is that everyone in the room must be able to read them. If you're not certain, there's one sure way to find out: Try it. Fire up the projector, call up the slide, walk to the back of the room, and see whether you can read it. If you can't, you need to make an adjustment.

Remember that everyone's eyesight might not be as good as yours. If you have perfect vision, squint a little when you get to the back of the room to see how the slide might appear to someone whose vision isn't perfect.

If a projector isn't handy, make sure you can read your slides from 10 or 15 feet away from your computer's monitor.

Avoid Small Text

If you can't read a slide from the back of the room, it's probably because the text is too small. The rule to live by is that 24-point type is the smallest you should use for text that you want people to read. A 12-point type might be perfectly readable in a Word document, but it's way too small for PowerPoint.

No More Than Five Bullets, Please

Have you ever noticed how David Letterman uses two slides to display his Top Ten lists? Dave's producers know that ten items is way too many for one screen. Five is just right. You might be able to slip in six now and again, but if you're up to seven or eight, try breaking the slide into two slides.

Avoid Excessive Verbiage Lending to Excessively Lengthy Text That Is Not Only Redundant but Also Repetitive and Reiterative

See what I mean? Maybe the heading should have been, "Be Brief."

Use Consistent Wording

One sign of an amateur presentation is wording in bullet lists that isn't grammatically consistent. Consider this list:

- Profits will be improved
- Expanding markets
- It will reduce the amount of overseas competition
- Production increase

Each list item uses a different grammatical construction. The same points made with consistent wording have a more natural flow and make a more compelling case:

- Improved profits
- Expanded markets
- Reduced overseas competition
- Increased production

Avoid Clashing Colors

The professionally chosen color schemes that come with PowerPoint are designed to create slides that are easy to read. If you venture away from them, be careful about choosing colors that are hard to read.

Watch the Line Endings

Sometimes, PowerPoint breaks a line at an awkward spot, which can make slides hard to read. For example, a bullet point might be one word too long to fit on a single line. When that happens, you might want to break the line elsewhere so the second line has more than one word. (Use Shift+Enter to create a line break that doesn't start a new paragraph.)

Alternatively, you might want to drag the right margin of the text placeholder to increase the margin width so that the line doesn't have to be broken at all.

Web addresses (URLs) are notoriously hard to squeeze onto a single line. If your presentation includes long URLs, pay special attention to how they fit.

Keep the Background Simple

Don't splash a bunch of distracting clip art on the background unless it's essential. The purpose of the background is to provide a well-defined visual space for the slide's content. All too often, presenters put up slides that have text displayed on top of pictures of the mountains or city skylines, which makes the text almost impossible to read.

Use Only Two Levels of Bullets

Sure, it's tempting to develop your subpoints into sub-subpoints and sub-sub-subpoints, but no one will be able to follow your logic. Don't make your slides more confusing than they need to be. If you need to make sub-sub-subpoints, you probably need a few more slides.

Keep Charts and Diagrams Simple

PowerPoint can create elaborate graphs that even the best statisticians will marvel at. However, the most effective graphs are simple pie charts with three or four slices and simple column charts with three or four columns. Likewise, pyramid, Venn, and other types of diagrams lose their impact when you add more than four or five elements.

If you remember only one rule when creating your presentations, remember this one: *Keep it simple, clean, and concise.*

Chapter 24

Ten Ways to Keep Your Audience Awake

. . . .

Nothing frightens a public speaker more than the prospect of the audience falling asleep during the speech. Here are some things you can do to prevent that from happening. (Yawn.)

Don't Forget Your Purpose

Too many presenters ramble on and on with no clear sense of purpose. The temptation is to throw in every clever quotation and every interesting tidbit you can muster that is even remotely related to the topic of your presentation. The reason that this temptation is so strong is that you most likely haven't identified what you hope to accomplish with your presentation. In other words, you haven't pinned down your *purpose.*

Don't confuse a presentation's title with its purpose. Suppose that you're asked to give a presentation to a prospective client on the advantages of your company's new, improved, deluxe model ChronSimplastic Infindibulator. Your purpose in this presentation is not to convey information about the new Infindibulator, but to persuade your client to buy one of the $65 million beasties. The title of your presentation might be *Infindibulators for the 21st Century,* but the purpose is "Convince these saps to buy one, or maybe two."

Don't Become a Slave to Your Slides

PowerPoint makes such beautiful slides that the temptation is to let them be the show. That's a big mistake. *You* are the show — not the slides. The slides are merely visual aids, designed to make your presentation more effective, not to steal the show.

Your slides should supplement your talk, not repeat it. If you find yourself just reading your slides, you need to rethink what you put on the slides. The slides should summarize key points, not become the script for your speech.

Don't Overwhelm Your Audience with Unnecessary Detail

On November 19, 1863, a crowd of 15,000 gathered in Gettysburg to hear Edward Everett, one of the greatest orators of the time. Mr. Everett spoke for two hours about the events that had transpired during the famous battle. When he finished, Abraham Lincoln rose to deliver a brief two-minute postscript that has become the most famous speech in American history.

If PowerPoint had been around in 1863, Everett probably would have spoken for four hours. PowerPoint practically begs you to talk too much. When you start typing bullets, you can't stop. Pretty soon, you have 40 slides for a 20-minute presentation. That's about 35 more than you probably need. Try to shoot for one slide for every two to five minutes of your presentation.

Don't Neglect Your Opening

As they say, you get only one opportunity to make a first impression. Don't waste it by telling a joke that has nothing to do with the topic, apologizing for your lack of preparation or nervousness, or listing your credentials. Don't pussyfoot around; get right to the point.

The best openings are those that capture the audience's attention with a provocative statement, a rhetorical question, or a compelling story. A joke is okay, but only if it sets the stage for the subject of your presentation.

Be Relevant

The objective of any presentation is to lead your audience to say, "Me, too!" Unfortunately, many presentations leave the audience thinking, "So what?"

The key to being relevant is giving your audience members what they need, and not what you think is interesting or important. The most persuasive presentations are those that present solutions to real problems rather than opinions about hypothetical problems.

Don't Forget the Altar Call

What would a Billy Graham crusade be without the altar call? A wasted opportunity.

The best presentations are the ones that entice your audience to action. That might mean buying your product, changing their lifestyles, or just being interested enough to do more research into your topic.

But the opportunity will be wasted if you don't invite your audience to respond in some way. If you're selling something (and we're all selling something!), make it clear how your audience can buy. Tell them the 800 number. Give them a handout with links of Web sites they can go to for more information. Ask everyone to sing *Just As I Am*. Do whatever it takes.

Practice, Practice, Practice

Back to good ol' Abe: Somehow a rumor got started that Abraham Lincoln hastily wrote the Gettysburg Address on the train, just before pulling into Gettysburg. In truth, Lincoln agonized for weeks over every word.

Practice, practice, practice. Work through the rough spots. Polish the opening and the closing and all the awkward transitions in between. Practice in front of a mirror. Videotape yourself. Time yourself.

Relax!

Don't worry! Be happy! Even the most gifted public speakers are scared silly every time they step up to the podium. Whether you're speaking to one person or 10,000, relax. In 20 minutes, it will all be over.

No matter how nervous you are, no one knows it except you. That is, unless you tell them. The number one rule of panic avoidance is to never apologize for your fears. Behind the podium, your knees might be knocking hard enough to bruise yourself, but no one else will notice. After you swab down your armpits and wipe the drool off your chin, people will say, "Weren't you nervous? You seemed so relaxed!"

Expect the Unexpected

Plan on things going wrong, because they will. The projector won't focus, the microphone goes dead, you'll drop your notes on the way to the podium. Who knows what else will happen?

Take things in stride, but be prepared for problems you can anticipate. Carry an extra set of notes in your pocket. Bring your own microphone if you have one. Have a backup projector ready if possible.

Don't Be Boring

An audience can overlook almost anything, but one thing they'll never forgive you for is boring them. Above all, do not bore your audience.

This guideline doesn't mean you have to tell jokes, jump up and down, or talk fast. Jokes, excessive jumping, and rapid speech can be unimaginably boring. If you obey the other instructions in this chapter — if you have a clear-cut purpose and stick to it, avoid unnecessary detail, and address real needs — you'll never be boring. Just be yourself and have fun. If you have fun, so will your audience.

Chapter 25

Ten Things That Often Go Wrong

The actual number of things that can go wrong when working with PowerPoint is probably closer to 10,000, but the following ten are among the things that go wrong most often.

1 Can't Find My File

You spent hours polishing that presentation, and now you can't find the file. You know that you saved it, but it's not there! The problem is probably one of two things: Either you saved the file in a different folder, or you used a different filename to save it than you intended. The solution? The most likely way to find your presentation is to check the list on the right side of the File menu. This list includes the presentations you've most recently worked on. If you don't find the presentation in that list, summon the Open dialog box (choose File⇨Open) and then click the My Recent Documents icon. This displays a larger list of recently used files. As a last resort, use the Windows search feature (Start⇨Search) to find the presentation.

I've Run Out of Hard Drive Space

Nothing is more frustrating than creating a fancy PowerPoint presentation and then discovering that you're completely out of hard drive space. What to do? Open a My Computer window (choose Start⇨My Computer) and rummage through your hard drive, looking for files you don't need. Delete enough files to free up a few megabytes and then press Alt+Tab to move back to PowerPoint and save your file. I did this recently: I had to delete a bunch of music files that I had accumulated to make my own CDs. (It was either them or the Word document files for the first few chapters of this book. Not an easy decision.)

If your hard drive is full and you can't find more than a few files to delete, try double-clicking the Recycle Bin icon and choosing File⇨Empty Recycle Bin. This often frees up additional hard drive space. If that doesn't work, choose Start⇨All Programs⇨Accessories⇨System Tools⇨Disk Cleanup. The Disk Cleanup program scans your hard drive for unnecessary files and offers to remove them for you. It can often free up many megabytes of hard drive space.

If you often run out of hard drive space, consider adding a larger hard drive to your computer. Nowadays, you can buy a 250GB hard drive for less than $100. If the thought of opening up your computer and installing a hard drive causes you to break out in a sweat, you can also get external drives that plug in to your computer's USB port.

I've Run Out of Memory

Many people still use computers with only 256MB of internal memory. Although you can run PowerPoint with as little as 256MB of memory, 512MB is a more reasonable minimum, and 2GB is ideal. The additional memory helps your computer to not give up and crash from the overload of open applications. Memory is cheap! Why not make sure you have enough?

PowerPoint Has Vanished!

You're working at your computer, minding your own business, when suddenly — whoosh! — PowerPoint disappears. What happened? Most likely, you clicked some area outside the PowerPoint window or you pressed Alt+Tab or Alt+Esc, which whisks you away to another program. To get PowerPoint back, press Alt+Tab. You might have to press Alt+Tab several times before PowerPoint comes back to life.

PowerPoint can also vanish into thin air if you use a screen-saver program. Try giving the mouse a nudge to see whether PowerPoint reappears.

I Accidentally Deleted a File

Just found out how to delete files and couldn't stop yourself, eh? Relax. It happens to everyone. Odds are that you can rescue the deleted file if you act quickly enough. Double-click the Recycle Bin icon that sits on your desktop. You can probably find the deleted file there. Copy it back to the folder where it belongs.

It Won't Let Me Edit That

No matter how hard you click, PowerPoint won't let you edit that doohickey on-screen. What gives? The doohickey is probably a part of the Slide Master. To edit it, click the View tab and then click the Slide Master button in the Presentation Views group. This step displays the Slide Master and enables you to edit it. However, the object you're trying to edit might be underneath another object. If so, move the other object aside temporarily. When you're done, drag the other object back into place.

Something Seems to Be Missing

You just read the chapter about SmartArt, but nothing happens when you try to insert a SmartArt diagram. Or worse, PowerPoint locks up when you try to insert SmartArt. Arghhhh!

It's possible that your PowerPoint installation has somehow become corrupted. Perhaps an important system file was accidentally deleted, or a problem has somehow managed to creep into the Windows Registry (the file that keeps track of settings for Windows as well as for programs you have installed on your computer).

Fear not! Office 2007 includes a self-healing feature that can diagnose and correct problems with your Office installation. To use it, click the Office button, choose PowerPoint Options, and then select the Resources tab and click the Diagnose button. Then follow the instructions that appear on-screen.

What Happened to My Clip Art?

You just purchased and installed an expensive clip art collection that has 500 stunning images from the Neapolitan Museum of Art, but you can't find them in the Media Gallery. Where did they go? Nowhere. You just have to tell Microsoft Clip Organizer about them. Fire up the Clip Organizer by clicking the Insert Picture button (in the Illustrations group of the Insert tab). Then, when the Clip Art task pane appears, click the Organize Clips link found at the bottom of the task pane. Then choose File⇨Add Clips to Organizer to add your pictures to the Clip Organizer.

I Can't Figure Out Where the X-Y-Z Command Went

If you're a long-time PowerPoint user, you've invested a lot of time finding where all of its important commands are hidden. Although the new user interface of PowerPoint 2007 is supposed to be easier to use, sometimes features are still hard to find. For example, PowerPoint's self-healing feature used to be available as the Help⇨Detect and Repair command. Now you have to navigate several layers deep to find this command.

Fortunately, PowerPoint's Help has a handy chart that lists the new location for all the old commands and toolbar buttons. To find this list, click the Help button (found at the top right of the PowerPoint window), click What's New, then click the link labeled Locations of PowerPoint 2003 Commands in PowerPoint 2007.

The Projector Doesn't Work

An LCD projector might not be working for many reasons. Assuming that the computer and projector are both plugged in and turned on and you have used the correct video cable to connect your computer to the projector, here are two common problems you should check:

- ✔ **Make sure your video input ports are working.** Most projectors have two or more video input ports. The projector must be configured to use the input port to which your computer is connected. Look for a button on the projector to set the input source. The projector might use a menu to set the input source: In that case, use the button that calls up the menu, scroll through the choices to find the video input source, and then select the input port to which your computer is connected.

- ✔ **If you're using a laptop, make sure that the external video port is activated.** Most laptops have a function key on the keyboard to do this. Also look for a key with an icon that represents a video monitor. You might have to hold down a function key (probably labeled "Fn") while you press the monitor key.

Chapter 26

Ten Best New Features of PowerPoint 2007

If you're an experienced PowerPoint user, you probably turned to this chapter first. Here you can find a brief description of the ten most significant new features of PowerPoint 2007, along with a reference to the chapter you can turn to for more information on the feature. (Actually, there are eleven listed here, but who's counting?)

The Ribbon

The most noticeable new feature of PowerPoint 2007 is the new user interface, which is centered around a gadget called *the Ribbon.* Gone are the old menus and toolbars. In its place, the Ribbon provides context-sensitive access to the tools you need most. Figure 26-1 shows the Ribbon in action.

Notice that across the top of the Ribbon is a series of tabs. These tabs are similar to the old menus of previous versions: Each tab provides access to a related set of commands. However, you access all the commands via graphical controls such as buttons, check boxes, drop-down lists, and galleries, rather than the boring text of old-fashioned menus.

The only real menu that's left in PowerPoint is the Office menu (also known as the *file* menu). It's the big orange, green, and blue icon at the top left of the screen. Click it and you'll see something that vaguely resembles the old File menu, with commands to open, save, print, and close files, plus a few other goodies.

If the Ribbon seems strange at first, take heart. I hated the Ribbon the first time I saw it. Hated it the second time too. It took me a good two months to get used to it. Now, when I go back to an old version of PowerPoint, I feel like Scotty from *Star Trek,* when he is sent back into time to the 1980's and tries to talk to a computer. When the computer doesn't respond, someone tells him to just use the keyboard. "How quaint," he says.

For more information about the Ribbon, see Chapter 1.

The Ribbon

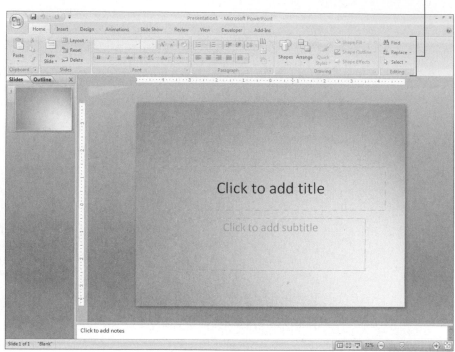

Figure 26-1:
The Ribbon
is the
centerpiece
of the new
user
interface.

The Quick Access Toolbar

The Quick Access toolbar (introduced in Chapter 1) is the closest thing you can find in PowerPoint to an old-style toolbar. It's a simple little toolbar that can hold the buttons you like to use the most. It is the *only* part of the PowerPoint user interface you can customize. In previous versions, you could customize almost everything. You drag toolbars around to different locations, hide toolbars, add or remove buttons from toolbars, and create new toolbars. In short, the old PowerPoint user interface was almost completely customizable. The new PowerPoint user interface is almost completely *not* customizable.

Why the change? Microsoft studied the logs of its support calls for Microsoft Office — millions of them, I suppose — and found that one of the top support calls they received was from people who *accidentally* customized the user interface and couldn't figure out how to get it back to normal. In fact, nearly all the users who had customized the user interface didn't do it on purpose. They did it by accidentally closing a toolbar or dragging it to a new location. And they couldn't figure out how to get the lost or displaced toolbars back.

Thus Microsoft decided that because very few users customized the user interface on purpose, but a lot of users did it by accident, the best solution would be to eliminate most of the customization you can do, at least from within the program. You can still customize the user interface if you want to, but you must do so outside of PowerPoint by editing an XML file that provides Ribbon customizations.

The one feature you *can* customize is the Quick Access toolbar, also known as the QAT. Here are the ways you can customize it:

- You can put it in one of two locations: above or below the Ribbon. To change the QAT's location, right-click it and choose Place Quick Access Toolbar Above/Below the Ribbon.

- You can add any button you want to the QAT. To do so, right-click the button and choose Add to Quick Access Toolbar.

- To remove a button from the QAT, right-click the button and choose Remove from Quick Access Toolbar.

Themes

Previous versions of PowerPoint had templates and Slide Masters as a way to help you create consistent and attractive presentations. Microsoft has taken this idea one step further with *themes,* which are sets of design elements you can apply to the slides in a presentation. Themes include color schemes, fonts, background styles, and design effects that are applied to shapes and other elements in the presentation.

Office comes with 20 predefined themes, which you can select from the Theme gallery shown in Figure 26-2. After you select a theme, you can customize it by tweaking the color scheme, font, and other elements that make up the theme.

Note that I said *Office*, not *PowerPoint*, comes with 20 predefined themes. Office themes work in Word, Excel, and PowerPoint. This makes it much easier to create documents, spreadsheets, and presentations with similar designs.

For more information about themes, check out Chapter 9.

Figure 26-2:
The Theme
gallery.

SharePoint Integration

If you work for a company that uses SharePoint, you'll be happy to discover that many new enhancements have been made to integrate SharePoint features with PowerPoint. Most notably, you can open a document stored in a SharePoint document library directly from PowerPoint, and you can check the document out so that others can't edit it while you're working on it.

For more information about SharePoint, see Chapter 19.

Slide Reuse

One of the most useful new features of PowerPoint is the ability to reuse slides. You can do that by stealing slides directly from another presentation or by creating a slide library that serves as a central repository for slides that can be reused. For example, suppose your company creates a "mission statement" slide that will appear in many presentations. Rather than create this slide in each presentation in which it appears, you can use a slide library to store the slide in a central location.

For more information, turn to Chapter 20.

Live Preview

This feature isn't covered specifically anywhere in this book, but it's one of the most useful new features of PowerPoint. In previous versions, whenever a formatting dialog box appeared, you'd have to twiddle with the dialog box and then click OK to see its effects. In PowerPoint 2007, a feature called Live Preview applies changes to the current slide immediately, even while a dialog box or gallery is open. Thus you can instantly see what effect changes will have on your slides without having to actually apply the change.

Improved WordArt

WordArt has been around for more than ten years, and this version contains the first major improvement that has been made to it. The improvement is a fundamental one. In previous versions of PowerPoint, WordArt objects were just that: separate objects. Now WordArt is just a type of formatting that can be applied to any text in PowerPoint. So you don't have to insert a separate object to create WordArt. Instead, you just type some text, select it, and then apply WordArt effects to the text.

Ironically, the new and improved version of WordArt is available only in PowerPoint 2007 and Excel 2007. Word 2007 still uses the old-style WordArt. Go figure!

For more information about WordArt, see Chapter 8.

Real Tables, at Last

Tables stunk in previous versions of PowerPoint. They were limited in size, and people had difficulties getting them to format and align right. They were very limited when compared with tables in Word.

Now, PowerPoint 2007 sports most of the same table features as Word. You can use the Draw Tables command just like in Word, and you can apply all of Word's fancy table formatting features to your PowerPoint tables. You can even merge cells! Hallelujah!

For more information about tables, see Chapter 17.

Real Charts!

Ding Dong, Microsoft Graph is Gone!

Well, it hasn't really been killed off. Microsoft left it in place so you can open old presentations that contain charts created with Microsoft Graph. But the good news is that charts created for PowerPoint now use exactly the same charting features as are available in Excel.

For more information about charts, see Chapter 14.

SmartArt

PowerPoint 2003 has a feature called the Diagram gallery that lets you create special types of charts that are essentially interchangeable. That is, you can quickly change from one diagram type to another, using the same text as labels for the elements of the diagram.

PowerPoint 2007 grows this feature to a new level, changing its name in the process to SmartArt. SmartArt diagrams can be formatted with any of the formatting features of regular shapes, which means you can apply backgrounds, fills, shadows, 3-D rotations, and a few new effects such as reflections and softened edges.

In addition, you can easily create a SmartArt diagram from standard bullet text. Figure 26-3 shows a typical SmartArt diagram.

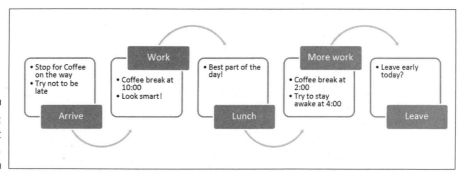

Figure 26-3:
A SmartArt
diagram.

The New Document Format

Last, but certainly not least, Microsoft has made a fundamental change to the PowerPoint document format. Enough so that, for the first time ever, Microsoft changed the filename extension for PowerPoint presentation files, from .ppt to .pptx. The *x* indicates that the file uses an XML format to store the presentation rather than a proprietary format.

This doesn't have much of an impact for ordinary PowerPoint users, except that Microsoft has managed to optimize the format so that presentation files now take up much less hard drive space than they used to, especially when they include large image files.

To save hard drive space, the files are compressed just like regular compressed .zip files. In fact, if you change the extension of a PowerPoint 2007 presentation from .pptx to .zip, you can open the file with Windows Explorer and see the various pieces that make up the internal structure of a presentation file. You can poke around and find some fascinating stuff. For example, each slide is actually stored as a separate XML document. You can open this document in Notepad and see the XML that's required to create the slide!

Index

SPORTS, FITNESS, PARENTING, RELIGION & SPIRITUALITY

0-471-76871-5

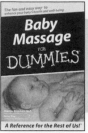

0-7645-7841-3

Also available:

- Catholicism For Dummies
  0-7645-5391-7
- Exercise Balls For Dummies
  0-7645-5623-1
- Fitness For Dummies
  0-7645-7851-0
- Football For Dummies
  0-7645-3936-1
- Judaism For Dummies
  0-7645-5299-6
- Potty Training For Dummies
  0-7645-5417-4
- Buddhism For Dummies
  0-7645-5359-3

- Pregnancy For Dummies
  0-7645-4483-7 †
- Ten Minute Tone-Ups For Dummies
  0-7645-7207-5
- NASCAR For Dummies
  0-7645-7681-X
- Religion For Dummies
  0-7645-5264-3
- Soccer For Dummies
  0-7645-5229-5
- Women in the Bible For Dummies
  0-7645-8475-8

TRAVEL

0-7645-7749-2

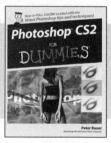

0-7645-6945-7

Also available:

- Alaska For Dummies
  0-7645-7746-8
- Cruise Vacations For Dummies
  0-7645-6941-4
- England For Dummies
  0-7645-4276-1
- Europe For Dummies
  0-7645-7529-5
- Germany For Dummies
  0-7645-7823-5
- Hawaii For Dummies
  0-7645-7402-7

- Italy For Dummies
  0-7645-7386-1
- Las Vegas For Dummies
  0-7645-7382-9
- London For Dummies
  0-7645-4277-X
- Paris For Dummies
  0-7645-7630-5
- RV Vacations For Dummies
  0-7645-4442-X
- Walt Disney World & Orlando
  For Dummies
  0-7645-9660-8

GRAPHICS, DESIGN & WEB DEVELOPMENT

0-7645-8815-X

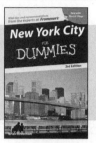

0-7645-9571-7

Also available:

- 3D Game Animation For Dummies
  0-7645-8789-7
- AutoCAD 2006 For Dummies
  0-7645-8925-3
- Building a Web Site For Dummies
  0-7645-7144-3
- Creating Web Pages For Dummies
  0-470-08030-2
- Creating Web Pages All-in-One Desk
  Reference For Dummies
  0-7645-4345-8
- Dreamweaver 8 For Dummies
  0-7645-9649-7

- InDesign CS2 For Dummies
  0-7645-9572-5
- Macromedia Flash 8 For Dummies
  0-7645-9691-8
- Photoshop CS2 and Digital
  Photography For Dummies
  0-7645-9580-6
- Photoshop Elements 4 For Dummies
  0-471-77483-9
- Syndicating Web Sites with RSS Feeds
  For Dummies
  0-7645-8848-6
- Yahoo! SiteBuilder For Dummies
  0-7645-9800-7

NETWORKING, SECURITY, PROGRAMMING & DATABASES

0-7645-7728-X

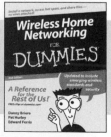

0-471-74940-0

Also available:

- Access 2007 For Dummies
  0-470-04612-0
- ASP.NET 2 For Dummies
  0-7645-7907-X
- C# 2005 For Dummies
  0-7645-9704-3
- Hacking For Dummies
  0-470-05235-X
- Hacking Wireless Networks
  For Dummies
  0-7645-9730-2
- Java For Dummies
  0-470-08716-1

- Microsoft SQL Server 2005 For Dummies
  0-7645-7755-7
- Networking All-in-One Desk Reference
  For Dummies
  0-7645-9939-9
- Preventing Identity Theft For Dummies
  0-7645-7336-5
- Telecom For Dummies
  0-471-77085-X
- Visual Studio 2005 All-in-One Desk
  Reference For Dummies
  0-7645-9775-2
- XML For Dummies
  0-7645-8845-1

HEALTH & SELF-HELP

0-7615 8450-2

0-7645-4149-8

Also available:
- Bipolar Disorder For Dummies
  0-7645-8451-0
- Chemotherapy and Radiation For Dummies
  0-7645-7832-4
- Controlling Cholesterol For Dummies
  0-7645-5440-9
- Diabetes For Dummies
  0-7645-6820-5* †
- Divorce For Dummies
  0-7645-8417-0 †

- Fibromyalgia For Dummies
  0-7645-5441-7
- Low-Calorie Dieting For Dummies
  0-7645-9905-4
- Meditation For Dummies
  0-471-77774-9
- Osteoporosis For Dummies
  0-7645-7621-6
- Overcoming Anxiety For Dummies
  0-7645-5447-6
- Reiki For Dummies
  0-7645-9907-0
- Stress Management For Dummies
  0-7645-5144-2

EDUCATION, HISTORY, REFERENCE & TEST PREPARATION

0-7645-8381-6

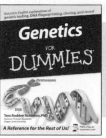

0-7645-9554-7

Also available:
- The ACT For Dummies
  0-7645-9652-7
- Algebra For Dummies
  0-7645-5325-9
- Algebra Workbook For Dummies
  0-7645-8467-7
- Astronomy For Dummies
  0-7645-8465-0
- Calculus For Dummies
  0-7645-2498-4
- Chemistry For Dummies
  0-7645-5430-1
- Forensics For Dummies
  0-7645-5580-4

- Freemasons For Dummies
  0-7645-9796-5
- French For Dummies
  0-7645-5193-0
- Geometry For Dummies
  0-7645-5324-0
- Organic Chemistry I For Dummies
  0-7645-6902-3
- The SAT I For Dummies
  0-7645-7193-1
- Spanish For Dummies
  0-7645-5194-9
- Statistics For Dummies
  0-7645-5423-9

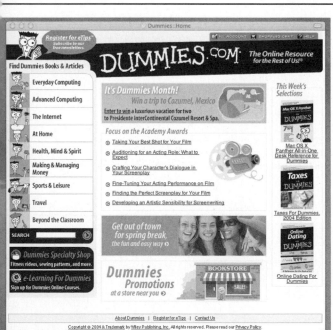

Get smart @ dummies.com®

- **Find a full list of Dummies titles**
- **Look into loads of FREE on-site articles**
- **Sign up for FREE eTips e-mailed to you weekly**
- **See what other products carry the Dummies name**
- **Shop directly from the Dummies bookstore**
- **Enter to win new prizes every month!**

* Separate Canadian edition also available
† Separate U.K. edition also available

Available wherever books are sold. For more information or to order direct: U.S. customers visit www.dummies.com or call 1-877-762-2974.
U.K. customers visit www.wileyeurope.com or call 0800 243407. Canadian customers visit www.wiley.ca or call 1-800-567-4797.